S0-CFR-707

Oyster Wars and the Public Trust

Oyster Wars and the Public Trust

Property, Law, and Ecology in New Jersey History

Bonnie J. McCay

THE UNIVERSITY OF ARIZONA PRESS / TUCSON

The University of Arizona Press

First printing

♾ This book is printed on acid-free, archival-quality paper.
Manufactured in the United States of America

03 02 01 00 99 98 6 5 4 3 2 1

Library of Congress Cataloging-in-Publication Data
McCay, Bonnie J.
Oyster wars and the public trust : property, law, and ecology in New Jersey history / Bonnie J. McCay.
p. cm.
Includes bibliographical references and index.
ISBN 0-8165-1804-1 (alk. paper)
1. Submerged lands—United States. 2. Fishery law and legislation—United States. 3. Commons—United States. 4. Oyster culture—Law and legislation—New Jersey. I. Title.
KF4627.M33 1998
346.7304′2—dc21 97-33776
CIP

British Library Cataloguing-in-Publication Data
A catalogue record for this book is available from the British Library.

Publication of this book is made possible in part by the proceeds of a permanent endowment created with the assistance of a Challenge Grant from the National Endowment for the Humanities, a federal agency.

Title page: Oystering at the opening of the public oyster beds at the "Graveling" on the Mullica River in New Jersey. (Drawing by the author)

Contents

Illustrations

Maps

Figures

Preface

Who can remember a time when oyster bars in New York City featured "York Bays," "Shrewsburies," "Chingaroras," and other specialties from New Jersey? Or, indeed, a time when going to oyster bars was the sophisticated and safe thing to do? Today, television and newspapers warn about the dangers of eating oysters even from the remote and seemingly less polluted waters of states such as Louisiana. My book is partly about this and other problems with oysters (and clams), but even more it is about culture, ecology, and law.

Pollution, concerns for public health, environmental deterioration, and overharvesting of natural oysters contributed to the demise and constriction of oystering in many parts of the world. In New Jersey, once a major center of oystering, the Delaware Bay and the Mullica River are the only places where oystering is done now, and recurrent epidemics of oyster diseases have nearly stopped it all. The story of how this came about is not, however, simply about the technical and economic dimensions of microbiology, shellfish, and sanitation; nor is it simply about the consequences of population growth and industrialization. It is also and necessarily, given the particulars of this history, about culture and a cultural problem about property. North American culture includes the idea of the free and equal right to go fishing and to use waters and beaches for transportation and pleasure. Yes, we might have to pay for parking, buy a license, and follow regulations imposed by our state and federal governments' fish and game agencies and the Coast Guard, but otherwise no one can keep us from the great rivers, bays, and oceans of our continent. It seems natural to claim these rights as human beings and as citizens.

By and large, Americans also accept the idea that problems flow from this situation: there may be too many speedboats in the bay to make sailing safe, the beaches will be too crowded on holiday weekends to be pleasurable, and fish are getting scarcer because too many people are going after them. This "open-access" problem, somewhat misleadingly titled the "tragedy of the commons," has become one of the most influential ideas proposed for why humans harm or destroy much that is valuable to them. It underpins policies in natural resource and environmental management that use the powers of government to limit how many people can be involved and how much they can do to or take from natural systems.

A long history of writing about people and nature would lead to the conclusion that free and open access is the natural, or at least prior, condition in most socionatural systems. In either case, the message is that the situation is ultimately disastrous unless people are restrained and access is limited. The point of this study, however, is that there are other sides to the question and that history, revealed in this study in legal cases, supports my point, even if succulent and safe oysters are hard to find.

The open-access explanation of problems of the commons supports policies that privatize some or all aspects of the use of natural resources. Contemporary examples include proposed sales of public lands, the creation of tradable permits for emission of pollutants, and carving up fisheries and forestry quotas into individual, transferable units. These are all new and controversial. Well, not so new. As will be seen, this policy has long been advocated and implemented for managing oysters but never completely and always with controversy, hence the "oyster wars" of the title.

Why is it so controversial to create private property in fish and oysters, rangelands, or rights to emit pollutants? Properly, the answer would depend on the specifics of the situation, but there are general answers as well, including the social, cultural, and economic values of maintaining some resources, places, and opportunities as "common property" to be shared by members of a community. The goal of this book is to explore this contested terrain through the lens of history and anthropology. By examining a series of conflicts—some involving enough planning, actors, and violence to be called "wars"—that have taken place over property rights in oysters, fish, and waterfront in the specific settings of New Jersey, I show the strength, persistence, and contours of claims for both common property and private property. By pointing to a long history of attempts to articulate and defend principles of free and equal access to certain "common" resources, I show how "unnatural" they are.

My work is grounded in ecological anthropology and human ecology, where I have specialized in studying maritime adaptations. In focusing on oyster wars and the evolving common law of New Jersey's courts, I continue traditions of cultural anthropology. In the spirit of Boas, Sapir, Kroeber, and other American anthropologists, I focus on a specialized domain of culture—sets of symbols structured through a special tradition concerning the bases for claiming property in oysters or other shellfish and the broader notion of "public trust," but with a holistic approach. In anthropology, the holistic, ethnographic approach has been enriched by ecological concerns and by political economy perspectives that call for greater appreciation of relationships of class and power and of the importance of larger geographic scales and globalized structures. Accordingly, in this study I contextualize legal decisions in relation to the social and ecological relations they touch upon, namely, the fisheries, shellfisheries, shipping, and other activities that use the riverbanks, beaches, channels, oyster beds, and fishing grounds of New Jersey. Moreover, I work within the more recent tradition in social analysis and cultural studies that insists upon the importance of social relations, conflict, and individual action in the construction of culture and the environment. The historical perspective I take is enhanced by appreciation of the dynamic and elusive nature of "tradition" and the extent to which culture is intentionally constructed by historical actors. All of this is part of what is loosely called "political ecology."

I do not pretend to be a legal historian, but I recognize parallels with and have benefited from the work of J. Willard Hurst (1960) and others who emphasize the embeddedness of American law in economic and social relations. The general concept of embeddedness is central also to my critique of models such as the "tragedy of the commons."

Acknowledgments

This book is a footnote that got away. It began when I was looking for information on the history of New Jersey's fisheries, with the support of the New Jersey Historical Commission and the Sea Grant College Program. It turned out that court cases were among the few sources of information. I had already been engaged in work on the problem of the commons in both Newfoundland and New Jersey, so what I read in the nineteenth-century case reports about the common law of fisheries and tidelands caught my attention. At first I used the cases merely as historical sources, concentrating on other work in New Jersey and Newfoundland that was supported by Sea Grant as well as the National Science Foundation, Rutgers University, and the New Jersey Agricultural Experiment Station. Over the years, as I returned to this extended footnote, I became interested in the cases as proper subjects of cultural anthropology and political ecology. After all, legal doctrines are sets of symbols and the meanings attached to them at different points of time and place; accordingly, they are what anthropologists mean by culture.

Acknowledgments are due everyone who helped me learn about and appreciate the past and present of New Jersey's fisheries and fishermen. I am particularly grateful to Clyde MacKenzie, George Moss, and Bill and Vivian Jenks. The Jenkses gave so much, including a chance to get my feet (and much else) wet, as it were, in both Shark River and the "culture of the commoners." Bill was also a collaborator in both writing about and planting shellfish. The fishing families of Belford, including the Egnatoviches and Isaaksens, also helped me better understand the historical questions posed in my work.

I am grateful to Hal Haskin, professor emeritus at Rutgers University, who, like MacKenzie, showed what a truly applied scientist can be, and to Susan Ford, Beverly Webster, and other members of the Haskin Shellfish Research Laboratory at Bivalve for the many ways they made me feel welcome and a colleague. Larry Taylor of Lafayette College in Pennsylvania graciously shared both observations and fieldnotes from his ethnographic work at Bivalve in 1983 that was part of a larger Sea Grant project on New Jersey fisheries. Carolyn Creed, who collaborated on studies of privatized fishing rights in the surf clam fisheries, is another professional to whom I owe so much. I am equally indebted to Steven

Rosen, who as a new graduate student in anthropology helped me enter the unfamiliar world of law libraries. His notes on the cases he found gave me my first clues that there might be a story in the law.

To those who read early drafts I extend both apologies for the problems and thanks for the advice, all of which I took to heart and some of which I followed. This group includes M. Estellie Smith, Sally Fairfax, Thomas K. Rudel, Andrew P. Vayda, Richard Merritt, John Sinton, Seth Macinko, Tom McGuire, and an anonymous reviewer. Camille Bevere, Geraldine Brustowicz, and June Needham of the Department of Human Ecology deserve special mention for their gracious and enthusiastic help in manuscript preparation (and editorial advice). I am grateful to Barbara Jones, who helped me check references, a most valued task. And, of course, I thank Christine Szuter at the University of Arizona Press, whose enthusiasm and patience have made it all possible.

The book is dedicated to my family, by whom I mean everyone to whom I should have been paying more attention while working on this project. My family includes Richard, Lori, Bill, Jim, and Jeanne Merritt, Caroline Benard, and Bernard and Jean McCay, for a start. It goes on to a newer generation, and it includes my colleagues and students at Rutgers as well as my friends. The book is about "common" versus "private" property rights; somewhere there should be "family" rights.

Introduction

This book is about conflicts over property rights in nineteenth- and twentieth-century New Jersey and about the resulting court cases and how they shaped local and American common law. It is a study in legal, ecological, and historical anthropology and in institutional change. The question posed is, Are tidal waters, the shores they lap, and the resources they hold common property, open to all, or private property, owned by a few? The answer has implications for much more than the oysters that raised these questions in nineteenth-century New Jersey, reaching to public advocacy and environmental law in the late twentieth century.

The question of property rights in nature is complex and problematic, capable even of leading to personal tragedy, as shown in the account of an eighteenth-century episode of conflict over ownership of coastal property that introduces this book. It shows the importance of common rights to fish, shellfish, and game animals to coastal inhabitants, but it also demonstrates how easy it was to lose those rights in a colonizing society that had commodified just about everything. The fiction of owning wild things and places was one thing; determining who the owners were and should be was another. That was the political, social, and legal question in the conflicts and court cases reviewed. The introductory story also introduces the Proprietors. Their claims to real estate figured large in New Jersey history; they played major roles in many of the court cases discussed, providing a contested basis for private title in lands brushed and covered by the tides. But first, Jacob Spicer and his tragedy of a privatized commons.

The Unnatural Privileges of Cape May

Jacob Spicer's will was read one night in 1765 at a Baptist meetinghouse in Cape May County, New Jersey. Spicer died at the age of forty-nine at his estate among the salt marshes, cedar bogs, and farmlands of this southernmost tip of the state. Grandson of one of the earliest English-speaking settlers who came to Cape May following whales, Spicer was a distinguished statesman and one of the richest men in what was still known as "West Jersey."[1] Nevertheless, he died a very unhappy man. His will requested that a pamphlet be written and distributed to all the citizens of the cape, based on the second verse of the second book of Psalms: "why do the heathen rage and the people imagine a vain thing?" (Stevens 1897: 139). What the people imagined was that Jacob Spicer was wrong in buying up the so-called natural privileges of Cape May. He spent the last decade of his life trying to justify and defend this acquisition, which privatized the "broken and sunken marshes, sounds, creeks, barren Lands" and "the natural privileges of fishing and fowling and all the articles of luxury and use to be obtained from the bay and the sounds" (Stevens 1897: 112).

That such "privileges" were even available for purchase was another expression of the way European culture transformed environmental relations in the New World: by perceiving and treating landscapes and natural resources as marketable commodities. The consequences for native Americans and ecosystems were profound, as Cronon (1983) and others have chronicled. Less well appreciated but evident in Spicer's saga are their implications for the settlers and their descendants. The hunting, fishing, and oystering lands and privileges of Cape May became commodities through the colony's system of land management. Divided into west and east provinces, New Jersey was one of several "proprietary" colonies of England, settled largely through real estate ventures organized by groups of shareholding investors and speculators.[2] The West Jersey Society held proprietary title to Cape May's land.[3] The Spicers were major buyers of the holdings of this group, expanding their estate from about 400 acres in 1696 (Stevens 1943) to over 2,342 unimproved acres in one township and probably more in others by 1751 (Stewart 1940). By that time most of the land had been sold off, and investors back in London gave instructions to their agent, a Dr. Johnson of Perth Amboy, to liquidate the West Jersey Society. All that remained were scattered "vacant lands" and the "natural privileges."

At first, Spicer and others tried to form a cooperative to buy and manage the disputed lands and privileges. In 1752, 141 freeholders formed an association, arguing that although the lands had little monetary value, something had to be done to prevent an individual from buying them up. That person would then be in a position "to monopolize the Fishery, oystering & which nature seems to have intended for a General blessing to the Poor, and [for] others who have bought the Lands and settled contiguous thereto" (Stevens 1897: 112).

This sentiment about the social value of fishing would be voiced during later incidents as well. But more than altruism was at stake; so were property values: "many of us the Subscribers having already given advanced prices for our Lands by reason of the vicinity of the said privileges, are now unwilling to be deprived thereof." The idea was that the association would buy up the natural privileges by taxing members' lands. Members and their descendants would hold equal shares as "tenants in common." In the association's plan, beaches, salt hay wetlands, cedar swamps, and other natural privilege properties "at the head or foot" of privately held land might be sold to contiguous owners, but "commonages of fishing & oystering" would remain open forever to all members of the association regardless of which individual owned the property.

It proved difficult to get people to agree on the value of "a right so endeared to the people as this" (Stevens 1897: 114), a problem recognizable today in the challenge of finding ways to ascertain the value of ecosystem goods and services. It was also difficult to keep everyone in agreement on the matter—the "contracting costs" (the cost, not necessarily in money, of getting a group of people to agree on an issue) that make it so difficult to enact major institutional change that affects natural resources (Johnson and Libecap 1982). Consequently, the association missed its chance.

In 1756 subscribers were dumbfounded and angered to find that one of their own, Jacob Spicer, had purchased all that remained of the West Jersey Society's proprietary holdings and for the paltry sum of £300. How this happened was a matter of speculation. When Dr. Johnson, the society's agent, died, he willed the society £1,000. It was rumored that he did this because of his guilt at having sold Spicer the land and use rights "at a time when the influence of the wine bottle had usurped the place of reason" (Stevens 1897: 115).

Spicer's 1759 memorandum book (reprinted in Stevens 1934) is dominated by requests that he sell swamp, sedge, marsh, and other lands that other residents wanted and, in many cases, had already surveyed. In 1761, Spicer barely got enough votes to be reelected to the colonial assembly; his popularity was waning, and, according to his biographer, he "was being severely condemned by the people for what they believed were a usurpation of their rights in purchasing the natural rights of the West Jersey Society" (Stevens 1897: 128–29). Spicer was denounced at a public meeting on March 26, 1761, when he was asked to sell the land and privileges to the community association and refused. His diary suggests the pride and selfishness that kept him from doing the public-spirited thing: "[i]f I should see a bargain to my advantage, then I told the people I should be inclined to sell them the natural privileges, if I should advance myself equally otherwise; but upon no other footing whatever, of which I would be the judge" (Stevens 1897: 129).[4] He was truly a modern man.

In a diary entry for April 15, 1761, commenting on a request to sell the natural privileges of the Upper Precinct of the county to its residents for a small amount, Spicer showed how torn he was about the matter:

> this was a delicate affair, that I did not know well how to conduct myself, for I was willing to please the people, and at the same time to do my posterity justice, and steer clear of reflection. Recollecting that old Mr. George Taylor, to the best of my memory, obtained a grant for the Five-Mile Beach and the Two-Mile Beach, and, if I mistake not, the cedar-swamps and pines for his own use and his son John Taylor reconveyed it for about £9, to buy his wife Margery a calico gown, for which he was derided for his simplicity. (Stevens 1935: 186)

Spicer was caught between his desire to do the right thing for the community at large, including his reputation as a citizen in that community, and his fear of being thought a fool. His greater inclination was to care for his own posterity as well as his reputation as a calculating, sensible businessman.

Spicer passed the property on to his son in 1762, three years before he died. Over thirty years later the son, also named Jacob Spicer, recognized the moral position of the larger community and returned the property to it. In 1795 the New Jersey Supreme Court confirmed that he had indeed full private property rights to the natural privileges of Cape May. Ironically, this was done to clarify the much-disputed title so that he could return the privileges to the community. Two months after the court decision, he deeded it all to separate associations made up of the inhabitants of the Lower, Middle, and Upper Townships of Cape May. In 1839 the state legislature recognized these associations as corporations with the power to enact and enforce regulations of this common property. The communal associations were sanctioned in 1844, 1859, and 1879 by the legislature.

True communal ownership conflicted, however, with a ruling that all such property belongs to the state on behalf of the citizens. As is evident in cases presented here, the right of proprietors to grant out tidewater lands and resources as they did fastlands was questioned and eventually denied by the courts. By 1897 it was understood that only the state could hold title in tidewater resources, and thus the Cape May common property associations went out of existence (Stevens 1897: 140). By that time, as we will see, both state and federal courts had decided that the relevant commoners in areas brushed by the tides were *all* citizens. This is the "public trust doctrine." The state became owner of tide-brushed lands and trustee of fishing, navigation, and other natural privileges.

The transience of the (unusual) Cape May experiment in communal management of coastal resources should not be surprising.[5] Communal sharing of privileges in and responsibilities toward nature, the basis of the moral economy of many rural societies, gradually disappeared as legally recognized property in England and America from the sixteenth century on (Coquillette 1979; Rose 1986). Rights of common pasture, rights of fishery, rights of estovers, and rights of way might still be claimed, but their chances in court against more "substantive" exclusive property rights were poor (Thompson 1976). Property increasingly became identified with exclusive possession, hastened by the success of the enclosure movement in England and contributing to the enclosure and sale of municipal common lands in colonial America (Coquillette 1979: 808–9). This made it more difficult for those with common or public use rights to bring action on others for harming the resources on which they depended. The air, running water, seas, and seashores became *res nullius,* owned by no one and thus available for untrammeled exploitation by everyone, particularly growing industries and municipalities. Legal protections for common use rights, as well as other traditional and agrarian uses, called "natural uses" in the courts, were replaced by utilitarian prodevelopment arguments for priority and the balancing tests of economic efficiency (Horwitz 1973). As common resources became "no one's property," many of the costs of development were then forced on society and the ecosystem, and there were few incentives to develop technologies to control pollution or overharvesting (Coquillette 1979: 820; see also Horwitz 1977: 77–78).

In this setting, the revival of communal property in Cape May is remarkable. On a broader scale it is less so, adding yet another case of resistance to forces of change that diminish the survival chances of people (e.g., Scott 1985). It is also echoed in the work of anthropologists and others that describes the reactions of villagers in non-Western nations to the commoditization of material goods, labor, and natural resources (Apparadurai 1986), including privatized fishing rights (Helgason and Pálsson 1996).

The social historian E. P. Thompson (1976) highlighted the role of law in these struggles, both as a tool of the elite who stand to benefit from the enclosure of common lands and waters and as a less reliable but sometimes available support for the more nebulous claims of ordinary and poor people. This is a major theme of my book. The contentious nature of Spicer's claim to Cape May's natural privileges is duplicated in other historical and contemporary situations, as shown in the court cases and anecdotes that form the substance of the book. Making commodities out of natural places and things—as distinct from places and things "improved" or "created" by human agency—remains a cultural or moral problem even in a capitalist, market-driven political economy. As I hope to show, this dilemma was expressed in New Jersey history, where the common law idea of public trust was recognized and shaped by the oyster wars.

The Public Trust Doctrine

The public trust doctrine is a very difficult and hence intriguing cultural artifact. It concerns the largely unarticulated (Reis 1991: 6) and diffuse rights (Sax 1980: 193) of the public, itself an unarticulated, amorphous, and elusive entity (Rose 1986). Its general meaning is self-evident: something is held by the government in trust for the public. Its original form, and its more precise rendering at law, concerns patently slippery, muddy, and intangible subjects: waterways and the shores lapped by them, usually tidal and navigable. With roots in Roman and English law, it grants common use rights for some purposes to the public. Here is how it was introduced in an important case of the California Supreme Court, *National Audubon Society v. Superior Court (Mono Lake),* in 1983: "[b]y the law of nature these things are common to mankind—the air, running water, the sea and consequently the shores of the sea" (Institutes of Justinian 2.1.1). From this origin in Roman law, the English common law evolved the concept of the public trust, under which the sovereign owns "all of its navigable waterways and the lands lying beneath them 'as trustee of a public trust for the benefit of the people' " (as excerpted in Plater, Abrams, and Goldfarb 1992: 386). The doctrine has been expanded in recent decades to emphasize the responsibilities of governments to protect public interests in recreation, water quality, and fragile and highly valued ecosystems.

The common law is tradition in the making, constructed through the peculiar set of social relations and culture known as case law. The public trust doctrine is a particularly apt example of the common law. It came about through centuries of conflicts over fishing rights and ownership of the beds of tidal and navigable waterways. It was created through the assertions of fishermen and other people with common rights against those claiming exclusive rights and through the thinking, writing, and persuasive skills of scholarly, imaginative, and sometimes nefarious specialists in the law. Eventually the legal fiction emerged in English common law that the tide-washed littoral and tidal rivers (and/or the beds of navigable rivers, a frequent matter of dispute) were owned by the monarchy (*Browne v. Kennedy* 1821: 208); however, they did not qualify as private property (*jus privatum*). Rather, the king's or queen's ownership was in his or her capacity as sovereign, and he or she held these places as *jus publicum,* subject to the common rights of fishing and navigation held by subjects of the kingdom. Some jurists also maintained that if these properties were granted to private persons, public use rights remained. For Americans the clincher, created by American courts deliberating on the conflicts over shellfish described in this book, is that after the American Revolution, the people became sovereign. Therefore, the people, through their representatives in state governments, hold not only certain common use rights but the property itself.

The public trust doctrine also came to be known as the state ownership doctrine and played a role in the management of fisheries as well as oil and gas, beach access, the protection of coastal dunes, and other matters (Burrowes 1988). American courts recognized that the submerged lands of all navigable waters below high-water mark, out to the three-mile limit of the territorial sea, are the property of the individual states rather than either private persons or the federal government. In legal theory the state does not own the fish and shellfish of those waters because they cannot be owned by anyone until captured, but U.S. policy stipulates that the individual states have management jurisdiction over the fisheries and shellfisheries and other extractive industries within three miles of the coastal baseline. The state governments should manage the public trust for the benefit of the people. Until 1976, when the United States joined other nations in declaring a two-hundred-nautical-mile band of extended fisheries jurisdiction and thereby created a zone of federal control, the states were the major players in fisheries management.

Like much else cultural and symbolic, the doctrine is ambiguous and multivalent. It is peculiar in challenging the dominance of private property in ways that would seem to favor the relatively poor and powerless at times when great fortunes and properties were being accumulated during the rise of industrial capitalism. It is an "unusual legal doctrine" (Sax 1980: 483; Stevens 1980; Rose 1986) that continues to support public interests and claims that are often vague, ill defined, and customary against private property claims that are more definite and precise. Historically, as students of common rights in agrarian England have shown, private claims have won out over public ones in courts of law (Thompson 1976: 339–40).

The public trust doctrine would seem to be a "behind the scenes" principle in Western culture. It is rarely codified in legislation. Most often it exists only by implication, in the legal sense: "[n]o legislation imposed it as common law, though the Magna Carta made reference to eliminating obstructions in coastal rivers. The doctrine was applied to the original states, and later to the western states through the equal footing doctrine, by implication. Thus *Illinois Central* itself [the landmark federal Supreme Court case] rested on an implied trust" (Wilkinson 1980: 299). It is also implied in private property through the idea, expressed in an 1887 case (*Mugler v. Kansas*), that "property in this country is held under the implied obligation that the owner's use of it shall not be injurious to the community" (cited in Belsky 1992: 73).

Another reason for seeing the public trust doctrine as a background principle derived from more general notions of Western culture is that although it is expressed and given shape in legal arguments and opinions, it cannot be easily pigeon-holed. In the leading environmental law text, it is treated as coequal with federal and state constitutions as among the "fundamental environmental rights" (Plater, Abrams, and Goldfarb 1992: 57). However, whether it is constitutional law, common law, or something else is an open question: "[t]here is little controversy about the existence of the public trust historically in the United States. But what, exactly, is it?" (Plater, Abrams, and Goldfarb 1992: 375). Common law is supposed to be subject to statutory law, but the public trust doctrine has been used to overturn a statutory enactment. "A number of courts and commentators have indicated that neither the federal government nor the state governments can act to abolish the public trust doctrine. . . . As trustees, the state sovereignties and federal government are bound by the terms of the trust" (Plater, Abrams, and Goldfarb 1992: 375). Does this mean that it is a principle of federal constitutional law? Is it a federal doctrine or just a state doctrine? Does it apply to federal government actions? In either case, what is its scope? It has already gone beyond the tidal waters and navigation and fishing issues, but how far can it go (Plater, Abrams, and Goldfarb 1992: 376)? These are all matters of uncertainty and dispute. Another set of questions concerns terms of the trust, particularly the degree to which a legislative body can change and alienate the use of public trust resources, a question central to the cases I review.

The persistence and revival of public claims to common property through the public trust doctrine are remarkable given the decline in legal recognition of *res communes* mentioned earlier. *Res communes* also included recognition of the inalienable property rights of freeholders against damages done by others to that property. The main English common law rule was "sic utere tuo ut alienum no laeda" [so use your own property as not to injure your neighbors] (Coquillette 1979: 775). The scope was eventually broadened to those with common rights, making it possible to at least think about the possibility that common-right fishermen and others might be able to go to court on nuisance grounds against those whose activities diminished their prospects, a topic that will appear in some of the cases to be discussed. However, in the eighteenth and nineteenth centuries the status of common rights had declined precipitously. More utilitarian ways of thinking had made their way into law chambers and courts, making it possible for owners of furnaces and factories to successfully argue for the greater social benefit of their activities against the acknowledged harm caused to adjacent property owners, much less common use right holders. These changes played a role in sundering relationships between individuals and their environments, thereby helping set the scene, as it were, for neoclassical tragedies of the commons.

The public trust doctrine played a role in this process, particularly during the mid–nineteenth century, when, as will be seen in the cases I review, courts interpreted state ownership to mean the right to alienate trust lands for private uses and when courts accepted "local custom" as adequate tests for making exception to the doctrine. On the other hand, the public trust doctrine, as well as the sentiments and actions of "commoners" such as the shellfishermen who appear in the oyster wars of New Jersey, helped keep alive the notion of state trusteeship as well as the idea that some things were too important to the society and the people within it to allow anyone to create barriers to their use. Ironically, it took an extreme act of alienation to revive the public trust doctrine and give it major stature in federal law: the giveaway of Chicago's waterfront on Lake Michigan to a railroad company.

Today as always the public trust doctrine is open to different readings. To some it means strictly that the states own the lands and waters below high-water mark and that the legislatures of the states may dispense with these lands if they deem it in the public interest. To others the trust part is more important than the state ownership part. State ownership functions as a trustee for public use rights of fishing, navigation, sunbathing, and other valued activities in coastal areas. In this reading, the people are the real owners; their elected representatives in the state are acting on their behalf, and public rights of fishing, navigation, and so on are inalienable rights.

Public Trust and the Commons

My interest in the public trust doctrine is incident to my research on common property regimes in marine fisheries and my concerns about the analytical model known as the tragedy of the commons. Dissatisfied with the assumption that the "natural" state of marine fisheries was the highly competitive, open-access scenario that resource economists and biologists saw as inevitably leading to resource decline and poverty, I joined many other social scientists in criticizing the model (McCay 1995a). To be precise, it is less a formal model than a powerful story. In *Property and Persuasion* (1994), Carol Rose emphasizes the importance of storytelling, of vivid narrative, to the task of persuading others about property relations. She pointed to the narrative of the tragedy of the commons as a case in point, objectified in the image of rustic village herders deciding to put cattle and sheep on the village commons and led by their lack of exclusive property rights into the tragedy of trodden and sparse overgrazed meadows (Hardin 1968, based on a similar analogy given in Lloyd 1833).

Economists and biologists are more likely to use graphs for persuasive power, including the now iconic one that shows how increases in the number of boats in a fishery would continue beyond the point of diminishing returns under open-access conditions, whereas a private owner would stop adding boats at the point of maximum profitability, or "rent," which was likely at some point before the line representing the state of the fish population began to go down (Gordon 1954; Scott 1955). Numerous fishing boats compete for a limited resource with little incentive to conserve it, because what is not taken today by one is likely to be taken today or later by another. Accordingly, as long as there is any profit at all to be made, more boats will come into the fishing grounds, and soon there will be no fish left; the "rent" created by nature is "dissipated" (Gordon 1954), a term charged with moral censure. The power of the fishery narrative is suggested by the fact that the social dilemma of open-access systems has come to be known as the "fisherman's problem" (McEvoy 1986), and a simulation game called "Fish Banks, Ltd." has become a popular tool for teaching about global environmental problems (Meadows, Fiddaman, and Shannon 1991). Within fisheries, the narrative has played a powerful role in defining both problem (open access) and solution (either stricter government control or increasingly privatized fishing rights).

I am among those whom Rose (1994: 289) defines as "neocommunitarians," positing an image of people coming to terms with each other and the resources upon which they depend. Our point is that the tragedy of the commons argument tends to ignore and in practice often thereby weakens communal systems of using and managing common resources (McCay 1978; McCay and Acheson 1987b; see also Ciriacy-Wantrup and Bishop 1975; Berkes 1989; Ostrom 1990; M. E. Smith 1984). The images and narratives used to give life to this argument include manorial courts agreeing on rules for "stinting" the number of animals allowed on village commons (Cox 1985; Hanna 1990), Swiss mountain villagers maintaining common rights and regulation of the high alpine pastures and forests (Netting 1976), inshore fishermen who successfully claim and defend exclusive territories (Acheson 1987), and the often elaborate systems of "sea tenure" found among the reefs and lagoons of the Pacific Islands (Johannes 1978, 1981).

There is, however, a danger in "romancing the commons." Most of the commercial fishing I have observed in both Canada (Newfoundland) and the United States (New Jersey) has a long history of open-access fishing, which only within the last decade or so has been curtailed by limited licensing. Moreover, many of the problems experienced in declining fish stocks have as much to do with outside factors, such as unmanageable climatic and oceanographic changes, poorly regulated foreign fishing, and coastal development, as they do with open access in the local fisheries. Although there are important, often informal systems of local-level regulation and self-governance in these fisheries, including the management systems of small cooperatives in New Jersey (McCay 1980, 1987), an exclusive focus on these systems is unfair to the reality of the majority of fisheries and, as I try to show in this book, the long history of struggle for freedom to fish. Open access can be recast (and likely tempered with regulations) as a common use right and the fisheries as cases of common property management, where the principle of equality is combined with notions of the need for flexibility and freedom on the part of those dependent on marine resources. As I have argued elsewhere (McCay 1989a), open access is Janus-faced: it can also be understood as a means of breaking down barriers on behalf of capitalist expansion in colonial development, trade, and fishing, with the help of consultants such as Hugo Grotius, working for the Dutch East Indies Company. In any case, it is rarely "natural." Although freedoms to fish and use the foreshores of tidal waters and navigable rivers are claimed as natural rights, they arise from specific political, social, and legal experiences. They have been created and recreated, shaped and challenged and reshaped in human encounters and deliberations. In the courts these claims became part of debates that led to the public trust doctrine.

In order to make my point, I too offer narratives, these of people fighting about common versus private rights in the "oyster wars" and other encounters in New Jersey.[6] In the chapters that follow, which are organized around court cases, I recount many events where common rights of fishing and state ownership of tidewater resources were challenged. Sometimes they were successfully defended, sometimes not. Sometimes they played a direct and important role in the process of crafting the public trust doctrine. Sometimes their outcomes were influenced by truncation of the "trust" part of that doctrine to allow alienation of the riparian commons to private hands. The accounts are also about the push toward privatization that accompanied the practice of oyster "planting" and was promoted as a way to create incentives for conservation and husbandry.

The book is thus about conflict and contradiction within the moral economies of fishery-dependent communities, focusing on how people used and helped shape the law to cope with social and ecological problems. The major actors begin with the "commoners": poor fishermen and others dependent on common use rights for at least part of their living, who used poaching, piracy, and test cases to protect their stakes in the resources of the tidal rivers, bays, and seas with their vehement claims to common fishery rights. The language of "rights" does not arise unless something is threatened, and in these events, the commoners felt threatened by a second kind of actor, the expanding class of oyster planters and shippers, whose business depended on enclosure of parts of the marine commons as well as continued access to naturally produced shellfish. They too often engineered test cases as a way to seek protection for their claims against the common-right fishermen. A third set of actors is made up of lawyers and judges, who had to make sense of these conflicts within the inherited framework of common, constitutional, and state law and to articulate reasons for their interpretations. Somewhere in these stories, lurking in the background, perhaps found in the clubs and offices and very persons of the lawyers and judges, are politicians and business investors. They are also in the background of a final group of actors, the peculiar people known as the Board of General Proprietors of East New Jersey, who claimed to be the real commoners, "tenants in common" of all of New Jersey's unallocated land, including the foreshores and tidewater lands, with the right and duty to survey and sell those properties to private owners.

The book contributes to the study of institutional change, a topic defined and claimed by "new institutionalists" in economics and economic history (e.g., North 1981), among others, but that is much broader than that (Powell and DiMaggio 1991; Douglas 1986, 1994). The emphasis on information and transaction costs—the costs of knowing what is happening, of making decisions individually and collectively, particularly with unreliable or spotty information, of monitoring behavior and gaining compliance with the rules, and so on—reopened economics to political economy (Williamson 1985; North 1990; Anderson and Hill 1977). It helped create incentives for collaboration among the many social sciences, economics, and history in exploring the causes and implications of institutional change, based on the axiom of rational action (see Little 1991). The "public choice" branch of political science, which brings economic tools to political issues, is a central focus of work on property rights institutions through the analytic and synthesizing work of the Workshop on Political Theory at Indiana University (Ostrom 1990; see also Bates 1992). Anthropologists are full-fledged participants in this discourse, particularly those like myself and James Acheson (McCay and Acheson 1987) who have worked within the paradigms of economic and ecological anthropology.[7]

In her discussion of the persuasive power of narrative imagery in property disputes, Rose (1994: 287) describes the "scarcity story" of institutional economics. In this story about the evolution of property rights, a resource becomes scarce in act 1; in act 2 people scramble to get it; in act 3 they get tangled up in conflicts about who gets what; "and, finally [act 4], they create property rights regimes, which make the conflicts go away, while the rights holders happily invest and trade" (Rose 1994: 287). The story gains vivid and hence persuasive life from accounts of the development of territoriality among Canadian Indian tribes within the North American fur trade (Demsetz 1967) and frontier conflicts over land, water, and mineral rights (Anderson and Hill 1977; Umbeck 1981).[8]

The tragedy of the commons variant is one with no act 4, or an act 4 where failure to come up with a private property regime results in worsened scarcity and conflict, bodies lying about the stage and the scenery in tatters. But if the play is about oystering communities, this need not be so. Privatization of shellfish beds, like enclosure of common fields and meadows and placement of barbed wire fences around the rangelands of the West, is more feasible than privatization of finfishing grounds. Moreover, it also has a long history of enthusiastic recommendation. In America (and the Old World), enclosure of oystering lands was deemed essential for the new practice of oyster culture, just as the enclosure of agrarian lands had long been advocated as necessary for agricultural progress. Some of the New Institutionalists in the general sense do this today as "free market environmentalists" (Anderson and Leal 1991) who advocate privatization or quasi-privatization of rights to use natural resources and ecosystem services. From this perspective the persistence of common property claims is problematic (Libecap 1989). I agree, but I also situate the problem in relationships of social class and political power and in the contested moral economies they engender, following more recent work in legal anthropology (Starr and Collier 1989a, 1989b) and political economy (e.g., Scott 1985) and a longer tradition in social history, where my indebtedness to E. P. Thompson is most obvious (Thompson 1966, 1975, 1978, 1991; see also Sider 1980, 1986). Political ecology is a relatively new label for these and related approaches as applied to environmental issues (Blaikie 1994).

The phrase "tragedy of the *commoners*" is useful in highlighting the disregard of social consequences in many natural resource management policies. Accounts of the roles of colonization and Westernization in destroying local sea tenure systems (Johannes 1978, 1981; Cordell 1989; McGoodwin 1990) have become powerful narratives in this regard. Also influential are accounts of parliamentary enclosure of common fields, pastures, wastelands, and even fish ponds in England that occasioned distress, protest, and covert and "illicit" claims on privatized lands (e.g., Reaney 1970; Hammond and Hammond 1920; Seebohm 1926; Tawney 1912; Turner 1984; Thompson 1966; cf. Hahn 1982 for the American South). Even more so, and more outrageous in the telling, are accounts of the Game Laws of the late seventeenth to nineteenth centuries that made the taking of everything from deer to rabbits the exclusive privilege of the elite and at times made poaching a hangable or transportable offense (Thompson 1975; Howkins

1979; Munsche 1981; Archer 1990). In the law courts of New Jersey these historical images, as well as that of the signing of the Magna Carta, the great charter of English liberties, played a major role in arguments for the public trust doctrine. Another story used by lawyers and judges who reflected on the consequences of privatization was the sweeping and dramatic evictions of Scots crofters in the great "clearances" of Highlands properties for sheep raising. These and other stories and images were important parts of an evolving and never singular culture of the commons in New Jersey and elsewhere in the New World, a culture that played a major role in constricting privatization, even of oysters.

Outline and Themes of the Book

My study is organized around court cases. Most are about oysters or clams; a few are about fish. Some are about waterfront development. Focusing on court cases and the law moves the study into the realms of legal anthropology, legal history, and environmental law, particularly as it relates to an understanding of the doctrine of public trust. By examining a series of conflicts—some involving enough planning, actors, and violence to be called "wars"—that have taken place over property rights in oysters, fish, and waterfront, I show the strength, persistence, and contours of claims for both common property and private property. I show how "unnatural" the notions of free and equal access to certain "common" resources are by pointing to the long history of attempts to articulate and defend them against privatization. As the New Jersey oyster wars and other conflicts I describe moved into the legal system (which most did, orchestrated as they were to that end), notions about natural rights were linked with other ideas by lawyers and judges, becoming the public trust doctrine. This doctrine took shape in New Jersey and surrounding states in the early nineteenth century, based, it was claimed, on Roman law, natural law, and English common law. However, it was a specifically American creation, and very problematic at that. The court cases reviewed show clearly that this doctrine could be reinterpreted and contorted to support privatization, as well as the notion that state governments "own" certain properties in trust for the people.

The courts that figure in this narrative are mainly the higher courts of the state of New Jersey (its supreme court, sometimes sitting as the court of errors and appeals), federal district courts, and the United States Supreme Court. The time span is from 1806 to about 1920, with excursions backward to the colonial era and even Roman times and forward to the 1990s. The approach is twofold. The first is to follow major court cases for both their content and their contributions to an evolving common law. By itself, that would constitute little more than a law review exercise. The second approach, more anthropological, is to explore the events, issues, and people behind the cases and decisions and how they might be connected with one another. Anglo-American case law treats court cases as discrete, chronologically related to one another through holdings and dicta and rulings but otherwise without connective tissue. This work, on the other hand, assumes and asserts the interdependence of the law and the lives and events that touch the law and are touched by what it does. The approach is similar to the extended case analysis, or situational analysis, that came to dominate the social anthropology of law in the 1960s and 1970s (see Greenhouse 1986; Starr and Collier 1989b). It uses disputes—here about rights to oysters and clams and fish—to gain access to larger or crosscutting domains of social structure or culture norms in conflict and consensus.

The first part of the book offers thematic and geographic orientation. It features two oyster wars, one that happened in a northern tidal river in 1808 between a common-right fisherman and an oyster planter and another, much larger event that took place in the Delaware Bay in 1821 between New Jersey and Pennsylvania oystermen. The chapters introduce the technology and describe some of the social and ecological conditions of oystering in nineteenth-century New Jersey, posing the question of why privatization of oyster beds was as halting and limited as it was. The 1808 incident shows a court grappling with the problem of property rights in tidal waters and an early expression of the long-standing fundamental principle at common law that the natural products and naturally productive places of the seas should be open to all. Both cases show fishing conflicts as "class acts," in the double sense of organized conflicts intended to bring matters to law courts and conflicts arising from and creating differences in social and economic class and power.

Wherever it is possible and seems important, I explore events that led up to and followed from the cases, as well as who was involved, what the issues meant in context, and how those contexts and events connect the cases. I do not simply identify and follow links between holdings, dicta, and so on, from one court opinion to the next. In the second section of the book, I do the former for two famous public trust cases, *Arnold v. Mundy* (1821) of the New Jersey Supreme Court and *Martin v. Waddell* (1842) of the United States Supreme Court. These cases provided much of the legal basis for the landmark public trust case in the United States, *Illinois Central* (1892). The oyster wars that gave rise to the cases took place in the Raritan River and Bay, part of the larger complex known as the New York Bays and hence the subject of boundary disputes between New Jersey and New York that colored and shaped the events depicted.

Figuring large in this account is the anachronistic Board of General Proprietors of East New Jersey. Their attempts to make good on their investments in New Jersey real estate after the major tracts had been surveyed and granted provided opportunities for those who wished to carve private property out of the riparian commons. But the major point is that in the middle decades of the nineteenth century, American legal treatise writers, particularly Joseph Angell (1826: 124–41), interpreted English tidewater and riparian law as if it were settled, when in fact they, their colleagues on and before jurisprudential benches, and ordinary people fighting over resources and rights were helping create that law.

The third part adds shad fishing and waterfront development to the topic of oysters and oyster planting. The "wars" revealed in cases of 1812, 1831, and 1884 were over private property rights to shad fishing on the Delaware River, which became the source of the legal construct of "local custom." These and other fishing rights cases played important roles in the ways judges ruled on waterfront and riparian property rights in the context of struggles for control of the New Jersey waterfront by industrial capitalists in the 1850s to 1870s. The "plot" is how legal interpretations under the rubric of local custom evolved such that a court could agree to enclosure of oystering commons despite the public trust doctrine, as it did in an 1874 case involving oystering in the Shark River.

In nineteenth-century New Jersey, "state ownership" came to be interpreted as more that of fee simple proprietor than that of public trustee. However, the state gradually regained its claims to ownership over submerged tidal and navigable lands, at least in the courts, and a series of riparian commissions were established to grant out state lands to private individuals. These became the vehicles for privatizing tidal lands and the subject of more oyster wars, the truly *big* wars of New Jersey's coastal history. As shown in the fourth part, they took place at the end of the nineteenth century and in the very early twentieth century in the Delaware Bay, the Mullica River and Tuckerton regions, and, although more in the form of guerrilla warfare, Raritan Bay.

The last part includes an update on the oystering saga in a discussion of comanagement within those fisheries, particularly after World War II. I also discuss more recent expressions of privatization in the fisheries: limited entry and an even larger step toward privatization of the very right to fish known as individual transferable quotas (ITQs). In the conclusion, I return to a question that scientists and other observers of the situation in shellfishing in New England, the Chesapeake Bay region, and New Jersey have asked over and over for the past century and longer. Why has it been so difficult for oyster fishermen, courts, and legislators to agree to change the dominant system of common rights to tidewater resources? In examining relationships between resistance to privatization and the public trust doctrine, I note three major meanings of the doctrine in the period under study. The first emphasizes common use rights, the second supports the notion of state ownership and a weakened sense of the inalienability of public rights, and the third revives the doctrine of public trust and expands its use with the rise of public advocacy and environmental law, pioneered by Joseph Sax (1970, 1971, 1980). Indeed, I was introduced to the idea of the public trust doctrine as an interesting and problematic cultural entity when I came upon the articles of Leonard Jaffee (1971, 1974). He delved into the arcane and complex history of the doctrine in order to clarify major legal and political controversies in New Jersey over beach access on the popular "Jersey shore," severe pollution of some of the state's rivers, and property claims in the swampy "meadowlands" of the otherwise industrialized northeastern corridor of New Jersey.

I hope to do for my readers what Jaffee did for me: suggest the relevance of the past, and the events that made up that past, for the present and the future. To begin that effort, I ask the reader to accept my argument for an essential linkage between questions about resistance to change in property rights and the meanings of the public trust doctrine. I hope to show that they are causally related in the intersection of contested claims to oystering and fishing rights and the deliberations of lawyers and judges about those claims and others concerning waterfront property.

Oyster Wars and the Public Trust

Part I Common, Private, and States' Rights in New Jersey Oystering

Introduction

Oyster planting, a truncated form of aquaculture described in chapter 1, set off major property rights conflicts as people objected to any inroads on their opportunities to take oysters and clams "in the wild." These conflicts generated most of the major shellfisheries court cases in New Jersey's higher courts. The courts' decisions were part of the answer to the question posed in this book. Why was privatization in the oyster business so hesitant and limited? It is an instance of the larger question of how institutions respond to individual incentives and choices; the somewhat narrower one of the actual processes by which property rights are changed; and the more specific one of "[t]he persistence of seemingly perverse property rights in the face of what would appear to be obvious alternatives" (Libecap 1989: 3).

The topic was and remains interesting. In the first chapter I suggest that this is less because of its role as yet another instance of a tragedy of the commons than because the shellfish industry of the region did not fit the basic requisites of modern capitalist industry. Expanding upon that argument also includes more of the contextual information about the political economy of the shellfisheries that is required to make sense of the court cases.

In chapter 2, I take some chronological liberty by jumping ahead to the 1820s to review two cases heard in a federal district court in Philadelphia. They had nothing to do with oyster planting but everything to do with the rights of a state and its citizens to regulate the fisheries. The cases, which centered on battles between New Jerseyans and Pennsylvanians over oystering on the rich beds of Delaware Bay in Maurice River Cove, highlight another theme of the book: collective action to protect the commons. Virtually all of the shellfishery court cases that made it to the higher courts are demonstrably "class acts" rather than simply incident to conflicts over oysters or clams. The actions were intended to "try the right," whatever that right might be. My term "class act" is a play, of course, on the other meaning of class, for most often the issue of right was tied to problems conceptualized as those between rich and poor, one social class and another.

The law plays a central role in any political economy, and what was most notable in the history examined is the extent to which the law could be used to protect common rights. The 1808 New Jersey Supreme Court case discussed in chapter 3 is the first of many where private rights to planted oysters were challenged. This early oyster war (actually more a skirmish) took place on the Shrewsbury River in the northern part of the state at a time when oyster planting was just getting started. Popular sentiment that the saltwater rivers were "common highways" was set against claims of exclusive rights to the fruits of one's labor, in this case, oysters that had been planted in the river from elsewhere. The common law principle recognized and shaped was the rule that protected the rights of commoners to natural shellfish grounds, allowing claims of private property in shellfish only in areas where oysters did not naturally grow. This principle set the stage for everything else. It became the sacred rule of the shellfisheries and remains so to this day. Many of the violent episodes recounted later in the book came about because someone allegedly broke it.

Chapter 1 Oystering in Eighteenth- and Nineteenth-Century New Jersey

The eastern oyster (*Crassostrea virginica*) is one of the most valuable foods and trade items of Atlantic coast tidewaters. Great kitchen middens of oyster shells testified to its role in American Indian diets and trade. European settlers and their descendants mined these middens and used the shells to make roads, ballast their ships, and lime their fields (Lockwood 1883: 224–25). Abundant and easy to acquire, large beds of oysters were once found almost everywhere, even in the now-degraded tidewaters of northern New Jersey and New York (Ingersoll 1887).

Oysters provided protein-rich food for New Jersey's colonists: "[f]rom far and near came the farmers to lay up the winter store of 'Chingaroras' [oysters found near Keyport on Raritan Bay]" (Lockwood 1883: 225). The commercial trade of oysters was important from the early eighteenth century on. Oystering supplemented the income of many coastal farmers: "[i]n the early days, oysters were free for gathering and every farmer from miles around owned oyster tongs and clam rakes and obtained part of his living from the bay" (Anonymous 1940). It also became a specialized trade or one of the many ways that "baymen" or "watermen" made a living. Oyster trade—to the growing urban centers and eventually even to Europe—grew with the colonies and the nation. Oystering was developed early because oysters, unlike fish, are easily captured by people with a primary orientation to the land, and, even more important, they can be shipped "in the shell" and remain in fairly good condition over long distances and times. By the late nineteenth century, New Jersey oystering was a multimillion-dollar industry, and the state ranked second only to Virginia in the value of oystering.

Fortunes were made, but all was not well. The ecological problems of oysters began once there was a market for them. The abundance of natural beds began to decline very soon after colonization because of intensified harvesting pressure and wasteful practices like dredging shells to make lime and fuel iron-making furnaces, thereby failing to return empty shells to the beds, where they serve as substrate or "cultch" for the attachment of oyster spat for the next generation. Added were localized problems due to predators, eelgrass, and disease as well as salinity changes due to the closure of inlets to the sea or changes in the flow of fresh water from the rivers.

Oyster Management, 1716 to 1820

The early political ecology of the fisheries of New Jersey and the larger region was almost entirely about oysters. One of the earliest oyster laws anywhere in America is the 1719 act of the colonial assembly of New Jersey "for the preserving of oysters in the province of New-Jersey":

> Whereas it is found by daily Experience, that the Oyster-beds within this Province are wasted and destroyed by strangers, and others at unreasonable times of the year, the Preservation of which will tend to the great benefit of the poor People, and others inhabiting this Province, Be it therefore Enacted by the Governour, Council and General Assembly, of this Province, and it is hereby Enacted by the Authority of the same, That no person or persons whatsoever shall Rake or gather up any Oysters or Shells from and off any of the Beds within the said Province, from the Tenth Day of *May* to the First Day of *September,* yearly and every year, after the Publication hereof. (Reprinted in Cushing 1978)

In addition to this long closed season, the colonists tried to keep nonresidents out of oystering:

> That no Person or persons . . . not residing within this Province . . . shall not, directly or indirectly, rake, gather up any Oysters or Shells within this Province, and put them on board any Canow, Periauger,[1] Flat, Scow, Boat or other Vessel whatsoever, not wholly belonging to and owned by persons who live within the said Province, under the Penalty of Seizing and Forfeiting of all such Canow, Periauger, Flat, Scow, Boat, or other Vessel, as shall be found doing the same, together with all the Oysters, shells, Oyster-Rakes, Tongs, Tackle, Furniture and Apparel thereto belonging.

The language and specifics of these provisions remained with very few changes (such as the onset and length of the closed season and the specification of the length of time one had to reside in New Jersey to be a resident) into and through the nineteenth century and on to the present.

In the colonial and early state period, prosecution and arrests relied almost entirely on interested citizens. In 1719 leading citizens of the province were named for each county to execute the act for His Majesty's Service.[2] Well into the nineteenth century the oyster management system relied on citizen's arrests, working with local justices of the peace, and confiscation and sale of the offenders' boats and gear, half the value of which went to the person who had gone to the trouble of seizing and prosecuting and half to either His Majesty, the local government, or the overseer of the poor. The numerous acts that followed that of 1719 bear testimony, often explicitly, to the ineffectiveness of these measures in protecting the oysters. Thus the 1769 act noted that the first act "hath not been sufficient to preserve the Oysters within the said colony; and that Practices are made Use of, not provided against by the said act, which, if permitted to continue, will in a short Time, destroy the Oysters in the Rivers and Bays of this Colony" (Bush 1986: 585). One problem was that people were working the oyster beds during the closed season (May 1 to September 1) under pretext of raking clams or other shellfish; the other was that large quantities of oysters were raked and taken up for the sole purpose of being burnt for the manufacture of lime. The act made it unlawful to do either and empowered local officials (mayors, aldermen, justices of the peace, etc.) to enforce the law.

After the Revolution, the new general assembly worked at updating and changing colonial laws. It got to oyster legislation in 1798, when it replaced and repealed previous acts. There was little substantial change. The legislature repeated the May to September closed season for harvesting and selling oysters, and it resurrected the residency rule of 1719.[3] The next omnibus bill of 1820 (New Jersey Laws, June 9, 1820) established many of the rules and regulations that would remain central to shellfish management into the early twentieth century.

The 1820 act, and an 1817 one that it incorporated, protected the rights of oyster planters who wished to claim exclusive rights (see below). Another important feature of the 1820 act, one that led to the court cases to be considered next, was its ban on the use of dredges in oystering. The state of Virginia had passed a similar law in 1811, and in 1820 the state of Maryland prohibited dredging in its waters as well as the transport of oysters from the state in ships not wholly owned for the preceding year by Maryland residents (Kennedy and Breisch 1983: 157). In New Jersey it was already illegal for nonresidents to harvest oysters and own vessels.

In all three states the legislatures were responding to changes in the ecology and industry of oystering (Ingersoll 1881). The oyster beds of New England had become badly depleted in the eighteenth century. Beginning around 1808 oyster schooners, many from Connecticut, traveled to New Jersey and Virginia to obtain oysters (both full-grown oysters and "plants," as discussed below) for the northern market. The legislatures were responding to local oystermen's concern about this new competition for oysters and perhaps markets. Big investors in the oyster business responded in turn, once rail connections and other transportation facilities improved, by opening branch packing plants in Baltimore in the mid-1830s and later in the towns of Delaware Bay. Investors also put capital into the dredge schooners, particularly those used in the region of Maurice River Cove, Delaware Bay, the site of the most abundant oyster beds of the region north of the Chesapeake Bay.

Taming the Wild Oyster: The Planting Business

Sometime in the 1700s, people began transplanting oysters to enhance their marketability. Oystering was a significant business in colonial and early republican times (Kochiss 1974; Ingersoll 1881), and the practice of oyster planting was an important adaptation to supply problems and demand opportunities of the trade. Closer to growing wildflowers in a cultivated field than to farming domesticated crops, oyster planting had nonetheless many of the attributes of agriculture and demanded the protection to investment afforded by private property.

Oysters, unlike many other resources of the sea, are sessile. They are responsive to human intervention and are prime candidates for mariculture. Their habitats can be bounded, improved, and defended, and people can manage them to improve growth, disease resistance, and other factors. Three cultivation methods are used to raise oysters. The first is intensive aquaculture or mariculture: human-managed breeding, hatching, and growing out of oysters. In New Jersey, it has been restricted to experimentation and laboratory culture, although by 1987 a community-based attempt to raise disease-resistant hatchery stock was under way in the Delaware Bay oystering town of Port Norris with the help of state and university scientists. In the past, oystermen at times happily reported that oysters they had planted had yielded spat, or larval forms, for another generation, and sanctuaries of adult oysters were created in Connecticut waters to provide larvae for "sets" on prepared shelled ground (Sweet 1941), but directed efforts at breeding oysters rarely took place. The oyster planting of this narrative refers to a more extensive system of mariculture, where naturally bred oysters are moved and managed to improve the conditions of their growth or to adjust to market conditions. These are maricultural systems in the sense that shifting wildflowers or other wild plants to a cultivated garden might be called horticulture.

There were two types of oyster planting, according to how long the oysters were expected to remain in their new homes: transplanting and bedding. Transplanting involved the shift of small, young oysters, called "seed" or "plants," from their original beds to new grounds, where they were left to grow to marketable size, usually for two to four years. It was hoped that their new environment would be more favorable to growth and the production of oysters of desired color, size, and/or flavor. Ideally, the seed was taken from native *local* oyster populations, although scarcity in native local stock often led planters to switch from the "hard" native stock to the "soft," less hardy seed from distant waters, usually to the south.

Reports from the end of the nineteenth century show that native oysters from the northern New Jersey/New York region were still very important to oyster planting despite a dramatic decline in their abundance, but also that planters were increasingly engaged in the second form of oyster planting, known as bedding. Sometimes also referred to as "laying down," in this practice mature oysters, at or near market size, were shifted—often over great distances—from one bed, usually the natural one, to another, a planted one, where they were left "to retain their life, or, if possible, to improve in vigor, size, and quality for a time, not to succeed one season of warm weather" (Ingersoll 1887: 520). Bedding is analogous to the end-of-the-line feedlot for livestock. As Ernest Ingersoll, a world-famous naturalist and author who wrote extensively about the oyster industry,[4] emphasized, it was not oyster *culture* but "only a device of trade to get fresh oysters and increase their size and flavor, which adds proportionate profit in selling" (Ingersoll 1887: 520–21). It also meant moving oysters closer to high-demand markets or taking advantage of extra time or labor to move oysters from outer to inner grounds so that when market conditions warranted their harvest they could be readily taken. The practice is said to have begun early in the nineteenth century, when New Englanders, confronted with the demise of oyster beds close to home, began to import oysters from the south, originally from Great Egg Harbor, New Jersey, but later, and most importantly, from the Chesapeake Bay (Ingersoll 1887: 521). The coastal trade in bedding oysters came to be known as the "Virginia trade." The state of Virginia outlawed all export of oysters for bedding and transplanting purposes at the close of the nineteenth century. Although an illicit trade continued for some time, New Jersey oystermen were increasingly forced to find other sources and to face the necessity of improving the management of the "native" stock.

A Brief Survey of Oyster Planting in New Jersey

Oyster planting spread throughout the bays of New Jersey in the first half of the nineteenth century, giving rise to the conflicts that led to the court cases

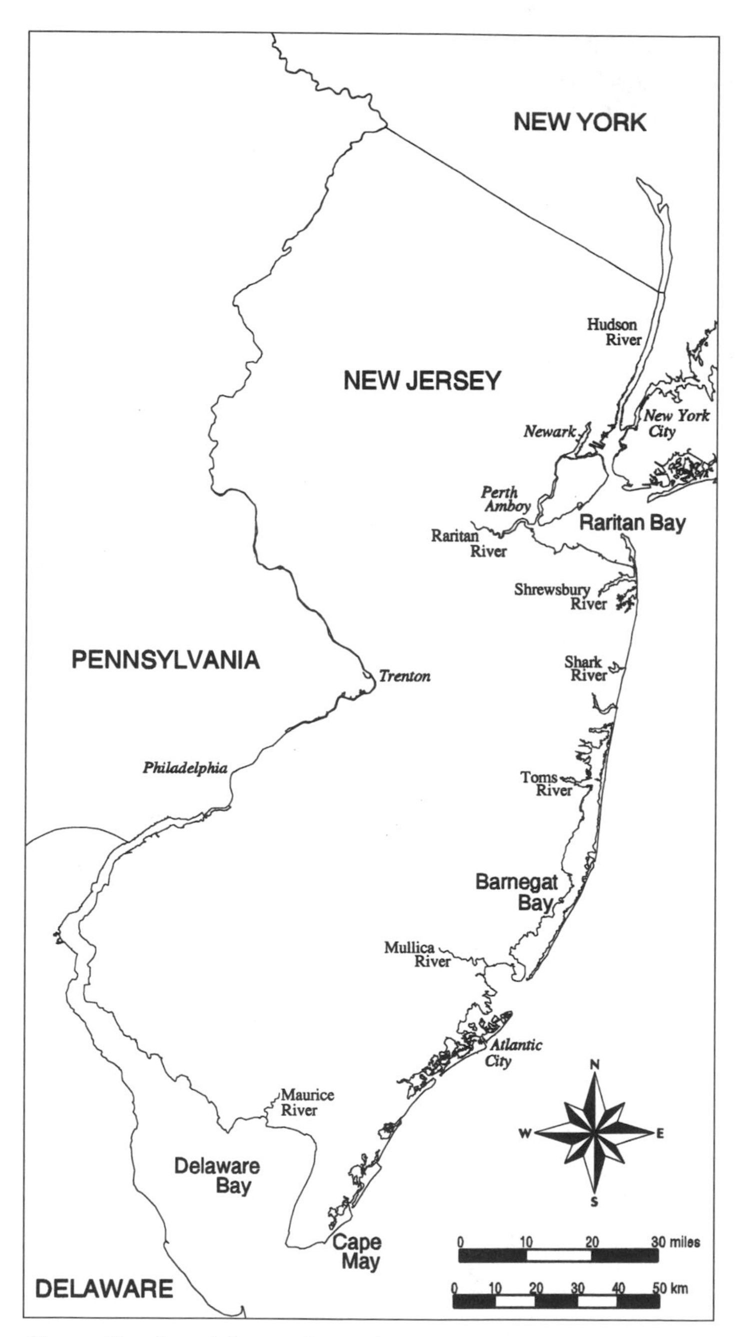

Map 1. New Jersey's bays and oystering areas.

portrayed in this book.[5] The major public trust cases, *Arnold v. Mundy* (1821) and *Martin et al. v. Waddell's Lessee* (1842), were about property rights in oysters in the Raritan River and Bay region, the early center of oystering (to be replaced in importance by the Delaware Bay as the nineteenth century went on). This was also the area of conflict between oyster planters and clammers and the site of a radical experiment in leasing private rights to natural oyster beds (chapter 11).

Oyster planting involved more than just transplanting seed or bedding plants. Reports on the Raritan Bay industry in the last two decades of the nineteenth century suggest its complexity (Ingersoll 1887; Hall 1894). It was based in Keyport and Perth Amboy, the sites of planting, shipping, and a few shucking enterprises, but included as well the activities of "seedmen" of South Amboy and numerous communities near Newark Bay (map 1). The town of Perth Amboy is important to this narrative. It is situated on an ancient Indian site for shellfishing and fishing at the mouths of the Raritan River and Arthur Kill, which separate New Jersey from Staten Island, New York. Oystering was its "chief business" by 1834 (Gordon 1834: 215). Perth Amboy was also the first capital of the province of East New Jersey and the location of the Board of General Proprietors, whose claims to real estate and governance provided controversial ways for people to gain private property in oyster beds.

Other major sites of oystering in the northern bays were the Shrewsbury and Navesink Rivers, large tidal rivers that flow into Sandy Hook Bay at Highlands, just inside the sandy peninsula that marks the end of the Upper and Lower New York Bays and the beginning of the Atlantic Ocean. These rivers were the location of the conflict that led to an 1808 case featured in chapter 3 that was a source of the ruling protecting natural oyster beds for common-right fishing. The oyster beds there were "owned" exclusively by farmers who owned land along the banks of the rivers and employed others to work their beds (Stainsby 1902: 19–20; Hall 1894: 478). The industry differed from that of the Raritan Bay, being an adjunct to farming rather than the focus of capital investment by specialized entrepreneurs in oystering. This was also true to the south, where many of the oyster planters were also farmers who took advantage of oystering beds bordering their lands and of farm labor during the off-season.

Shark River, one of the small inlets connected with tidal rivers along the northern coast of New Jersey, was the site of oyster planting at least by the 1860s (Stainsby 1902: 25). Shark River planters imported seed from Barnegat Bay and also engaged in attempts to cultivate their own, using tin cans as cultch for oyster spat (Hall 1894: 482). They worked within an unusual local management system whereby the country freeholders leased lots on the river. Shark River was the subject of *Wooley v. Campbell* (1874), in which the New Jersey Supreme Court

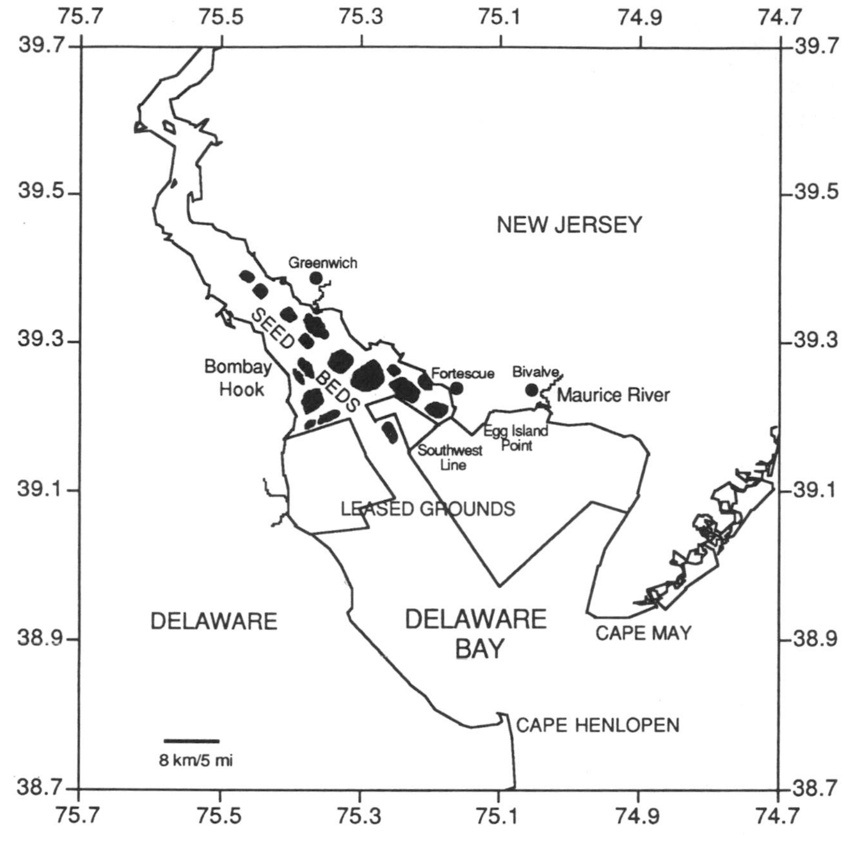

Map 2. Oyster seed beds and leased grounds, Delaware Bay. (Courtesy of Susan E. Ford, Haskin Shellfish Research Laboratory, Port Norris, N.J.)

upheld the rights of planters to the oysters found on their leaseholds even where natural oysters and clams might also be found (see chapter 8).

Moving down the coast, we come next to the broad, shoal expanses of Barnegat Bay, the largest of New Jersey's coastal bays: about twenty-seven miles long and from one to four miles wide. Like the others, it was created by barrier islands or peninsulas and is hydrologically dominated by the workings of narrow inlets to the sea. Immediately to the south and adjoining it is Little Egg Harbor or Tuckerton Bay, a continuation of Barnegat Bay, followed by a large expanse known as Great Bay. The region encompasses the shorelines of Ocean and Atlantic Counties and historically depended heavily on clamming and oystering, as well as other forms of "baying," often combined with logging, mining, shipbuilding, and other uses of the pine barrens of this part of the state. It was the site of several important conflicts leading to court cases and major policy changes, including *Townsend v. Brown* (1853) (see chapter 8) and a violent encounter over a private claim by the Sooy brothers in 1907 (chapter 10).

Small-scale oystering was also done in the small coves and bays of Cape May, but the largest industry was in the Delaware Bay. The great Delaware Bay oyster business benefited from the existence of extensive although scattered natural beds of oysters throughout the Maurice River Cove region, but especially in the "upper bay," north of Egg Island Point (map 2). Sloops and schooners worked the natural oyster beds in less saline waters "up the bay" and transplanted oysters to the planting grounds within Maurice River Cove. Delaware Bay was the site of armed conflict in the 1880s and 1890s, in response to attempts by some oystermen to create private property in areas known as natural oyster beds (chapter 9).

The class structure of oystering included a proletariat of tongers, shuckers, and others who worked for the large firms, owners of which were at the other end of the socioeconomic scale (mostly in the Raritan and Delaware Bay regions, often controlled by urban capitalists). In between were independent tongers and small-scale planters who might do clamming and other baying activities as well (mainly in the tidal rivers and coastal regions). This "yeomanry" was particularly dependent on common use rights and hence quick to respond to infringements of those rights.

Stalled Evolution and Imperfect Capitalism

By the end of the nineteenth century, vast amounts of submarine terrain surrounding New Jersey's shores were used to cultivate oysters through the technique of oyster planting. However, commentators like Ansley Hall, a statistical agent for the newly formed United States Fish Commission, argued that cultivation should and could be expanded further (Hall 1894). Pollution, disease, predation, and other environmental problems eventually limited the growth and finally spelled the end of oystering and oyster planting in much of the state. But a major obstacle in the nineteenth century was social conflict over property rights, succinctly described by Hall:

> In New Jersey the natural oyster grounds have always been carefully exempted from private ownership, and any system of oyster cultivation involving proprietary rights in them has been unfavorably regarded. The planters have succeeded in acquiring a

> legal right to hold non-producing areas, for the purpose of planting oysters, as against the individual citizen, but not as against the state; and even this advantage has, in some sections, been gained in the face of strenuous opposition. (Hall 1894: 465–66)

Many others then and since observed the same problem. A late-nineteenth-century nature writer (Stevenson 1894) depicted the evolutionary stages of development experienced by the oyster industries of the world in the terms familiar in his time. At first the natural oyster beds were held as public property and easily met demand. At the end, they were so depleted that the industry came to depend entirely on cultivated grounds and private property. The transitional stages are several. Natural beds, for example, served as seed beds for increasingly important private grounds. By the end of the nineteenth century most of the European oyster fisheries were at Stevenson's final phase, fully privatized and dependent on cultivation techniques, and some of the U.S. oystering areas were moving into that phase. What was interesting and disturbing to participants and observers of the time was that Maryland, New Jersey, and many other shellfisheries areas of the United States remained stuck at an early phase of that transition. The theme was echoed in Isaiah Bowman's presidential address to the American Association for the Advancement of Science in 1940, when he listed the failure of oyster culture (in large part because of resistance to privatization) as one of the three scientific failures of the world, the other two being peacekeeping and the erosion of tropical lands (Bowman 1940).

Why was oyster culture so problematic? One way to answer this question is to suggest that the shellfish industry was a cultural anomaly, a problem of imperfect capitalism in the midst of a society increasingly dominated by the forces, relations, and ideologies of industrial capitalism. From New England to the Chesapeake Bay, oystering and clamming developed through the nineteenth century and into the twentieth century in a way that defied expectations about the course of capitalist growth. The same might be said of finfishing, but it was easier to understand why changing property rights would be difficult there, given the mobility of fish; oystering was another story.

Nonetheless, conditions in New Jersey's shellfish industry clearly did not fit some of the basic prerequisites of modern capitalism even as well as agriculture did. According to Max Weber (1961: 172–73), the first requirement is the existence of a large number of wage laborers, free and forced to dispose of their labor power on the open market. The oyster industry in many urban and rural regions had access to such wage laborers, but open access and common rights to fishing and shellfishing meant that large numbers of people were not really forced to engage in wage labor. Independent artisanal production, such as tonging for wild oysters and clams and "progging" about the bays, was an option. The local terms "bayman" and "waterman" connote such independence.[6]

Another prerequisite of industrial capitalism is "[a]n absence of restrictions upon economic exchange on the market: in particular, the removal of status monopolies on production and consumption (such as existed, in extreme form, in the Indian caste system)" (Giddens 1971: 179). In the eastern seaboard shellfisheries there were no monopolies on the consumption of shellfish. However, there were status monopolies of a sort, or at least the potential for them, through local and state laws that attempted to exclude corporations and the more entrepreneurial planters from access to oystering lands. Thus, nineteenth-century oyster legislation would create Jeffersonian communities of independent, self-sufficient smallholders and grant them monopolies on the production of oysters for market. I say the potential, because in most cases the laws were not enforced, and in fact production and marketing were directly and indirectly controlled by large, powerful firms situated in New York, Philadelphia, Baltimore, and other urban centers.

A third prerequisite, according to Weber, is the use of technology that is constructed and organized on the basis of rational principles, particularly mechanization. The shellfisheries are glaring exceptions. The "Luddite-like" (Gersuny and Poggie 1974) fish and shellfish regulations that emerged throughout the northeastern states in the nineteenth and twentieth centuries slowed and even prevented the development of harvesting technology. Among the regulations that constrained oyster planting was the rule that no oysters could be planted and then rightfully claimed as private property on beds where oysters were known to naturally grow, a rule that was accepted as American common law through cases such as the 1808 New Jersey Supreme Court case of *Shepard and Layton v. Leverson* (chapter 3). Eventually, natural oyster and clam beds were demarcated as preserves of public or common fishing rights, even though, as will be shown through an examination of later court cases, ways were found to enclose even those "commons."

An important rule, variable in detail from place to place but to similar effect everywhere, forbade the holding of private property such as leaseholds by corporations. Yet another set limits to the size of the holding of any one individual (e.g., two acres or five acres). Finally, in all the northeastern states laws restricted the technology of oyster harvesting. In many shellfishing areas, only the simplest of tools—one's hands and toes, a long-handled rake, or pincerlike tongs—can be used, keeping shellfishing a job for people with strong arms and backs willing to work extremely hard for long hours on the water.

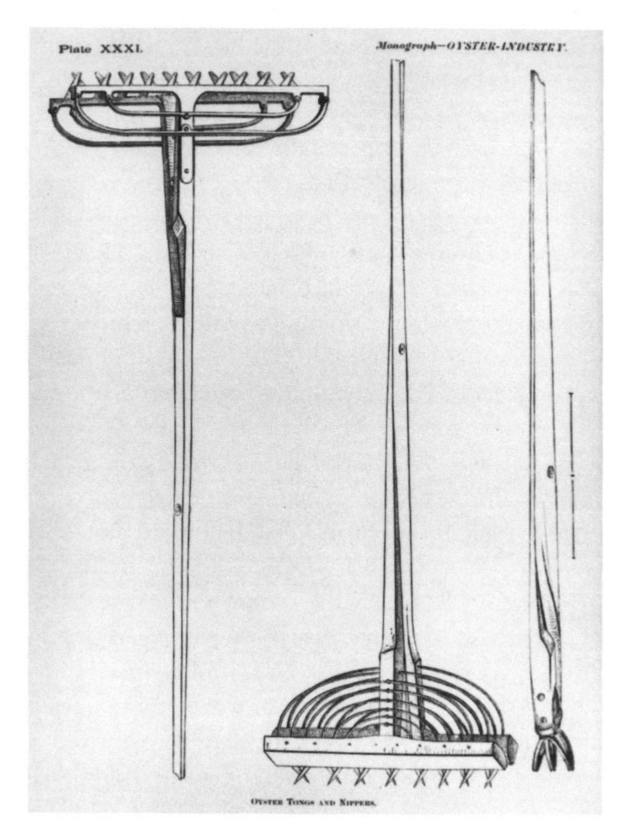

Figure 1. Oyster tongs and nippers. (Ingersoll 1887: pl. 238)

Opposition to mechanization in shellfishing began in the early nineteenth century, and in some regions, such as parts of Maryland, the bays of Long Island, and the Atlantic coast of New Jersey, it resulted in laws that remain and are actively supported to this day. Communities tried to regulate the use of harvesting techniques to protect the oysters and to protect one class of oystermen from another. An extreme example appeared in the 1820 New Jersey laws: on parts of the Navesink River of Monmouth County there was an old law against using any means of taking oysters other than "by wading in and picking [them] up by hand." More important, by 1820 the use of shellfish dredges was forbidden in all New Jersey waters. In 1846 exceptions, significant ones, were made for "planted" beds and the oyster beds of Delaware Bay, and until the 1960s the use of sail-powered dredges, but not motor-powered ones, was also allowed in Raritan and Sandy Hook Bays. But otherwise, the use of dredges for clams or oysters is still against the law, a rule that is passionately and sometimes violently upheld. These and other regulations are thought of as conservation measures, but what they do is distribute the catch among a greater number of people (McHugh 1972) and help keep shellfishing unattractive to big business. They were and are very disturbing to economists and investors in shellfishing who want more efficient operations (see also chapter 13).

A fourth characteristic of industrial capitalism in Weber's scheme is detachment of the productive enterprise from the household. In the shellfisheries priority was given to small-scale enterprises, although in Raritan Bay and Delaware Bay these were eventually marginalized in competition with large ones. The former usually involved a man working on the water alone or with his brothers or sons, although in some specialized industries, such as late-nineteenth-century soft-shell clamming, it was a cottage industry. However, wherever leasing or other means of private property were possible or the business of harvesting was run from large vessels allowed to use dredges (and later steam power), the productive enterprise was often "detached" from the household, organized in partnerships and companies. Nonetheless, fishing of all kinds, including shellfishing in the bays but also deep- and distant-water fishing, remains a small business that is usually run by families. Moreover, excepting the Delaware Bay region, opposition to participation of large corporations (and technology) in shellfishing is fervent and effective to this day. Even without such opposition, the "petty commodity" mode of production has generally endured in fishing while it has disappeared in land-based activities. Holders of capital find it safer to invest in less risky industries or focus on marketing and processing, leaving harvesting to small firms and families (McCay 1981a).

In the development of industrial capitalism, capital itself became constituted as separate from and superior to labor (and land). Here, too, shellfishing is problematic. Capital and labor were not clearly separated in all cases, and capital was not necessarily in a superior position with regard to ownership and the ability to extract rent or create profits. Everyone had a common right to the resource rent of the common property fisheries. This is, of course, the economic problem of the commons: in an open-access situation, and in the presence of market or other incentives, the existence of "free" rent from nature will continue to attract people and tools ("effort") until there is very little available to anyone—the oyster beds are depleted, fish and profits are gone.

The shellfish business is exceptional, however, in that there are few technical barriers to creating and enforcing private property claims and hence capturing resource rent, in comparison with fisheries for dispersed, unpredictable, and migratory species. So this condition did not have to continue, and from the start of truly commercial operations in the early nineteenth century, whether and under what circumstances private claims could be upheld would become the subject of contests on the water and in the courts.

Max Weber and others recognized the role of the modern state and its rational, legal administration in making modern capitalism possible. One of the ways that the state did this was through laws and the machinery of enforcement to protect private property and hence support the class positions of those with property and the workings of a market that depended on private property rights. But, again, the shellfish industry—like the sea fisheries in general—was exceptional. The situation was variable, complicated, and changing in the Atlantic states, but generally the state laws were interpreted as protecting the common rights of citizens to fish and shellfish and to tidewater lands. Rationalized largely by the legitimacy of tradition or English common law, but also by recourse to notions of equity (especially the particular needs of the poor), this principle set the stage for everything else. Accordingly, when the state was called upon to support the private property claims of oyster planters, it had to do so contingent on the protection of common rights, a fact that played a major role in curtailing planting and hence "modern capitalism" in the shellfish business.

Colonies and then states claimed management jurisdiction a long time before there was any explicit talk of "state ownership" or "public trust." A common management tool was a residency rule: excluding nonresidents from a particular fishery. The early history of oyster management is based on this and other regulatory tools, most of which had little effect in part due to the difficulty of keeping out defiant nonresidents.

The next chapter discusses two cases that had nothing to do with oyster planting but everything to do with the rights of a state and its citizens to regulate the fisheries. Their context includes, as we have seen, a long history of colonial and state attempts to manage access to the valuable oyster and shad fisheries, with closed seasons, restrictions on technology, and residency rules. The case that centered on battles between New Jerseyans and Pennsylvanians over oystering rights on the rich beds of Delaware Bay in Maurice River Cove highlights another theme of the book: collective action to protect the commons. Virtually all of the shellfishery court cases that made it to the higher courts are demonstrably class acts, rather than simply incident to conflicts over oysters or clams.

Chapter 2 Oyster Wars and States' Rights

In the early 1820s a group of oystermen from Leesburg, New Jersey, tried to take matters into their own hands to enforce new rules about oystering in Maurice River Cove, Delaware Bay. The court cases that followed resulted in support for state control over fisheries, including the right to impose residency restrictions. Using the powers of the state to impose restrictions and regulate access was not simple. For one thing, the state of New Jersey did not have Leviathan powers, certainly not for fisheries.[1] The acts passed by the legislature often ratified decisions that were really local in genesis, scope, and enforcement. Nonetheless, the courts were critical actors in the process, and people seemed quick to take their disputes to them. For another, use of the U.S. Constitution to challenge state statutes in both state and federal supreme courts became common in the early nineteenth century, playing an important role in the decline of legislative supremacy and creating a more even balance of power among legislative, executive, and judicial branches (Friedman 1973: 107). In New Jersey, the constitutionality challenge from Pennsylvanians engaged in oystering in Delaware Bay came very soon after the omnibus shellfishery laws were passed in 1820.

The federal circuit court case that arose from the challenge, *Corfield v. Coryell* (1825), was cited in nineteenth-century treatises on the law of tidewaters (e.g., Angell 1826) and is used today as legal support for state residency rules (e.g., Anonymous 1982). It affirmed states' rights to impose residency rules in the fisheries, using the interesting argument that just as owners of "private fisheries" had exclusive rights, so co-owners of common property fisheries had exclusive rights. But let us first turn to the case as it appeared in a lower court, the federal district court, in 1822.

Keen v. Rice

An anonymous advocate of the New Jersey side of the conflict wrote and published a lengthy report of the 1822 federal district court trial that is unusual for the extent to which it captured dialect, dialogue, style, and humor in the courtroom. The judges were named Ingersoll and M'Kean. John Keen, the plaintiff, claimed damages for assault and battery, false imprisonment, and the seizure and conversion of his boat against Philip Rice, the defendant. Keen was represented by two other Ingersolls: Charles and Joseph. Rice was represented by Condy, Newcomb and M'Ilvaine, Esquires.

The dispute was about access to the rich oyster beds of the Delaware Bay, the most extensive, productive, and enduring oystering area of New Jersey, fringed by the low-lying and marshy lands of Cape May, Cumberland, and Salem Counties on the New Jersey side, the state of Delaware on the other side, and Pennsylvania upriver. The principal planting grounds are in Maurice River Cove, defined as that part of the New Jersey side of Delaware Bay that lies between Egg Island Point and Cape May Point, with extensions offshore (Hall 1894: 495) (map 2). However, at the time of the conflict in question, this cove was used for natural oystering, not transplanting. Oyster planting was probably not done in the Delaware Bay until the 1840s and not on a major scale until after 1856 (Hall 1894: 499). Prior to that time, Jerseyside baymen concentrated on working the natural beds of oysters in the numerous creeks that meander through the marshlands that fringe the bay, especially to the north of Egg Island Point. Fortesque and Greenwich were principal ports for the oystermen. Many were farmers who supplemented their incomes by oystering, but with the rise of oyster planting in midcentury, oystering often became a principal if not full-time occupation (Hall 1894: 499).

On June 9, 1820, the New Jersey legislature established a closed season for raking or gathering oysters (from May 1 to September 1), prohibited dredging for oysters, and made it unlawful for a nonresident to take oysters from state waters. John Keen was the captain and Edward Corfield, a Philadelphia lawyer, the owner of the *Hiram,* a sloop outfitted for oyster dredging. The *Hiram* and its crew were arrested in the act of breaking all three rules. On May 15, 1821—out of season—the *Hiram* and two other boats were dredging for oysters—an illegal practice—in what were—contestably—New Jersey waters. The crew of the *Independence,* a Leesburg, New Jersey, schooner owned by Philip Rice but captained by Daniel Coryell, took it upon themselves to "enforce obedience to the oyster laws of New-Jersey." They seized all three Philadelphia boats and sold the *Hiram*.

Keen's attorney emphasized the warlike nature of the encounter:

> 40 or 50 men belonging to the township of Maurice River, fitted out a small vessel, called the *Independence,* armed with a swivel and a quantity of muskets, for a cruise

> against the [Pennsylvania] oyster boats. They embarked at Leesburg, and sailing down Maurice River, soon overhauled the objects of the expedition. On discovering the hostile aspect of the *Independence,* most of the oystermen precipitately fled. The *Hiram,* however, of which the plaintiff [Keen] was commander, being tardy in her movements, and threatened with a broadside in case of a moment's delay to come under the lee of the *Independence,* was with two others captured, and after being manned by a prize crew from the victors, sent up to Leesburg for condemnation. (*Keen v. Rice* 1822: 3–4)

A major issue in the 1822 trial was the intent and behavior of the owner and crew of the *Independence,* the New Jersey boat sent out to enforce the 1820 act. Keen's attorney called upon witnesses to emphasize the aggressive way the boat and crew were overtaken by the Jersey men. They called the *Independence* a "pirate." One said that when it approached, it hoisted the U.S. flag, and a command to fire was given. There was no discharge, but when taken aboard the *Independence,* the crew of the *Hiram* found, "in addition to the swivel and small arms, a large quantity of sharpened wood, to be used as boarding pikes." Clearly, the Maurice River men were prepared for a fight. The Maurice River men were also reported to have said on the return to Leesburg that they "regretted that the *Yorkers* had been permitted to escape without a single shot" (*Keen v. Rice* 1822: 4). The victory was celebrated by the New Jersey community as if it had been a victory of warfare: "[o]n arriving at Leesburg with the prizes, several salutes were fired from the swivel and musquettry, accompanied by triumphant cheering" (*Keen v. Rice* 1822: 4).

Witnesses on the Jersey side of the case tempered the narrative. They said they were merely taking precautions against a possible attempt to resist arrest and in fact had little other than the wooden boarding pikes to use. They had neither bayonets nor balls. The swivel, a small mounted cannon, was, according to one of the witnesses, "a nasty, noisy, ugly, disagreeable thing, fit only to waste good powder, and keep folks from hearing one another" (*Keen v. Rice* 1822: 6). Crew on the *Hiram* who served as witnesses for the Philadelphian plaintiff against the Maurice River men of New Jersey were not entirely helpful to the plaintiff's case. One was asked why the *Hiram,* out of the three dredge boats captured, was the only one condemned by the local New Jersey court. Disdain for lawyers is said to have been particularly intense in the early period of the new nation (Friedman 1973: 81–84). It surely figured here: "he sturdily persisted that it arose from a discovery . . . that she belonged to 'Squire *Corfield,* a lawyer in *Philadelphia,* and they wished to give him *a chance to law it to his heart's content.* The other vessels (as this witness remarked) not being the property of *lawyers,* were immediately discharged. This intelligent account of a judicial proceeding excited no little merriment" (*Keen v. Rice* 1822: 5, emphasis in original). However, the plaintiff's counsel persisted in the charge that the Maurice River men had caused severe damage using unlawful procedure: "[f]or this unheard of aggression, there was no warrant, or shadow of authority. The plaintiff, on his arrival, was frightened away by a shameful imposition, and the next day his vessel was condemned by a tribunal of the most extraordinary character" (*Keen v. Rice* 1822: 3–4; the text does not explain what was extraordinary about it).

The trial proceeded with more "merriment" and clever banter. Among the rhetorical "pleasantries" was counsel Ingersoll's account of the damages experienced by John Keen, erstwhile captain of the *Hiram,* after having been taken to Leesburg, New Jersey, in defeat. Keen not only lost the use of his vessel for the whole summer but apparently could not even go near it or venture out because of the rumor—a "shameful fabrication," said his attorney—that he was in danger of arrest for another offense. The Maurice River community treated him well, he admitted, but the "personal civility he had met with, and his freedom from actual abuse, were only an aggravation of his injuries. It was beheading him with a silver hatchet" (*Keen v. Rice* 1822: 9).

Finally M'Ilvaine, counsel for the New Jersey men, said enough, this is serious. The inquiry was important not only because of damages on either side "but as a question of right, resulting from the legislation of a neighboring state, and in which the feelings of thousands were interested" (*Keen v. Rice* 1822: 9–10). The question of right was whether the state of New Jersey had the right to pass and enforce oystering laws, and the main question of fact was whether the legislative power of the state extended to the place in Maurice River Cove where the *Independence* captured the *Hiram.* The larger question of right was whether the oyster beds should be protected to benefit oystermen and consumers or lost to rapacious greed.

M'Ilvaine recounted the history of New Jersey in relation to the oyster beds and observed that repeated efforts had been made to preserve them but with little success. With the coming of the dredge and the fourteen hundred men that the Philadelphians said depended on the Delaware Bay oyster beds, severe measures were necessary:

> Impunity had encouraged the rapacious, and the last instrument that was wanted, to complete their destruction, was the *dredge.* Stronger measures than had been formerly resorted to, now became indispensable; 1400 men, it had been said [by plaintiff's counsel], procured their subsistence from the fisheries in the Bay, and one of them, at least, had been blessed with a family of ten children. If all the 1400 had been equally favored, it was time for New Jersey to defend her coasts, or she might

> shortly be *dredged* by these *lords of the sea* from one end to the other. (*Keen v. Rice* 1822: 11)

He went on to say that the Oyster Act, called by the plaintiff's side "illiberal and monopolizing," was instead "an act of preservation" that would benefit not only the New Jersey citizens engaged in oystering but "all who indulged themselves in the luxury of oysters" wherever they lived.

The important technical and political question concerned how far to sea New Jersey's authority and jurisdiction went. The Philadelphians claimed that it went no farther than low-water mark, that the rest was "open sea" and hence federal water. The New Jersey lawyers contended that after the Revolution New Jersey had the same territorial rights to the sea as other nations, to the middle of rivers and to a cannon shot or three leagues from the shore at sea. New Jersey never ceded its *general* jurisdiction to the United States, although Congress could legislate to manage *admiralty* jurisdiction as well as interstate commerce.[2] This question had come up in New York during a steamboat controversy, where state courts established the right of the state to management of its own waters. But the constitutionality of this holding was not established by the United States Supreme Court until 1845 (*Pollard's Lessee v. Hagan*).

The defense for the New Jersey patriots, M'Ilvaine, took pains to point out the propriety of their behavior. Both the crew of the *Independence* and the local court that had condemned the *Hiram* behaved with great civility and respect for person, property, and law. The threats of firing "were but jest, and the salutes an innocent exhibition of the hilarity of the moment" (*Keen v. Rice* 1822: 19). The local court did its duty in seizing and condemning the two offending nonresident oyster-dredging sloops. The court behaved wisely and fairly by deciding to let one of the offending dredgers go, because the owners and crew were poor, "and they were discharged, with the very tools and profits of their offending" (*Keen v. Rice* 1822: 19–20). The *Hiram,* on the other hand, was owned by someone who could afford the loss and the cost of a legal battle. In his summation, M'Ilvaine tried to show how ludicrous the case really was: John Keen was asking for damages when the boat he captained was interrupted in violation of the laws of both New Jersey and Pennsylvania during the summer closed season. John Keen was saved from a Jersey jail because of the advice of his captors to lay low. He had lost a vessel that was not his own and claimed damages for the loss of a summer's oystering work that was illegal because by law the summer was the closed season for oystering (*Keen v. Rice* 1822: 22).

The legal importance of the case (and more particularly its successor, on appeal) had little directly to do with oystering but everything to do with sovereignty and jurisdiction and the responsibility of the state as a resource manager. Another attorney for the New Jersey side, Condy, followed up M'Ilvaine with a discourse on the law of nations, the power and duty of the sovereign to protect common property fisheries, and the particular need for such because of the rise and destructiveness of dredging. The territorial issue was the longstanding one of the boundary between Pennsylvania and New Jersey. Condy was followed by J. R. Ingersoll, one of two Ingersolls on the Pennsylvania side, who argued that the state of New Jersey had never before tried to exercise jurisdiction below low-water mark without the consent of neighboring states.[3] The system agreed to in the most recent interstate compact, that of 1783, was one of "concurrent jurisdiction," which also implied concurrent fishing rights. "But the people of Maurice River had taken another view of the subject. They were disposed for *experiment,* and the Plaintiff and his vessel became the victims of their *error*" (*Keen v. Rice* 1822: 25).

Yet a third Ingersoll, president of the district court in Philadelphia, charged the jury. Playing his own small role in the nineteenth-century change in relationships between judge and jury (cf. Horwitz 1971: 323), Jared Ingersoll took care of the legal questions himself and left the jury to deal only with the barest of facts. He told the jury that he had already made up his mind that Maurice River Cove was within the territorial jurisdiction of the state of New Jersey and that the oyster beds on which the *Hiram* was working illegally were properly the subject of state regulation. He told the jury to ignore some of the fine points raised by the plaintiff concerning the intention of the state legislature and not to worry about the question of whether a warrant was required. Instead, they had simply to decide on whether Philip Rice, the owner of the *Independence,* participated in the capture of the *Hiram,* and if he had participated, had he done so for a *lawful purpose,* whether or not the boat was afterward lawfully used. It took the jury only fifteen minutes to decide that Rice, the owner of the New Jersey vessel, should be acquitted.

Corfield v. Coryell

The contest had only just begun, judging from the fact that the legislature of New Jersey appropriated funds to help cover the legal expenses of the Delaware Bay oystermen in 1822, 1823, and 1825. In 1825 the legislature appropriated another $325.70 for "the purpose of a final settlement" to be paid to one Israel Stratton, Esq., for the above purpose. *Keen v. Rice* resurfaced that year in federal circuit court in Philadelphia as *Corfield v. Coryell* (or Carrall). John Keen's claims for damages had been very shaky, so in the higher court the lawyer and owner of the vessel, Corfield, became the plaintiff trying for damages. The defendant was switched too, the other way: the captain, John Coryell, rather than the owner, Philip Rice, who had been acquitted earlier.

The circuit court decided to ignore Corfield's plea for damages and instead dealt with the constitutional issues.[4] The court upheld states' rights to use residency rules in marine resource management. It distinguished common property fishing rights from the class of general rights protected by the U.S. Constitution. The circuit court observed that while the power to regulate commerce was ceded by the states to Congress, this was not so for ownership of fisheries and oyster beds within a state's boundaries.[5] These "are the common property of the citizens of that State, and were not ceded to the United States by the power granted to Congress to regulate commerce" (*Corfield v. Coryell* 1825: 5), recognizing the then recent New Jersey ruling of *Arnold v. Mundy,* which established the public trust doctrine (chapter 4). The court also noted that state regulations of oystering did not interfere with either navigation or trade.

Two clauses of the U.S. Constitution were invoked. The eighth section of the first article of the Constitution, the "commerce clause," grants to Congress the power to regulate commerce with foreign nations and among the several states and with the Indian tribes. The second section of the fourth article, the "privileges and immunities clause," declares that the citizens of each state are entitled to all the privileges and immunities of citizens in the several states. These clauses are often used, as they were then, to challenge state residency rules about fisheries and hunting. But the 1825 circuit court decided that the "right of fishing" was *not* one of the "fundamental" privileges and immunities referred to in the U.S. Constitution. The court cast fishing rights as exclusive, not public. Its reasoning was that private fisheries, where they existed (and important ones were found on the Delaware River as well as in England; see chapter 7), are exclusive to individuals; by analogy, then, the common fisheries are exclusive to the "tenants in common" of each state.[6] This interpretation made the states the equivalent of English manors or towns. The holders of the common right of fishing "are so exclusively entitled to the use of it that it cannot be enjoyed by others without the tacit consent, or the express permission of the sovereign who has the power to regulate its use" (*Corfield v. Coryell* 1825: 7). The legislature, representing the sovereign people of the state, thus has the power to decide whether to allow nonresidents to harvest fish and shellfish and under what conditions.

Strengthening this argument was the more familiar one about the need to exclude others in order to protect material resources. Presaging later courts, the

1825 circuit court also felt that the need to manage oyster beds might justify residency requirements: "[t]he oyster beds belonging [to] a State may be abundantly sufficient for the use of the citizens of that State, but might be totally exhausted and destroyed, if the legislature could not so regulate the use of them as to exclude the citizens of the other States from taking them, except under such limitations and restrictions as the laws might prescribe" (*Corfield v. Coryell* 1825: 8–9).

Residency: An Open Question

Corfield v. Coryell was the first of many cases in the nineteenth century to uphold residency restrictions under the concept of state ownership or public trust of tidewater and other wild resources (Anonymous 1982: 4). In 1876 the United States Supreme Court upheld a Virginia statute that prohibited citizens of other states from planting oysters in the tidal beds of Virginia on the grounds that the state owned the beds, tidewaters, and even the fish "so far as they are capable of ownership while running" (*McCready v. Commonwealth of Virginia* 1876: 394). The state could appropriate the oyster beds for exclusive use of its citizens because such action was "in effect nothing more than a regulation of the use by the people of their common property" (*McCready v. Commonwealth of Virginia* 1876: 395). This argument rested on a distinction between "public" and "common" fisheries similar to that found in the New Jersey case. The court held that fishing rights are not "mere" privileges and immunities of citizenship but are genuine property rights. Citizens of one state do not have vested interests in the common property of citizens of another state. Therefore, the state can give exclusive use of oyster-planting lands to its own citizens, in this case, Virginians. It is "not different in principle from that of planting corn upon dry land held in the same way."

Nonetheless, challenges to residency laws continued, especially in the Delaware Bay, where they were part of long-standing disputes over state boundaries and compounded by struggles for control over oystering. To a large extent the oyster industry of that region of New Jersey was developed by Philadelphia and other Pennsylvania capital (Del Sordo 1985; Ingersoll 1887). Residency requirements were constantly being challenged by Pennsylvanians as well as oystermen from across the bay in Delaware, and many, often violent oyster wars ensued. The local management systems depended on those requirements and were weakened by difficulties enforcing them.

The residency issue is intricately tied to the more general one of the meaning of state ownership, a major topic in the public trust cases that will follow. Do states "own" fish, shellfish, and wildlife to the extent of being able to determine who enjoys and profits from them? Is ownership a metaphor for state responsibility to manage those resources? And is it the kind of ownership that includes the right to sell off the rights? The first two issues have been reopened in recent cases. For example, in *Douglas v. Seacoast Products, Inc.* (1977), while the state of Virginia maintained its right to regulate and limit access to the menhaden within its waters, the United States Supreme Court took a much narrower view of state ownership and hence residency. It referred to state ownership as a "19th century legal fiction expressing the importance to its people that a State have the power to preserve and regulate the exploitation of an important resource" (cited in Anonymous 1982: 5; see also Lewis and Strand 1978). The court stated that "ownership" of fish and wildlife is "pure fantasy" until they have been captured. Other cases show that residency requirements are even more open to challenge under the privileges and immunities clause than they were in the 1820s. States now may have to persuade the courts that discrimination against nonresidents is necessary to meet biological conservation objectives (Anonymous 1982: 10–11).

The events behind the two cases reviewed show concerted, intentional social action to protect common rights in New Jersey's oyster beds, the layman's version of what became the public trust doctrine of the courts around the same time, as we will see (chapters 4–6). The question concerned which citizens held common rights where. It was also tinged, as in other cases, with a question of social class: wealthy urban investors and their employees versus the humbler watermen of South Jersey. Class-mediated property claims figured large throughout the shellfisheries, particularly where oyster planting had begun. Responses to oyster planting by fishermen who challenged any inroads on their opportunities to take oysters and clams in the wild generated most of the major fisheries court cases in the postrevolutionary history of New Jersey's higher courts. The 1808 New Jersey Supreme Court case to be discussed in chapter 3 is the first of many in which private rights to planted oysters were challenged. This early oyster war took place on a tidal river in the northern part of the state at a time when oyster planting was just beginning, and through it a sacred principle of shellfish property rights and management was created.

Chapter 3 River Pirates of the Shrewsbury

On a tidal river in northern New Jersey, sometime before 1808, two men took about a thousand oysters that had been planted in that river by another man. Were they thieves or simply exercising a common right? What rights were created by the act of transplanting oysters? What was available to protect the rights of the oyster planter?

The questions came up in February 1808 in the first fisheries case heard by New Jersey's highest court, the supreme court.[1] The chief justice was Andrew Kirkpatrick, and the other two justices were William Pennington and William Rossell, all three of whom appeared in later cases described in this narrative. They met to decide on an "action of trover and conversion" (taking property that belongs to someone else and converting it to one's own use). It had been sent to them *on certiorari* from the district court of common pleas in Monmouth.

The original plaintiff in the appeal was Leverson, who had been planting oysters in a bed in the North (Navesink) River in Shrewsbury Township at the northern end of New Jersey's coast. His attorney was Ewing. The plaintiffs "in error" (that is, formerly the defendants, but *on certiorari* coming as plaintiffs) were Shepard, Jr., and Layton, and their attorneys were Hunter and Stockton.[2]

Shepard and Layton were accused of taking a thousand oysters from Leverson, for which they had been ordered to pay three dollars. They appealed to the court of common pleas, which backed the first decision. Still dissatisfied, they took the case to the top. Evidently Leverson was also interested in getting this settled at law: Ewing, his attorney, explained that "[t]he action . . . was brought to try the right to plant oysters in the river" (*Shepard and Layton v. Leverson* 1808: 370). This would be the first of many conflicts engineered to "try" both common and private rights in New Jersey's tidewaters. Doubtless behind them were hundreds of incidents, detected and undetected, punished or gotten away with, that did not come to the formal legal system or, if they did, were resolved in local courts.

One of the reasons the lawyers and judges involved appear to have been interested in these otherwise petty cases—three dollars' worth of oysters!—is that they raised major questions about property rights, and property rights were viewed as the core of society. Oysters and their cultivation are difficult to fit into land-based categories and philosophies of property.

Given the early date and relatively remote place, it is a safe bet that Mr. Leverson was engaged in "transplanting," not "bedding." In any case, he had a definite interest in protecting his labors by claiming exclusive rights to their fruits.

To the Case

In the New Jersey Supreme Court, at its Monmouth Pleas in 1808, Mr. Ewing argued on the side of Leverson, the oyster planter, using *Blackstone's Commentaries* on the common law to support his contention that oysters were a special case in the law concerning wild things. Unlike a deer caught in a forest, which becomes the hunter's property unless he lets it go, whereby he abandons his property, "the act of planting the oysters in the river, was not an act by which an intention can be presumed to abandon them." He chose an agricultural analogy to buttress his argument: "the case of feeding cattle in the highway." One does not intend to let others claim the cattle when they are let loose to graze along the highway. He also argued that Leverson "had a right to appropriate what was common to his own use" (*Shepard and Layton v. Leverson* 1808: 370), implying John Locke's labor theory of property: that one could claim exclusive rights to what one has labored to produce or harvest.

Mr. Hunter argued in favor of Shepard and Layton, countering the cattle analogy with another: planting oysters was more like "sowing grass seed in a common." The act of placing oysters in the river "was abandoning the property in them, and . . . the defendant had no right to appropriate the place where the oysters were put to his own use." The river was common to all, including Shepard and Layton, and therefore Leverson was placing his oysters in Shepard and Layton's river! Moreover (this was a point seconded by Richard Stockton, the other attorney on the side of the commoners), if the planter's exclusive rights are established, then the common rights of others are extinguished: Leverson's act "was a destruction of the right of others, for the whole of the river might be thus appropriated."

Justice Rossell had nothing to say except that he affirmed the lower court's ruling that Shepard and Layton had taken Leverson's property. (Much later, in 1837, Rossell would appear as a judge in the federal district court, supporting private property rights in Raritan Bay; see chapter 5.) However, both Kirkpatrick and Pennington dwelt at some length with the question in ways that presage their later roles in defining the public trust doctrine (chapters 4 and 5).

Kirkpatrick introduced his opinion with a brief discussion of tidewater property issues that might come up if the case turned on the question of whether a "several fishery" could be created.[3] "Several" means exclusive, and there had been no claim as such in this case: "[h]ere, the plaintiff has thrown his oysters into a public river, where all the inhabitants have a common right of fishery" (*Shepard and Layton v. Leverson* 1808: 371).

Kirkpatrick's remarks provide contextual evidence for the very early spread of oyster planting in New Jersey. They also show that he acknowledged the economic importance of the activity and its need for protection but refused to allow that to weigh against the general principle of common rights, a principle he would bring to the center of the public trust doctrine in 1821:

> I am informed that this business of planting oysters in these waters has been carried to great extent; that the beds now there, claimed by individuals on this principle, are numerous, and of great value; that this right has been recognized by a sort of tacit consent, and the property protected by mutual forbearance. And as it has a tendency to increase the quantity of oysters, and at the same time, with little or no injury to others, to promote the interest of those engaged in it, I wish it could have been supported and rendered permanent, but upon the whole case, I can see no principle upon which that can be done. I am of opinion,
>
> 1st. That in a common fishery, such as this is stated in the case to be, no man can appropriate to himself any particular shoal, bed, or spot, to the exclusion of others.
>
> 2d. That this throwing, or as it is called in the case, this planting of these oysters, was a returning of them to their proper element, to mix with their kind; that it was in contemplation of law, a complete abandonment. (*Shepard and Layton v. Leverson* 1808: 373)

Nature Is to Culture as . . .

William Pennington also commented on the case. He addressed the question of whether Leverson had particular rights to the oysters he planted in the river because he planted them at a spot where "there were no oysters to be found" (*Shepard and Layton v. Leverson* 1808: 374). This fact was also addressed by Kirkpatrick. The attention they gave it reflected and helped give support to a general principle, one that still remains in the region's shellfisheries, that private property may be created out of the commons only where the commons is barren. The fundamental structural principle (Lévi-Strauss 1963) is that productive nature is to common rights as barren nature is to private rights. Common rights should not be extinguished by claims to private property, but if there are no fish or shellfish available for the commoners, then private rights can and should be exercised to make barren grounds productive.

Pennington allowed for this principle but denied that it applied in this case. Although the exact spot where Leverson planted his oysters had no other oysters at the time, the larger river was one where oysters were found naturally. When the oysters he planted grew, there would be no good way to distinguish them from the others: "[t]his case would resemble the case of a stranger voluntarily throwing his grain or money into my heap, when, from the difficulty of separation, caused by his own folly, I would be entitled to the whole" (*Shepard and Layton v. Leverson* 1808: 374–75).

Kirkpatrick too brought a critical perspective to the notion that planting on barren ground was adequate basis for claiming exclusive property in the oysters planted:

> The oyster, like other animals, propagates its own species; it does so, particularly, as the case states, in this river. It does not appear when this bed was planted; it does not appear, whether the oysters taken by the defendant were of the old stock, or of the young brood, or whether of either one or the other; the spawn of another bed, higher up the stream, might have lodged here and formed these; they are in no way identified, *they have no ear mark,* they cannot be distinguished. (*Shepard and Layton v. Leverson* 1808: 372, emphasis in original)

The chief justice took an unusually dynamic view of oyster biology, adopting an argument of one of the attorneys, that planting oysters "was a destruction of the right of others, for the whole of the river might be thus appropriated" (*Shepard and Layton v. Leverson* 1808: 370). Kirkpatrick observed that although the particular spot upon which Leverson dumped his oysters might have been barren, the facts that the rest of the river had natural oyster beds here and there and that oyster spawn moved about before it settled on firm substrate as spat meant there was no way to distinguish between the oysters Leverson had planted and those that had grown from natural larvae on that very spot of ground. Moreover, Kirkpatrick opined, Leverson could unfairly lay claim to the entire river if he were allowed to maintain private property in the oysters he planted, because *their* offspring would move about and settle as spat on other beds, which he or other oyster planters could thus claim as their own: "[t]he oyster, though once settled in the sand, is incapable of locomotion, yet from its mode of propagation, may people a whole river. Could it be said then, that the first planter might, by this means, secure to himself the oyster fishery in the whole extent of this water? And yet, if he can appropriate one spot, why not another, and another, and another?" (*Shepard and Layton v. Leverson* 1808: 373).

Class and the Social Relations of Oystering on the Shrewsbury

In *Shepard and Layton* the impetus was to protect the commoners against a threatening technology, oyster planting. At stake were not just oysters or even a technology but certain social patterns of production. What was threatening about oyster planting was less the set of tools used (which might involve little more than hands, a pair of tongs, maybe a crude dredge, and a small open boat) than the fact that, to protect their investments, oyster planters claimed private property in both the oysters they had transplanted and the ground they used. In so doing, they encroached upon the commoners, those depending on wild stocks. The baymen poached oysters and used the law to try to stop the encroachments taking place. The planters tried to get political and legal help to protect their investments. The situation was patently one of conflict, as recognized by observers much later: "[t]here is no denial to be made of the fact that the oystermen of this State are composed of two distinct factions whose interests seem to continually clash, and who have been increasingly warring with each other . . . , viz., the planters and the tongers" (New Jersey Oyster and Shell Commission 1901: 105).

Technologies of oystering and property rights are intertwined with social relations of production such that debates about property rights are also—although not always explicitly—debates about the nature of work and the distribution of rewards. The relations of production in wild oystering, where, at least in shallower waters, a solitary tonger might work independently, were different from those of highly developed oyster planting, where the solitary tonger was likely to become a wage laborer on a dredge boat or an oyster shucker or packer on a piecework basis onshore: the difference between artisanal or petty commodity and capitalist social relations of production.

Social class came to separate tongers from planters throughout the range of oystering but rarely more obviously than on the Shrewsbury. The North, or Navesink, and the Shrewsbury Rivers of the northern coast of New Jersey are large, interconnected estuaries. By the latter half of the nineteenth century they were very important centers of three fishing industries: oyster planting, crabbing, and clamming for the soft clam (*Mya avenaria*). Eeling, fishing, and harvesting of the hard clam (*Mercenaria mercenaria*) were also done on "the Shrewsbury" (a generic term for both rivers). For a while, during one of the times in which there was a direct inlet to the sea rather than along Sandy Hook, around which one had to voyage to get to the ocean, people who lived in scattered farms and small villages on these rivers also fished for bluefish, cod, and other finfish in the ocean. However, the closure of this inlet in 1848 made it difficult, although not impossible (boats were dragged over the narrow barrier beach to the sea), and soon the small "fish-landing" community of Nauvoo was founded in the area of present Sea Bright. "The Shrewsbury" became almost entirely a "bayman" or "riverman" habitat.

The rivers go inland great distances, into some of the richest farming country of the coastal plain of northern New Jersey. While some baymen owned or tenanted small farms, the majority worked seasonally or occasionally for prosperous farmers or were hired on barges and ships that transported farm produce and shellfish, crabs, and fish out to Sandy Hook Bay and thence a short sail across the New York Bays to Manhattan and market. The oyster planters of the Shrewsbury were generally prosperous farmers who hired their farm laborers or baymen to work the oyster grounds, in contrast to the oyster planters of Raritan Bay to the northwest and Delaware Bay to the south, where planting was a more specialized and heavily capitalized activity. The heady development of the fisheries of the Shrewsbury in the latter half of the nineteenth century was due not only to abundant natural resources but also, and especially, to the proximity of this rich estuary to a major consumer market, New York City. The natural graces and proximity of the Shrewsbury and Navesink also drew the elite of the metropolises of New York and northern New Jersey who built summer "cottages" that were really mansions, just as the nearby barrier beach became the "Riviera" of the Middle Atlantic. Social class differences were extreme, and the baymen and other fishermen were truly marginal.

The Spirits of Shepard and Layton

In later court cases the law concerning "natural" beds and oyster culture was based on less dynamic views of oyster biology. It is probable that, with increased experience in oyster planting, people came to recognize the unlikelihood of the "peopling" of an entire river by the offspring of oysters planted in one spot. Planters found that, no matter how hard they tried, they rarely got a "natural set" out of oysters that they had transplanted from another place.

No matter to Shepard, Layton, and other Shrewsbury rivermen: the common right of fishery was secured for the time being. The court decision also clarified that what was required for an action of trespass was showing that the oysters taken by people fishing under common right were actually planted on a barren piece of tidal land, and this required clear staking as well as agreement about whether the land was indeed naturally bereft of oysters. So oyster planters had guidance, too, and they prospered in the Shrewsbury River system, gradually taking over the entire system as their activities and those of the commoners depleted the natural oyster beds.

Within about forty years after the 1808 court case, the natural oyster beds of the Shrewsbury River system had virtually disappeared (Hall 1894; Ingersoll 1887; Stainsby 1902). By the mid–nineteenth century the only oysters there were transplanted small seed from the Raritan River and Newark Bay and larger plants from Long Island Sound or the Chesapeake Bay. By the end of the nineteenth century, the native Shrewsbury oysters were "practically extinct," and transplanting oysters seemed not to work either because of changes in the barrier beach system that protected the Shrewsbury and Navesink Rivers from the higher salinity of the sea (New Jersey Oyster Commission 1902: 9). The 1901 reported catch of the Shrewsbury River system was worth $7,168. In 1853 it had been worth about $200,000 (Stainsby 1902: 23). This tragedy of the commons was not entirely due to overharvesting. By the end of the nineteenth century sewage from the town of Red Bank and from smaller villages and individual homes was recognized as the source of disease-carrying shellfish; farm practices added to the effects of storms on coastal morphology to silt up shellfish beds and alter other natural parameters.

In 1902 the fifteen planters left in the area pleaded for legislative help, according to the report of an investigative committee led by William Stainsby (Stainsby 1902: 22). Their problems had been many. They lost mightily from the parasitic oyster drill (believed to have come in a shipment of seed from Connecticut), from the high cost of imported oyster seed, and from disastrous changes in the salinity of parts of the river occasioned by a storm that erected a sand barrier across the mouth of the river and another that had created a new inlet through Sandy Hook. The predations of the baymen made oyster planting difficult too: "[b]ut although strange enemies to oyster life, and unlooked for causes of destruction to it come and go, the river pirate or oyster thief is with us always" (Stainsby 1902: 22).

The "pirates" were people who claimed to have common right to the planted oysters, and thus they carried out their "depredations" quite openly. The spirits of Shepard and Layton haunted the river long after the extinction of the native oysters. The people fishing under common right (whom I sometimes call "commoners") had no natural oysters left but retained their audacity as river pirates and their flexibility as baymen, constructing a subculture that remains today in coastal towns of the vicinity (McCay 1981b, 1984).

At the turn of this century the subculture of the commoners was particularly creative, working with the old structural rule that declares that natural grounds are common property while barren ones can be private property. According to Stainsby, the river pirates refused to acknowledge any claim to private property in the river other than a lease system sanctioned by the legislature, a system that had been created for the other oystermen in the state by this time. For some reason, the Shrewsbury oyster planters had failed to obtain help from the legislature, so the pirates chose to interpret the law creatively. Elsewhere in the state, leases of oyster-planting ground from the state were allowed only where there were no natural oyster beds. Leases did not exist on the Navesink and Shrewsbury; ergo, these must be natural oyster beds: "[t]hese people take the ground that the planters having no leases, makes all oyster deposits here natural beds, from which all, regardless of who has planted the seed, have an equal right to take oysters" (Stainsby 1902: 22). No matter that the last truly "natural" oystering was reported in 1868 (Stainsby 1902: 21)!

Without help from the state legislature, including not only laws but funds for watchmen and patrols, which were rarely adequate to the task but kept things lively, the planters had only their own defenses: "[t]he enterprising planter who sows the seed, without which the river would soon become barren of oyster life, is often obliged to rely on his shot gun to aid him in gathering the crop for which he has expended his labor and money. This state of things exists at the present time" (Stainsby 1902: 21).

The pirates played no small role in this decline, interpreted in 1902 as "almost to the point of extinction." Elsewhere in the state, pirates also evoked outcries of suffering and loss from oyster planters and those who solicited their opinions. Their actions—"theft" from planted beds and the political and legal action they took to obstruct the development of state-sanctioned private tenure for the planters—were widely blamed for the slow and uncertain development of New Jersey's oystering industry.

The major obstacle to privatization in New Jersey and elsewhere was the refusal of oystermen and clammers fishing "under common right" to acknowledge claims of planters to either the oysters they had planted or the submarine ground on which they were planted, or both. Property claims are only as good as the local social agreements that encourage compliance with them and the legal system available to enforce them. Both were problematic for oyster planters. Planters had trouble defending their claims to oystering grounds and the oysters they planted on them. Apart from some state leaseholds as early as 1824 in the Raritan Bay area (chapter 5) and by the 1860s in Shark River (chapter 8), property rights in cultivated beds depended on poorly defined riparian rights, court interpretations of various rules that developed, and "the flimsy right of occupation." These claims were continuously subject to dispute. It was not until 1899 that the state set up a comprehensive and enforceable system of protection for planters as well as a way to manage conflicts between planters, tongers, and clammers. It was first established in the Delaware Bay/Maurice River Cove Industry. In 1902 it was extended to the Raritan Bay and Ocean County (Barnegat and Tuckerton Bays), in 1905 to Atlantic County, and in 1907 to Cape May County. Oyster planting grew long before good protection was available, but it was held in check by insecurity of tenure and the claims of people objecting to privatization of oysters and shellfishing grounds in the bays.

Tongers like Shepard and Layton were afraid of losing ground, literally and figuratively, to the planters. Much more was at stake, including access to markets, the social relations of production, and the nature of community, but the focus in courts and the legislature was on oysters and oyster grounds. The planters, in turn, bemoaned the losses they experienced from poaching and from lost opportunities because of the obstacles the tongers placed before their attempts to expand planting. There, too, more was at stake; to the above list should be added the moral claims of "progress" and "science," usually on the side of the planters, against the morality of "independence" and "self-sufficiency," usually on the side of the tongers. The conflict has never been the subject of a movie or novel, but it was as intense as and very similar to those that triggered the range wars of the Far West. The outcome varied; in the Raritan and Delaware Bays, where the resource base and locational factors attracted large capital, the tongers did less well than they did on the coast. But they persisted everywhere, not without help from the courts and the evolving public trust doctrine.

The common law principle recognized and shaped in *Shepard and Layton* was the rule that protected the rights of commoners to natural shellfish grounds by allowing claims of private property in shellfish only in areas where oysters did not naturally grow. This principle set the stage for everything else. It became the sacred rule of the shellfisheries. It was built into most shellfish statutes, was upheld by later court cases (see *State v. Taylor* 1858),[4] and is central to the state's shellfish-ground leasing policy today. Many of the violent episodes recounted later came about because someone allegedly violated it.

But the legal principle did not resolve conflicts between planters and tongers. *Shepard and Layton* confirmed that oyster planters could not expect any legal support for their claims to exclusive property in oysters that they planted on beds where oysters naturally grew. However, much was unsettled. Leverson had been foolhardy for not clearly staking his oysters. By not staking them he made it difficult to tell whether the oysters taken by the rivermen were the ones he planted or others. It was not clear whether staked oysters could remain private property or whether they too were "abandoned" to the commoners. As we will see, the Raritan River case to be discussed next had little to add to this question, because a farmer had been foolish enough to plant on a natural oyster bed even though he staked his claim.

The next chapter features a far more famous case that addressed a second major issue—who could own underwater land and under what conditions—and became the basic statement about public trust in New Jersey. What the 1821 Raritan River case, *Arnold v. Mundy,* addressed that was left in doubt by the Shrewsbury case was whether a person could also have exclusive property in the submarine land used for oyster planting. Leverson, the oyster planter in the Shrewsbury case, did not claim ownership of the river bottom, nor did he seem to be a riverside farm owner. He was "merely a wayfaring man, who dropt his oysters in a navigable river," and according to one of Arnold's lawyers, "[a]t the time when that case was decided it seemed quite clear, from the anxiety manifested by the judges to protect planted oysters, that if he had been owner of the soil he would have been successful" (*Arnold v. Mundy* 1821: 49). Arnold, on the other hand, was anything but a wayfaring man; he was a man of property, at least 175 acres of it. The question was whether he had even more, under salt water.

Part II The Public Trust Doctrine

Introduction

As the oyster wars and other conflicts I describe moved into the legal system (which most did, orchestrated as they were to that end), lawyers and judges linked notions about natural rights with other ideas that together became the public trust doctrine. This doctrine took shape in New Jersey and surrounding states in the early nineteenth century, based, it was claimed, on Roman law, natural law, and English common law. However, it was a specifically American creation, and very problematic at that.

An anachronistic institution is involved in the events and my narrative of them: the Board of General Proprietors of East New Jersey, whose attempts to make good on their investments in New Jersey real estate after the major tracts had been surveyed and granted provided opportunities for those who wished to carve private property out of the riparian commons. But the major point of this section is that in the middle decades of the nineteenth century American legal treatise writers, particularly Roger Angell (1826: 124–41), interpreted English tidewater and riparian law as if it were settled, when in fact they, their colleagues on and before jurisprudential benches, and ordinary people fighting over resources and rights were helping create that law.

Chapter 4, then, describes the 1818 attempts by oystermen to "try the right" on the Raritan River against a farmer who had fenced off the oyster bed in front of his farm. This led to the state supreme court case of *Arnold v. Mundy* (1821), where Chief Justice Kirkpatrick applied his understanding of the public trust doctrine to the common law of New Jersey. The "sovereign" was the owner of lands under mean high tidewater; since the American Revolution the people were sovereign, and thus they were owners through their representatives in state government. The text of the case also shows contested views of law and history. What was the meaning of the colonization of New Jersey? Was it a business transaction through the Proprietors? Or was it also the creation of a society and recognition of a culture that included a "birthright" such as the liberty to obtain food and livelihood from the waters?

Chapter 5 shows the tight linkage of events to the United States Supreme Court case of *Martin v. Waddell* (1842), as the Proprietors and their associates tried to establish property rights to waterfront and submerged lands as against the state. My attempt to contextualize these cases also unearthed another oyster war, in 1827, over the question of interstate boundaries and residency rules that had also figured in the 1822 case discussed in chapter 2, but this time between New Jersey and New York. Although the Proprietors were successful in lower federal court against the state-ownership rule of the public trust doctrine, at the Supreme Court, Chief Justice Roger Taney repeated most of what Kirkpatrick had said. This chapter also develops the argument that the public trust doctrine, in its American form, was indeed a cultural invention although at the time legitimized as one of the features of English common law deemed important to the new nation.

Chapter 4 *Arnold v. Mundy* and the Public Trust Doctrine

One day in 1818 Benajah Mundy led a fleet of oyster skiffs on the Raritan River. Their destination was a spot marked by some slender willow twigs not far from the riverbank in Amboy Township. This was an area of once spectacular and still, at that time, impressive shellfishing, especially for oysters, part of the "Great Beds" that extended from several miles up this slow, meandering river out into Raritan Bay.

Mundy and his gang used their long-handled, scissorlike oyster tongs to take up some of this succulent, prized shellfish, but not for market. Their intent (it was said—how do we know otherwise?) was to "try the right," to take a contested matter to court. Robert Arnold, the farmer who had put up the twigs and (he claimed) planted the oysters that Mundy and the others tonged, was also eager to try the right. This was one among many instances of trying the right, a tactic somewhere between nefarious lawbreaking and civil disobedience that had the intent or consequence of bringing hotly contested matters to court, where, the contestants hoped and expected, their problems would be resolved.

The court cases that ensued from the Mundy / Arnold confrontation led to the first major articulation of the public trust doctrine in America: not only do people have common rights of fishing and navigation on tidal and navigable waters, but the state, acting as trustee for the people, owns the tide-washed and submerged lands. This did not settle the question. Over twenty years later a closely related conflict between a New York lawyer and a group of men who had state leases to oyster lands in the same area led to the United States Supreme Court's decision of *Martin v. Waddell* (1842), which affirmed the New Jersey court's interpretation. This chapter and the next explore the context and content of both cases, the causal linkage between them, and the novelty of the public trust doctrine.

The Social and Ecological Situation on the Raritan

The immediate context of the raid by Mundy and his crew was the decline in natural oysters and the rise of oyster planting. The oyster beds at issue were part of the complex known as the Great Beds, which lay between Staten Island, New York, and the Raritan River area of New Jersey. They were about a mile across, located in Raritan Bay just beyond the mouth of the Raritan River, and reaching about five miles up the river (Hall 1894; MacKenzie 1991a: 8). Around 1700 the colonies of New York and New Jersey agreed on a boundary that split the Great Beds in two. Signs of decline from heavy harvesting were evident even then, and the eighteenth century saw numerous laws intended to protect the oyster beds, or at least protect them from exploitation by outsiders (Ingersoll 1881). The laws did not protect the oysters. Natural beds declined, but the location, so close to New York City and other urban centers, made the area attractive to the practice of laying down seed oysters taken from other areas for a season or so of growth before marketing, as described in chapter 1. At the time of the Mundy/Arnold confrontation, however, an active fishery for the natural oysters continued, although the Great Beds were no longer so great. It was possible to argue, as Arnold's lawyer did, that the common-right fishermen had exhausted them and that private property would ensure survival of the industry:

> The oysters on the open beds are nearly exhausted; the rakers have become so numerous that oysters are not permitted to attain any maturity; they are small and worthless—hence the price of those fit for use is greatly enhanced; but if this reasonable use of a man's own soil is permitted and protected, every land owner on the shores of our bays and salt rivers will have an oyster-bed; the quantity brought into market will bring down the price, so that the poor as well as the rich may eat and be glad. (*Arnold v. Mundy* 1821: 49)

The Dispute between Arnold and the Woodbridge Tongers

Conflicts over oystering rights on the Raritan River and in Raritan Bay were not new. The case report indicates that at least from the late 1780s landowners had been staking off and trying to defend oyster beds in front of their farms, and over the same period commoners had been objecting to and defying these claims. Robert Arnold bought his 175-acre farm in 1814 from Joseph Coddington.[1] Coddington first staked off the oyster beds in front of the farm around 1790 and continued to do so over the decades, but to little avail: "[t]he people had always claimed their rights [when] Coddington was in possession . . . under a claim of common right" (*Arnold v. Mundy* 1821: 2). Sometimes they used the local courts to uphold their claims. Mostly they used tenacity and a willingness to fight: "during his time there, [Coddington had] claimed the exclusive right of taking oysters upon the bed so staked off; but the people had always disputed that right, had entered upon it, and taken oysters from it, when they pleased, and if opposed by Coddington, that the strongest usually prevailed" (*Arnold v. Mundy* 1821: 65).

After Robert Arnold bought the riverside farm he staked off an even larger claim in the river, between thirty-five and forty-five acres, and got into the new business of oyster planting: "[a]fter the plaintiff purchased, he bought oysters, and planted them on the beds, and staked it off. It appeared that he was at considerable expense in planting, and bought several boat loads, and claimed an exclusive right as far as he had planted, and oysters without his leave" (*Arnold v. Mundy* 1821: 2). The stakes were slender willow poles that extended below low-water mark but posed no obstacle to small craft. The oyster bed was about fifty yards beyond low-water mark, separated from the shore by a shallow mud flat, and was sometimes bare at extremely low tide. The problem was that it was a bed that had always had oysters on it as long as people could recall, a natural bed of oysters to which people claimed common right.

Having a "fishery" attached to a farm was, apparently, local practice and custom, as shown in this advertisement for a neighboring farm in the 1810 *New York Gazette*: "[f]or sale and possession given immediately. That beautiful farm at Amboy, known by the name of the Brighton Farm . . . , containing about 110 acres. There are several handsome building spots on this farm, and an excellent orchard, and the fishery on the Raritan, in front of the farm, and appertaining to it, very valuable for laying down oysters" (quoted in McGinnis 1959). However, people seemed no more inclined to respect Arnold's claim to exclusive oystering on the bed than they had Coddington's. Consequently, Arnold went to the Board of General Proprietors of East New Jersey, headquartered at Perth Amboy, for a survey of the tidewater land adjacent to his farm to support his claim that the oyster bed went with the farm. Recall that the Proprietors were the syndicate that had received East New Jersey (the northeast half of the state) from the duke of York in the 1680s to sell to settlers. A survey from the Proprietors was the basis for secure title, at least on land.

Arnold v. Mundy involves more than a clash between claims of private rights and public or common rights, although it is usually cited that way. First, as will be seen in more detail below, the claim of private rights through the Proprietors had special wrinkles. Second, so did the claim of common rights. We have a tendency to think of common property as the equivalent of public property, but it can represent exclusive rights granted to a specific group of people (McCay and Acheson 1987a). So in this case, Richard Stockton, Arnold's lawyer, said this: "it is well known that the Woodbridge men claimed the right of fishing *not as a right of common, but under their grant from the proprietors commonly called the Woodbridge charter*" (*Arnold v. Mundy* 1821: 61, emphasis in original).

Woodbridge was one of a small group of townships in the colony that had received its own charter from one of the original Proprietors. Its 1669 charter purportedly guaranteed townspeople the common right of fishing within the metes and bounds of the town, like charters elsewhere in the colonies, including Long Island, and was among the most "liberal" of all the colonial charters in the degree of self-government granted (Whitehead 1897: 107).[2] Unfortunately, Arnold's 1818 survey from the Proprietors showed that the oyster bed in front of his farm was not within the boundaries of the Woodbridge charter. It was then, Stockton asserted, that the Woodbridge men decided to raid the oyster bed using the claim of common right of fishing instead of township rights: "the defendant came, at the head of a small *fleet* of *skiffs*, and took away these oysters, avowedly to try the right" (*Arnold v. Mundy* 1821: 2, emphasis in original).

Benajah Mundy took the oysters in 1818 not as a lonely pirate but as the leader of a "fleet of skiffs." This was *social* action, intended not to grab a few oysters but to get the attention of the courts. The Woodbridge men claimed that they took the oysters "merely with a view of trying the plaintiff's pretended right, and not with a view of injuring the bed or taking the oysters further than was necessary for the purpose" (*Arnold v. Mundy* 1821: 2). Arnold sued Mundy for damages at a special Middlesex County circuit court in December 1819. Mundy pleaded not guilty. His defense was based on the argument that the site was a public navigable river, where oysters naturally grow, and that "all the citizens of the state had a common right to take oysters therein" (*Arnold v. Mundy* 1821: 2). The issues were not quite that simple. Once elevated to the higher courts, they became whether the Board of General Proprietors of East New Jersey had any right to sell tidewater lands and whether common rights of fishing applied to navigable and tidal waters against such claims.

To account for the inventiveness of the American version of the public trust doctrine, of which more below, Kirkpatrick has been posthumously described as both obscure and unprepared for this case (MacGrady 1975: 610). But he was not at all obscure; he was one of the more learned jurists of his day, especially where matters of property were concerned (Elmer 1872), including tidewater law. He may or may not have been unprepared: he was clearly very concerned about the weighty implications of a decision in the case as it bore on questions of title throughout New Jersey. At the outset, at the Middlesex circuit of the court in December 1819, he said that he preferred not to consider the matters presented. Instead, he offered to simply take a verdict for damages (*Arnold v. Mundy* 1821: 9). Though but an oyster tonger, Benajah Mundy could not be put off. He declined Kirkpatrick's offer of a verdict for damages, and his attorneys called for the opinion of the court, which was for "nonsuit" (i.e., Arnold had no case, and thus the suit for trespass had to be dismissed). Arnold's attorneys objected, and in May 1821 they appeared before the state supreme court to reargue their case. A new trial was granted, and in November 1821 the case reappeared, Kirkpatrick presiding, where he delivered his final opinion. He prefaced his opinion with an apology for not having given as much time as he would have liked to consider the issues of the case given both illness and a trip abroad on other official duties (*Arnold v. Mundy* 1821: 69–70). The apology was modest, hardly evidence of unpreparedness. Besides, the attorneys on both sides had covered most of the relevant doctrinal and case law.

The Public Trust Ruling

The questions were, Who owned the tidal and navigable waters and the soil beneath and washed by them, and what was the scope of the common right of fishery? Here is Chief Justice Kirkpatrick's famous opinion on these matters:

> Upon the whole, therefore, I am of opinion . . . that the navigable rivers in which the tide ebbs and flows, the ports, the bays, the coasts of the sea, including both the water and the land under the water, for the purpose of passing and repassing, navigation, fishing, fowling, sustenance, and all the other uses of the water and its products (a few things excepted) are common to all the citizens, and that each has a right to use them according to his necessities, subject only to the laws which regulate that use; that the property, indeed, strictly speaking, is vested in the sovereign, but it is vested in him not for his own use, but for the use of the citizen, that is, for his [the citizen's] direct and immediate enjoyment. (*Arnold v. Mundy* 1821: 77)

His authorities were "the law of nature, which is the only true foundation of all the social rights; . . . the civil law, which formerly governed almost the whole civilized world, and which is still the foundation of the polity of almost every nation in Europe; . . . the common law of England, of which our ancestors boasted, and to which it were well if we ourselves paid a more sacred regard" (*Arnold v. Mundy* 1821: 77). Kirkpatrick argued that these authorities supported the idea that the sovereign could not use his or her powers to take away common rights:

> since [the Magna Carta] no king of England has had the power of granting away these common rights, and thereby despoiling the subject of enjoyment of them . . . when Charles II took possession of this country, by his right of discovery, he took possession of it in his sovereign capacity; . . . he could not, and never did, so grant what is called the *common property* as to convert it into private property; . . . these

> royalties . . . passed to the duke of York, as the governor of the province exercising the royal authority for the public benefit, and not as the proprietor of the soil, and for his own private use. (*Arnold v. Mundy* 1821: 77, emphasis in original)

With the American Revolution, sovereignty passed to the people, and exercise of the responsibility of holding public property went to the legislature:

> upon the Revolution, all these royal rights became vested in the people of New Jersey as the sovereign of the country, and are now in their hands; and . . . they, having, themselves, both the legal title and the usufruct, may make such disposition of them, and such regulation concerning them, as they think fit; that this power of disposition and regulation must be exercised by them in their sovereign capacity; that the legislature is their rightful representative in this respect. (*Arnold v. Mundy* 1821: 78)

Kirkpatrick listed the many things that a legislature might do:

> the legislature, in the exercise of this power, may lawfully erect ports, harbours, basins, docks, and wharves on the coasts of the sea and in the arms thereof, and in the navigable rivers; . . . may bank off those waters and reclaim the land upon the shores; . . . may build dams, locks, and bridges . . . ; may clear and improve fishing places, to increase the product of the fishery; . . . may create, enlarge, and improve oyster beds, by planting oysters therein in order to procure a more ample supply. (*Arnold v. Mundy* 1821: 78)

But Kirkpatrick also emphasized that parts of the public trust were inalienable, and he linked their inalienability to the broader cause of freedom.

The Significance of Raiding an Oyster Bed

Arnold v. Mundy is regarded as a landmark case in New Jersey riparian and tidewater jurisprudence as well as American wildlife and public trust law (Lund 1980), even though it was more often ignored than followed (Jaffee 1971, 1974), as we shall see. The significance of the case was not merely the result of clever invention by lawyers and judges, nor does it simply derive from later use (and pointed nonuse) by other lawyers and judges and scholars as part of American common law. Its significance also lay behind the action that took the protagonists to court. Its importance was premeditated by the actors and redefined, at another level, by the courts.

The parties to the dispute on the Raritan River had specific concerns about rights to oysters that were shaped by their recent experience. Both sides acted to try the right, Mundy and the other Woodbridge men by deciding to raid that bed of oysters to bring the conflict to the courts, Arnold by having the survey done and planting oysters in a natural bed. The growing number of oyster planters in the area felt that their claims to property in the fruits of their enterprise were insecure. One of them, a Captain Lewis, was indicted (and acquitted by a jury) for threatening to kill trespassers with a loaded pistol a few years earlier (*Arnold v. Mundy* 1821: 49). Oyster planters wanted legal confirmation of their private property rights just as the Woodbridge men wanted legal confirmation of their common property rights.

The immediate question was whether Arnold had a right to exclusive use of the oyster bed in front of his farm. The court decided that he did not, that the only right he held was the same right held by Mundy, the other Woodbridge men, and all people of the state: the "common right of fishing." Neither riverside property ownership nor title through an official survey blessed by the Proprietors nor the act of planting (especially because it was done on a natural bed) conferred private property in the oysters or the oyster bed upon Arnold.

In its social and ecological context, the decision seems anomalous. In 1818 the oystermen of the Raritan region were on the brink of profound social change in part because of their own role in causing ecological change. It would not be long before the skiffmen of the Raritan River, like Benajah Mundy and his colleagues, would be known as "seeders," who sold the small natural oysters they could tong or rake to oyster planters for much less money than what the planters would eventually realize on the market. They would be transformed from independent oystermen to seeders producing for the planters and, in the off-season, working for the planters on their beds. And they would be forced by their position to overharvest the seed oyster beds (see chapter 11). But, for the moment of 1818 to 1821, they could and did fight for their legal rights to common property oystering, perhaps unaware of the larger processes in which they were involved but mightily annoyed by anyone who dared to carve a private fiefdom out of the commons.

It was evident that oysters needed protection from the inexorable dynamic of depletion of common resources and that oyster-planting appeared to be an alternative to extinction of the oystering trade. In addition, if some imagination is allowed, Robert Arnold must have presented himself as a civilized, law-abiding citizen in contrast to a grubby and piratical bunch of rivermen. There were, however, larger questions at stake, at least in the court's reading of the situation:

> It is a fact, as singular as it was unexpected in the jurisprudence of our state, that the taking a few bushels of oysters . . . should involve in it questions momentous in their

> nature, as well as in their magnitude; calling forth the talents, learning, and industry of our bar; affecting the rights of all our citizens, and embracing, in their investigation, the laws of nations and of England, the relative rights of sovereign and subjects, as well as the municipal regulations of our own country. (*Arnold v. Mundy* 1821: 78)

Little wonder that Kirkpatrick hesitated to rule.

Culture and History in *Arnold v. Mundy*

Tidewater property law is particularly obscure, and anything to do with shellfish would seem too mundane to be interesting. But the discourse of lawyers and judges in *Arnold v. Mundy* was anything but obscure or mundane, addressing as it did very fundamental questions about New Jersey and the new United States of America. Central was the question of whether English common law or a new law, appropriate to the new land, should apply. Ironically, as will be discussed in the next chapter, those who argued for English common law actually crafted a "local" law, for there were problems in representing and interpreting English common law. Surrounding that question was a clash in the all-American values of freedom, on the one hand, and private property, on the other. Robert Arnold and other oyster planters rested their case and their enterprises on the sanctity of private property and its role in entrepreneurship as well as in managing natural resources. Mundy and the other Woodbridge men rested their claim for common rights within a larger set of freedoms secured in the Magna Carta and reclaimed in colonial and revolutionary experiences.

The Great Charter: Of General Liberties or Special Privileges?

The Magna Carta is often used as a common law source of free rights of fishing, particularly chapter 33 of the 1215 version, which reads: "[a]ll fish-weirs shall be removed from the Thames, the Medway, and throughout the whole of England, except on the sea coast." Thus, Mundy's lawyers argued that, regardless of what happened before or since the Magna Carta was signed at Runnymede, it was the great charter of rights and liberties for all English people, and free fishing was one of those rights.

However, one could interpret English common law as having negated the fishery provisions of the Magna Carta by allowing the sovereign to grant "several," or exclusive, fisheries, as well as recognizing the validity of grants made before 1215. This was the tack taken by Arnold's lawyers. From this perspective, the pertinent history was post–Magna Carta, when the law had played a part in the solidification of a society founded on secure title to private property. The ancestors "brought [to America] the common law purified from its local dross" (*Arnold v. Mundy* 1821: 23), which they called the "folk law." This was a new and different land. The landscape itself contrasted with that of England, where tidal and navigable rivers were one and the same. In America, the notion that common property rights adhered to tidal and navigable rivers was inappropriate because great rivers and lakes were navigable far beyond the tidal tongues of salt water. Accordingly, English common law on fisheries, founded on English geography, was limited to English society: "[e]verything of a mere local origin was left on the other side of the ocean, and we have gradually substituted in its place a local common law of our own. Our ancestors brought the folk law merely, as contradistinguished from the *jus coronae* and the local common law of England" (*Arnold v. Mundy* 1821: 23). Thus, the provisions in Magna Carta that were often cited as support for the common right of fishing, such as that all weirs must be put down on the Thames, had no particular meaning for Americans.

Each side presented a different image of what the signing of the Magna Carta was all about to add narrative persuasion to their arguments. To strengthen their point that the particulars of the Magna Carta did not apply to American tidewaters and fisheries, Arnold's lawyers drew a picture of Runnymede as the field of encounter between two self-seeking groups of actors: the Saxon nobles and barons and the Norman conquerors. The Saxon barons were "bold, turbulent, rapacious, and oppressive" (*Arnold v. Mundy* 1821: 26), no defenders of the rights of common folk or a free people. Only happenstance and changed political and social contexts led the folk to see the Magna Carta as a common law document securing political and personal liberty and common property rights: "[t]he barons armed themselves not to support the rights of the people, but to protect their own usurpations upon the rights of both monarch and people, and, in the collision between the two oppressors, some principles of liberty were struck out" (*Arnold v. Mundy* 1821: 25).

Mundy's lawyers—and the majority of New Jersey's highest court—took another, equally plausible view. To argue that English common law did apply and that its foundation in the Magna Carta was high principled and protective of freedoms, they portrayed the Saxon barons as "great men *et tota communitas Angliae*" who used their power to force a return to Saxon liberties, to restore "common law and common right" (*Arnold v. Mundy* 1821: 39). The events leading to the Magna Carta were not just a power play between rapacious self-seeking barons and tyrannical self-seeking kings in which the commoners were left to glean scanty liberties. The Saxon barons forced the king to sign the

Magna Carta for higher motives, to secure "many important principles" and to keep the king "from preventing the people of their rights." It was far more than a "local" document or a mere source of "folk law": "Magna Carta, then, was the great fundamental law of England, binding alike on prince, noble, and peasant; securing rights and their infringement."

It was also the common law brought to America with the colonists and secured through the American Revolution. Conjuring a vivid and powerful image, Mundy's lawyers suggested that Arnold's attempt to claim a superior law of private property in the Raritan River was no more and no less than what the Norman conquerors tried to do in England. The situation was exactly the same. The best way to handle the fact that in England common rights of fishery, like those of hunting, had been extinguished was to see this as a recurrence of what the barons at Runnymede had sought to constrain through the Magna Carta. As Chief Justice Kirkpatrick observed, "[I]t seems pretty clear that it has always been considered as an encroachment upon the 'common rights of the people' " (*Arnold v. Mundy* 1821: 73). Thus, the relevant history began with the Saxons and the Magna Carta and involved a recurrent struggle to maintain and reclaim the imagined liberties of the Saxon community. However true it might be that Americans were selective in using the common law of England, its general principles and their birthright included the Magna Carta. It was far from "local." It *was* the folk law. It established that "the people have a vested right, *communis piscariae*" (*Arnold v. Mundy* 1821: 38), in the sea and its arms and in navigable rivers. Robert Arnold had no right to usurp the common fishery on the Raritan River. Nor did the Proprietors of East New Jersey.

The court's choice of the principled interpretation of the Magna Carta may be understood in light of colonial and revolutionary experiences. Debates about the meaning of the Magna Carta and the relevance of English common law in America took place within a long history of concern in the American colonies and new states about rights to hunt and fish (Tober 1981), as well as confusion about laws concerning forests, wild game, and fish (Lund 1975, 1980: 21–24). Regardless of—or in reaction to—the reality of few places for public fishing in England, in many American colonies care was taken to include the right of fishing as among the rights afforded to colonists as British subjects. In the early days of the Massachusetts Bay Colony public interest in certain waters was recognized in, for example, Massachusetts's "great pond" ordinance of 1641, which guaranteed the right to fish and fowl in ponds larger than ten acres in size, and similar acts of the colonies of New Hampshire and Maine (Angell 1826: 39–40). The Body of Liberties of the Massachusetts Bay Colony was, at least in later interpretation, even more explicitly defiant of the English situation. It contained an article whose "great purpose . . . was to declare a great principle of public right, to abolish the forest laws, the game laws, and the laws designed to secure several and exclusive fisheries, and to make them all free" (*Commonwealth v. Cyrus Alger* 1851: 68). It was not enough to claim English common law as the birthright of the colonists. They knew the law well enough and tried to secure some "Saxon" liberties against it.

Certain of the early charters, grants, and acts of assembly or of groups of proprietors also specified the free right to take fish and shellfish. In the 1683 charter of Rhode Island and the Providence Plantations, "[t]he relations of the fishermen to the owners of the shores were defined with great minuteness, and were calculated to make all the fish of the sea, and all the molluscous denizens of the muddy tide-flats, as available as possible to every citizen" (Ingersoll 1881: 47). William Penn's 1693 charter for Pennsylvania assured colonists free and equal access to fish as well as wild game (Tober 1981: 19). The royal charter to Lord Baltimore is another case: Baltimore became owner of the soil covered by water subject to the common right of fishing (*Browne v. Kennedy* 1821). And *Arnold v. Mundy* might have been an extremely different case if it had taken place in the Delaware River or Bay, part of the region known in colonial days as West Jersey, as opposed to East Jersey, which included the Raritan River. In 1767 the predominantly Quaker Proprietors of West Jersey made a grant of the common right of fishery to all inhabitants, referring to English common law. But there was no such provision in East ("north") Jersey (Board of Proprietors of East New-Jersey 1837: 4), making *Arnold v. Mundy* the difficult case that it was.

Real Estate Venture or New Society?

The conflict over tidewater rights and oysters also brought forth opposing views on New Jersey history. On Arnold's side (and the side of the Proprietors) was the view that New Jersey was colonized as a vast real estate development. Charles II gave New Jersey away to encourage settlement (especially by dissidents). By his 1664 grant to the duke of York and thence to Berkley and Carteret, he granted the land "to individuals. It was no longer the property of the nation; their lawful agent had alienated it" (*Arnold v. Mundy* 1821: 20). The twenty-four Proprietors who later took over ownership and administration of the colony surveyed and granted title to private property and retained title to whatever was not conveyed.

This was a land in which private property was not only sacred but the only kind of property that existed. Anything not entitled to individuals was residual and could be converted into private property, including tidal rivers and arms of the sea and, as we have seen in the story of Jacob Spicer of Cape May, all "natural privileges." The settlers had to have known and understood that this was a land of private property, even those among the colonists "who prate about the rights of the people, and common right, and other imposing terms" (*Arnold v. Mundy* 1821: 20). They would not have endured the privations and dangers of the Atlantic crossing and the wilderness without having inquired into how this colony was set up. It was the businesslike colonization of a "howling wilderness."

Kirkpatrick agreed with the Woodbridge oystermen's lawyers in seeing New Jersey as more than a real estate development, in seeing it as a civilized land where rights mattered. Settlers were attracted by letters from friends and advertisements of the Proprietors that loudly and proudly described the abundance of fish and oysters and the freedom to take them (*Arnold v. Mundy* 1821: 91–92; see Wacker 1975 for accounts). Once they arrived, they had to be able to obtain food and livelihood from the waters, and hence they brought their ancient common rights of fishery with them to the new land. To say that "they knew nothing of their birth right . . . and that liberty, which they so highly valued, was confined to the grants and concessions" (*Arnold v. Mundy* 1821: 92) was an insult to the memory of the early settlers and the Proprietors.

Moreover, these documents of colonization were not business transactions. The king's charter to his brother the duke of York was not a "mere private conveyance" but a "great state paper," and the duke and his heirs in New Jersey acted as "qualified sovereigns" (*Arnold v. Mundy* 1821: 34–35). They had no more powers than the king of England had to alienate resources from the commons. The Proprietors of New Jersey were indeed "tenants in common of the soil," able to grant private property through surveys and registration of title. But they were bound by the limited notion of sovereignty over the navigable, tidal rivers and seas and could not use their tenancy to take away the common right of fishery. New Jersey was not only a business but a society and a culture. Private property was one basis of propriety and hence culture; in a civilized land of people with an English birthright, common property was another.

Kirkpatrick's ruling fit into several developing trends of the early nineteenth century and was pivotal in the recognition of the inherent and inalienably public nature of some resources, namely, waterways. It was also known as the most important case of his career (Elmer 1872: 308). It may, however, have contributed to a movement against him that led to his failure to be reappointed by the assembly in 1824, a most unusual event for a state supreme court judge. One of his biographers, L. Q. C. Elmer, clearly did not agree with Kirkpatrick's refusal to listen to newer ideas and arguments, and he, like other younger members of the bar, resented Kirkpatrick's failure to listen patiently to their arguments instead of checking them with "caustic severity." Is it coincidence that it was in

1824, when Elmer happened to be speaker of the house of assembly, that Kirkpatrick was bitterly disappointed at not being reappointed to his position on the state's supreme court? Is it possible that broader-based dissatisfaction with his ruling in *Arnold v. Mundy* also played a role in his dismissal? 1824 also was the year that the most prestigious lawyers of New York, New Jersey, and Pennsylvania were called upon by the Proprietors of East New Jersey to consider the challenge to that ruling (Board of General Proprietors of the Eastern Division of New Jersey 1825). As will be shown in the next chapter, it eventually, but not without struggle, led to recognition of the public trust doctrine by federal courts too, becoming the law of the land.

Chapter 5 Proprietors, Oyster Wars, and the Invention of Tradition

The claims of the Proprietors, countered by the claims of common-right oystermen and others, formed the crucible for invention of the public trust doctrine. The relationship of the Proprietors to governance was a contentious part of the seventeenth- and eighteenth-century history of New Jersey and a central question in the nineteenth-century tidelands court cases. Between 1699 and 1702 the English crown (Queen Anne) and the Board of General Proprietors of East New Jersey negotiated a surrender of the Proprietors' powers of government. The nineteenth-century court cases dwelt on this because it could be interpreted to mean that the Proprietors also surrendered their rights to lands and waters below high tide, if English common law granted those to the sovereign in his capacity as trustee for public rights (*jus publicum*). The Proprietors insisted that this was not the case, that this was plain old property and hence theirs to allocate.

In all other proprietary colonies, after the American Revolution the new state governments bought out the Proprietors' rights. Not so in New Jersey, although this was brought up many times (see, for example, Parker 1885). In the first half of the nineteenth century the Proprietors still owned New Jersey land as tenants in common and were the source of title to all land in the state that had not already been granted either by the Proprietors or through special "king's grants" (Pomfret 1964). Although the power of the Proprietors had declined, they were still present in politics as they were in law and business. They were still willing to use political and legal resources to secure and expand their positions. However, the possibilities of proprietorship had shrunk. During the latter half of the eighteenth century the Proprietors had "lost interest in trying to win their war with the common man and adopted a policy of getting rid of their remaining land as profitably and expeditiously as possible" (Fleming 1977: 36). Their major interest became that of making money out of finding, surveying, and selling unallocated land.

By the early nineteenth century much of the valuable upland had been taken up one way or the other, making leftover interstices of patents and grants and the tidelands among the few ways the Proprietors could profit from their shares. Kirkpatrick's court in 1821 thought that Robert Arnold's claim to the oyster bed adjacent to his farm on the banks of the Raritan River, based on a survey and title from the Proprietors, was the first claim of this kind. It was not, but it was part of a practice that would increase as the riverfront property of New Jersey gained value for industrial and transportation purposes and the Jersey beaches became the "Riviera of the Atlantic."[1]

The Proprietors are part of the background needed to account for the fact that two of the most important public trust cases in the United States are parts of a causally linked sequence of events. Lawyers and judges are prone to cite either *Arnold v. Mundy* or *Martin v. Waddell* or both, and books dealing with the public trust doctrine or wildlife and fisheries law might do the same without recognizing the extent to which one deliberately followed the other, not to mention their contexts.

Responses to *Arnold v. Mundy*

Three clear responses to Kirkpatrick's *Arnold v. Mundy* decision and opinion occurred by 1825, only four years after the decision. First, some oyster planters went to the state legislature for special provisions to support their claims in oyster beds. Others convinced the state to use its "ownership" to set up leasing systems for oyster planting. Finally, those very dissatisfied with the ruling against the Proprietors of East New Jersey, with its several political and economic implications, began to plot another legal assault that led to the United States Supreme Court.

The 1820 act "for the preservation of clams and oysters" (chapter 1) was the first in New Jersey (and the United States; see Kennedy and Breisch 1983: 157) to include a provision supporting exclusive rights in planted oysters. That provision was for a small area on the coast of southern New Jersey, between Great Egg Harbor and Little Egg Harbor Rivers; like all such laws thereafter, rights of navigation and fishing on natural oyster beds were protected. Right after the *Arnold v. Mundy* decision, a similar act was passed that allowed owners of meadow and other lands along the shores of Elizabeth Township, fringing then oyster-rich Newark Bay and Staten Island Sound, to stake out oyster-planting grounds (New Jersey Laws, December 8, 1823).

In 1824, the legislature went further, exercising state ownership of tidewater lands by allowing people to lease them for the purpose of planting oysters. It was a way for the members of the assembly to respect Kirkpatrick's ruling about state ownership while responding to the pleas of oyster planters. It first happened in the waters of Raritan Bay off Perth Amboy and South Amboy (New Jersey Laws, November 25, 1824, December 27, 1824), in the midst of the domain of Benajah Mundy and the common-right oystermen and of Robert Arnold, riparian claimants, and the Proprietors (who were headquartered in Perth Amboy). The acts encompassed the Great Beds of the Raritan River and Bay as far as Cheesequake Creek, in Keyport, South Amboy Township. Both riparian landowners and landless oystermen could apply, but landowners had priority, giving strength to claims of waterfront owners that became "local custom" in later courts (chapter 7). As usual, persons fishing under common right were protected. The leasing system was administered by the county, but rental fees of between two and five dollars an acre depending on the quality of the "land" eventually went to the state. In 1834 the legislature extended the system for ten more years, after which time the system disappeared; state protection for the claims of planters was not revived in this region until the turn of the century.

The 1825 Challenge to Kirkpatrick's Ruling

The Board of General Proprietors of East New Jersey began to plot a legal challenge soon after *Arnold v. Mundy*. In 1825, the very year that Kirkpatrick was forced to leave the state supreme court, the Proprietors commissioned and published an intellectual challenge and some consulting advice from eminent lawyers: "The Case of the Proprietors of East New-Jersey, with the Opinions of Counsel on the Same," printed in Newark, New Jersey. James Kent, Peter Jay, and Elias Van Arsdale were among the authors. Kent held the highest position, that of chancellor, in New York State's equity courts and was the writer of the nineteenth century's most influential set of legal commentaries (Kent 1826). Why would he bother about title to muddy bottom? One reason is that oystering was indeed very profitable, and investments in oyster-planting lands were attractive even to distinguished men. For example, over $30,000 were invested in a forty-eight-acre plot in the Raritan Bay lease grounds within three years after the leasing system had begun (Ogden 1828). In addition, consulting paid. It was not unusual for leading jurists to be paid for their opinions. Kent often received consulting fees even when there might be conflicts of interest (Horwitz 1977: 137–38). Further, the economic and political stakes were higher than the case itself suggests. The Elizabeth and Raritan Bay oyster-planting regimes were caught up in conflicts between the oystermen of New Jersey and those of neighboring Staten Island, and these were fueled by long-standing boundary conflicts between the states. Behind the legislative acts and foregrounded in conflicts in the water and the courts was the fact that New York claimed ownership to high-water mark on the New Jersey shores of the Hudson River, the Arthur Kill, and Raritan Bay. Indeed, New Jersey was squeezed at both ends, by New York at these northeastern margins and by Pennsylvania and Delaware, which made similar claims at the southwestern margins. The stakes were very high, involving among other things steam, tug, and ferry service, the industrial development of waterfront property, and the creation of new cities.[2] The conflict raged until 1834, when Congress ratified an agreement engineered by the United States Supreme Court, whereby jurisdiction was split at a line down the middle of the Hudson River through New York Harbor, but New York retained jurisdiction over Ellis Island and several other islands on the New Jersey side of the line. New Jersey got control of the land underwater. The dispute lingers, revived in the late 1990s in a Supreme Court hearing of New Jersey's attempt to gain control of the land that has accreted to Ellis Island, the historic immigration center, in areas once underwater (MacFarquhar 1996, 1997).

One can only speculate about how the move against *Arnold v. Mundy* by the Proprietors and others fit into charged political situations. The challenge mounted by the Proprietors was also against the state, within which the likes of Federalists were losing power to more democratic and lower-class claims as well as to the growing political and bureaucratic interests of state legislatures and city governments (Fleming 1977). The interests of the Proprietors as proprietors were important as well; they were attracted to "gores" or pockets, sometimes tiny, of unsurveyed land and to the tidal and submerged lands as sources of revenue.

The text of the 1825 booklet commissioned by the Proprietors shows the determination of the lawyers to get a test case to the federal courts, which the Proprietors believed would be more objective about the question of state property rights than were state courts. Jay advised that one of the parties to the suit that might be undertaken to test the ruling of *Arnold v. Mundy* should be a citizen of a state other than New Jersey so that the suit could be initiated in the federal circuit court rather than the state courts (Board of General Proprietors of the Eastern Division of New Jersey 1825: 16). It is probably no accident that ten years later the person who claimed title through the Proprietors and challenged the leases held by New Jersey oystermen in waters off Perth Amboy was a New Yorker. But first, another oyster war.

A Perth Amboy Oyster War

Oyster planting developed prodigiously in Raritan Bay, based in both Staten Island (New York) and New Jersey ports (see MacKenzie 1991a: 61–82). Thomas Gordon, who had just finished his work as the first gazetteer of the state, referred to the wealth of the industry and the state leaseholds:

> the chief business of [Perth Amboy] is the oyster fishery. The shell-fish are abundant in the bay, and the bottom is so favourable to their growth, that large numbers are transplanted thither, not only from the river above, but also from Virginia. A capital of more than $40,000 is said to be thus employed, yielding an annual profit of more than $20,000. The state of New Jersey has leased about 250 acres of land, covered with water, here, in small lots, of a few acres each, whose tenants rear oysters upon them. (Gordon 1834: 215)

Masked in this enthusiastic report was the fact that planting had come to almost totally replace the natural oyster beds. However, Gordon did mention another kind of trouble. New Yorkers raided the Perth Amboy oyster-planting grounds, and boats were destroyed along the Perth Amboy shore (Gordon 1834: 215; see also McGinnis 1959).

Then and thereafter, theft from shellfish beds often had an interstate component (MacKenzie 1991a). But more than petty theft was involved; again, taking oysters and clams could be a "class act" of organized resistance to incursions on rights. A pamphlet (Ogden 1828) shows that the raids and riots began about 1827 and were initially focused on the oystering grounds of a state-chartered company, the Oyster Company of Perth Amboy, whose president was O. W. Ogden (relative of a former governor who was a renowned Federalist, monopolist, and part of a proprietary family). According to a testimonial given to the state legislature by Ogden in 1828, twenty-four men, each holding two-acre lots, received legislative approval to form a company "for the more easy management of their business." The legislature let them hold a forty-eight-acre lot for twenty years, rather than the two-acre and ten-year limit of the original law. In turn they agreed to pay increased rent.

Because of the residency rules for leasing systems in Perth Amboy, South Amboy, and Elizabeth, the people of Staten Island were no longer able to participate in oystering in areas very close to their ports, at least not directly or legally.[3] Moreover, they must have shared concern about monopolistic tendencies in the business with Jersey-side baymen. In any case, they vented their organized wrath on Ogden's corporation. On September 2, 1827[?], Ogden reported that "riots" began:

Figure 2. Enclosed dock for oyster vessels, Perth Amboy, New Jersey. (Ingersoll 1887: pl. 239)

> [About fifty] schooners, sloops, and pittiaguers, in hostile array, with flags flying, denoting commanders of different grades . . . filled with a great multitude of people . . . and armed with swivels, guns, and other weapons of offence, entered into the Bay of Amboy, and anchored in regular order within the jurisdiction of the state of New York, with the avowed purpose, openly declared, of going on to this forty-eight acre lot, and of taking and carrying away therefrom all the oysters they could there find. (Ogden 1828: 5)

Ogden said that he went over to Staten Island to warn people of the dire consequences that would follow any attempt to take oysters from the lots. The people he found there had just come in from their threatening foray. They were not impressed by his recital of the company's rights under New Jersey law. They consulted with each other and told him that they would go ahead with their plans. And they did:

> shortly afterwards, on the same day, a great number of canoes and small craft, amounting to more than one hundred and fifty, fully manned from the said fleet, with oyster tongs on board each boat, spread themselves over this forty-eight acre

> lot; and the men on board of these small boats, without the least color or pretence of right whatever, under the cover and protection of the said armed fleet, from time to time, for two weeks and more, riotously and forcibly plundered this planted oyster bed, and continued so to do while the oysters there growing were worth the taking up, . . . and loaded therewith, from time to time, the large vessels in which they had come . . . using, in the mean time, threats of retaliation in case of forcible resistance, even to the burning of the good city of Perth Amboy, to the great terror and dismay of its peaceable inhabitants. (Ogden 1828: 6)

Ogden and others in the company went to the county justice of the peace and then to the sheriff's office for warrants, but neither constables nor *posse comitatus* were able or willing to serve papers on the "rioters." Omitting to first read the Riot Act, the posse used a fieldpiece to disperse the marauders. They returned the next day. The grand jury of the county indicted everyone whose name could be learned, but nothing could be done because they were not residents of New Jersey. Ogden pleaded for legislative relief to protect the property of oyster planters (he claimed that his company lost $30,000 to the rioters) and to preserve the peace (Ogden 1828: 8). The state legislature apparently did little to help. By 1834 the situation was still very tense, and more riots may have taken place: "conflicting claims have induced vexatious disputes, and even alarming riots, which have prevented the quiet enjoyment of the tenants, and the collection of rents" (Gordon 1834: 215). Somewhere along the line Ogden got the Proprietors to survey and grant him ten acres of land in the area (New Jersey Riparian Committee 1882: 67). But it took a New Yorker to do the same and bring the matter to federal courts.

Waddell's Claim through the Proprietors

Into the fray appeared William Coventry H. Waddell, a lawyer and businessman from New York. In 1834 he went to Perth Amboy to have a survey made "under the authority of the Proprietors, and duly recorded in the proper office." The terrain surveyed was one hundred acres in Raritan Bay. He registered his claim with the Proprietors and leased it to one "John Den" for the purpose of oyster planting. John Den was a legal fiction, required for the common law action of ejectment.[4] Not only did Waddell challenge state ownership by making his claim through the Proprietors, but his one-hundred-acre claim directly took on the existing state leasing regime. In the fictitious name of John Den, Waddell filed an action for ejectment in April 1835 in the federal circuit court for the district of New Jersey against seven Perth Amboy planters: Merrit Martin, Smith Martin,

Abraham Webb, Abraham Bloodgood, Solomon Russ, Joseph W. Reckless, and Lawrence Kearney. They were the "Martin and Others" of subsequent court cases, and they were—not at all fictitiously—lessees of the state.

It could be argued that Waddell was simply an entrepreneur who saw the continued uncertainty about tidewater rights as an opportunity to stake a large tideland claim, but his claim was far larger than any oysterman could reasonably use and a direct challenge to the state-sanctioned leaseholders. It seems very unlikely that Waddell was interested only in oystering, given his other financial and legal entanglements.[5] It also appears that he was one of the Proprietors of East New Jersey, at least by 1843, a year after the Supreme Court decision on this case (New Jersey Riparian Committee 1882: 73). The circumstantial evidence also includes the fact that Waddell's New York citizenship made it possible to move the case out of state courts and into federal courts. This fit the strategy set up ten years before when the Proprietors obtained advice from Kent, Jay, and Van Arsdale in the 1825 pamphlet.

In 1837 the federal circuit court for the district of New Jersey in the third circuit heard the case as *John Den ex dem. William C. H. Waddell v. Merrit Martin and Others*. At the core of the issue again was the right of the Proprietors, as against the state, to grant property rights in tidewater lands. Merrit and Smith Martin and their colleagues defended their right to the oystering grounds first through the common right of fishery and second through their exclusive rights by leases from the state. Waddell, on the other hand, claimed his "by a regular deduction of title from the king, and by a deed from the proprietors . . . granted to him in fee" (*John Den ex dem. William C. H. Waddell v. Merrit Martin and Others* 1837: 62).

The composition of the court was in the Proprietors' favor: presiding were Henry Baldwin and William Rossell. Rossell had been on the courts of *Shepard v. Leverson* in 1808 and *Arnold v. Mundy* in 1821, where he forcefully dissented on the side of the Proprietors and private property. Baldwin gave the opinion in favor of a riverside landowner and against a common-right fisherman in an 1831 shad-fishing case (chapter 6) and gave an equally forceful opinion in favor of landed property and the Proprietors in this 1837 case. Their ruling in 1837 was consistent: Waddell had exclusive rights to the one hundred disputed acres of Raritan Bay that he had surveyed because he obtained it through the Proprietors, who held all lands, including tidewaters, upon their grant from the duke of York in 1664. They also held that if there was a common right of fishing, it was extinguished by the exclusive right of the Proprietors and the plaintiff, Waddell. Accordingly, the state had no right or title; any grant or lease from the state was void (*John Den ex dem. William C. H. Waddell v. Merrit Martin and Others* 1837: 64).

Enthused by their first court victory on riparian rights, the Proprietors immediately had the decision published by a Trenton printer (Board of Proprietors of East New-Jersey 1837). It reasserted the general and specific powers of the Proprietors against those of the state and called into question attempts on the part of the state legislature to regulate not only fisheries but also wharf construction, reclamation, and other matters central to industrial development along the waterfront.

The United States Supreme Court, 1842: The Public Trust Affirmed

The federal district court decision was the first in which an exclusive claim to tidal lands through the Proprietors had withstood the test of law or legislative sanction. The state and the Perth Amboy planters appealed the verdict to the United States Supreme Court. On appeal it was known as *Martin et al. v. Waddell's Lessee,* or *Martin v. Waddell.* In 1842 Chief Justice Roger Taney's Supreme Court voted 8 to 2 to overturn the district court's decision in favor of the state, common rights of fishery, and the state's leaseholders. For the first time the Supreme Court recognized the public trust doctrine.

The arguments and issues of the case, even the language, were almost identical to those of *Arnold v. Mundy.*[6] Following Kirkpatrick, the court reaffirmed that English common law was applicable and preserved the right of common fishery in tidal, navigable waters. It also held that the state, as representative of the sovereign people, was the only legal "owner" of tidal, navigable lands and resources. It followed Kirkpatrick again in taking the high moral ground about the meaning of the "letters patent" given by King George II to his brother: they "were intended to be a trust for the common use of the new community about to be established" rather than "private property to be parcelled out and sold to individuals, for his own [the duke of York's] benefit" (*Martin et al. v. Waddell's Lessee* 1842: 411). The king of England did not give the dominion and "propriety" to his brother James for forty beaverskins a year solely as real estate to be divested. Creating a market for that real estate—attracting and keeping settlers—meant providing many of the customary rights of British subjects. Some of that dominion, namely, the sea, its arms, and creeks, remained the property of the sovereign to be used for public benefit.

Chief Justice Taney (better known for his infamous decision in the Dred Scott case, which contributed to the Civil War) followed Kirkpatrick in taking a decidedly liberal, contextualized view: "in deciding a question like this we must not look merely to the strict technical meaning of the words of the letters patent. The laws and institutions of England, the history of the times, the object of the charter, the contemporaneous construction given to it, and the usages under it, for the century and more which has since elapsed, are all entitled to consideration and weight" (*Martin et al. v. Waddell's Lessee* 1842: 411). Those letters were intended to help the duke of York establish a colony on the newly discovered Atlantic lands that would be made up of British citizens who would expect the laws and usages of England, as "applicable to their situations." Accordingly, they expected the principle of the "public common of piscary belonging to the common people of England." Taney referred back to *Arnold,* where Benajah Mundy's attorney had also noted that "[t]he use of fisheries and rivers, as common property, was peculiarly applicable to their situations" (*Martin et al. v. Waddell's Lessee* 1842: 382).

Taney said there really was no question about whether people had common property rights in navigable waters. They clearly had. But the question that had preoccupied this court, the lower courts, the state courts, and many more in America and abroad was whether the king, after the Magna Carta, had the right to grant exclusive rights to the soil of navigable rivers. Thereby contributing to subsequent legal confusion, Taney refused to delve into the question as such, observing that the very fact of six hundred years of debate about the right of the king to do so "would of itself show how fixed has been the policy of that government on this subject . . . ; and how carefully it has preserved this common right for the benefit of the public" (*Martin et al. v. Waddell's Lessee* 1842: 412–13).

Taney broadened the scope of the public trust doctrine by placing New Jersey practice within the context of the practice of other colonies. He also gave weight to ordinary practice and common usage. He pointed out that the people of New Jersey from 1702, when the surrender of powers of government was made by the Proprietors, had "exercised and enjoyed the rights of fishery, for shell-fish and floating fish, as a common and undoubted right, without opposition or remonstrance from the Proprietors" at least until 1818, when Robert Arnold tried to use a grant from the Proprietors to force the Woodbridge oystermen off the oyster beds in front of his farm.[7] In this he was influenced by Mr. Wood, attorney for the Perth Amboy leaseholders (as he had been for the Woodbridge tongers). Wood noted that the oyster fisheries were always protected as common, that "[t]he acts recite the rights of the poor to take oysters, and protect them from encroachment by citizens of other states; all founded on the idea of common rights" (*Martin et al. v. Waddell's Lessee* 1842: 388). He went on to note that the few grants made by the Proprietors in tidewater lands were confined to banks or margins of public rivers, and there was no pretense of claims to exclusive fishing or oystering rights.[8]

For these and other reasons, the Supreme Court overturned the lower court's decision in favor of the state and its citizens and the public trust. Following *Arnold v. Mundy,* the majority of the Supreme Court justices reaffirmed that English common law was applicable and preserved the right of common fishery in tidal, navigable waters. It held that the state, as representative of the sovereign people, was the only legal "owner" of tidal, navigable lands and resources. At common law the "dominion and property in navigable waters, and in the lands under them, [were] held by the king as a public trust" (*Martin et al. v. Waddell's Lessee* 1842: 263). From that premise, Taney went on to say that "when the Revolution took place, the people of each state became themselves sovereign; and in that character hold the absolute right to all their navigable waters and the soils under them for their own common use" (*Martin et al. v. Waddell's Lessee* 1842: 262–63).

Thus was born in federal law the public trust doctrine, which holds that states own submerged soil and foreshore of all navigable/tidal bodies of water. In *Pollard's Lessee v. Hagan* (1845), Taney's Court expanded it to the new states. It is firmly embedded now in American case law through its use in *Illinois Central Railway Company v. State of Illinois* (1892), which is the official "landmark" case, serving as it did to apply the doctrine and clarify the trust aspect of state ownership, one of the issues that was murky in Taney's decision. That case will be discussed in chapter 8 in the context of the development of a "fee simple" theory about state ownership versus public trust.

Inventing Legal Tradition

Some of the vigorous debate after the American Revolution about the relevance of English common law in America appears in these Raritan oyster rights cases, as we have seen. The primary complaint of those who wanted to codify an entirely new set of laws for America was the perceived irrationality and arbitrariness of common law. American legal treatise writers, who began their work in the 1820s, tried to reduce common law to "seemingly coherent, intelligible, and logical systems" (MacGrady 1975: 547). But "the common law had little to fear. It was as little threatened as the English language. The courts continued to operate, continued to do business; they used the only law that they knew" (Friedman 1973: 95). In the process they also constructed the common law anew as they responded to issues brought to the courts by people exercising and claiming conflicting rights.

Kirkpatrick's and Taney's construction of the public trust doctrine was that the English crown was the absolute owner of the foreshore, submerged beds, and waters of tidal and/or navigable waters. For certain purposes, an inalienable public trust, deriving from the *jus publicum* as opposed to the *jus privatum,* is attached to that ownership. In revolutionary North America, the crown's title passed to the people of the states to be held in trust for them by their representative governments after the Revolution. However, in 1821 there was virtually no support in English common law for the absolute claim of state or crown ownership of lands below high-water mark. That idea did not really find its way into English common law until sometime *after* its promulgation in American law.

I will note only the highlights of what is necessarily a very complex analysis. It is a story of doctrinal invention, and reinvention, and invention again, a story that, when carried out more thoroughly than possible in this space, shows not only appreciation of the dynamic and elusive nature of "tradition" but also specific examples of how culture is intentionally, as well as mistakenly, constructed by historical actors (Hobsbawm and Ranger 1983; Ohnuki-Tierney 1990). Unless otherwise indicated, my source is largely MacGrady (1975), who in turn relies heavily on Moore (1888), who showed how dubious were claims that the origins of the public trust doctrine were clearly in Roman and early English law.

First, although Roman law is frequently cited as the source of the public trust doctrine (e.g., Sax 1980: 185), it had nothing to say about sovereign ownership of the foreshores or submerged soils of ocean frontage, bays, and rivers. It offered instead the notion of *res communes,* those things that were "common to all . . . but owned by no one, namely, the great flowing waters, the sea, and its shores" (Johnson and Johnson 1975: 84, from the Institutes of Justinian). Connecting common rights with ownership was an English invention that took place sometime between 1250 and 1256, when Bracton wrote on these matters. English legal theory insisted upon ownership of all things, making the Roman category of *res communes* a problem and eventually contributing to the idea that the sovereign owned many things otherwise common to all.

The notion that the Magna Carta supports common rights of fishing can also be seen as a later interpretation (Jaffee 1971: 585–88). As a writer for the *Yale Law Review* said, over the years the provisions of the Magna Carta and other early charters have been "expanded . . . almost unrecognizably" in common law to mean a public right of fishery (Anonymous 1970: 767). They were held by seventeenth- to twentieth-century authorities to mean that the only private fisheries allowed in England were those granted prior to the Magna Carta. After King John's reign, the doctrine goes, the crown was restrained by public rights of navigation and fishing from granting private fisheries. However, by 1215 just about all of England's tidewater and navigable river territory was in the hands of manors, town corporations, and individuals, making the oft-cited common fishing rights of English law an effective but pitiable fiction. In English common *practice,* regardless of what the common law was believed to say about sovereign ownership and public rights, "the beds and shores of virtually all navigable waters, tidal and nontidal, were privately owned" (Anonymous 1970: 767) by the time of the Magna Carta and later.

Digges and the Fishing Grants

In any case, the Magna Carta, which predated Bracton, said nothing about sovereign ownership of tidal and navigable things or places. Some scholars assume that the king held those lands as part of the feudal system (e.g., Jaffee 1971: 579). But others suggest that chapter 33 meant little more than that the barons wanted to restore untrammeled navigation on rivers that had become cluttered with stationary fish traps. The Magna Carta was reinterpreted to meet changing needs at later times (MacGrady 1975, following Moore 1888; Johnson and Johnson 1975). The idea that tide-washed shorelines and the bottoms of navigable rivers are owned by the sovereign, which is central to the public trust doctrine, gained substance through greed, corruption, and some legal creativity. Thomas Digges, an otherwise obscure writer, was commissioned by Queen Elizabeth to help the monarchy raise money. He developed a theory that the shore, like the sea itself, was part of the great "waste" of the kingdom never granted out, and that no one could hold title to the shore unless he could prove an express grant from the king. The logic of his theory was easily acceptable in England; it was a straight analogy to the system of rights to common wastelands in manorial estates. The lord owned the lands subject to the use rights of tenants, who had, nonetheless, to prove their rights unless they were clearly attached to the soil. This *prima facie* rule, or rebuttable presumption, was soon used by "title hunters," Digges among them, who obtained "fishing grants" from the crown that allowed them to question the title of present occupants and blackmail them in order to raise money for the crown's depleted treasury.

The crown and title hunters profited, but Parliament and courts objected, so that it could hardly be said that the rule became common law right away. Juries were particularly skeptical of the claim. Digges himself lost every jury verdict in attempts to enforce his "fishing grants," and from 1574 to 1888 no English jury gave a verdict for the crown against use of the foreshore by the subject even though the number of "fishing grants" on the Patent Rolls during the reigns of

Elizabeth, James I, and Charles I (to ca. 1649) equaled half or more of all lands in the kingdom. It took the imprimatur of a seventeenth-century English jurist, Sir Matthew Hale, to make this common law.

Matthew Hale: On the Face of It

American jurists and treatise writers probably knew nothing about Digges. Instead they depended on Hale's *De Juris Maris,* which was written in 1667 but not published until 1787 in *Hargrave's Tracts*. Hale used and refined Digges's thesis; as authority he cited three doubtful cases. *Attorney-General v. Philpott* (1631) upheld Digges's rule and paved the way for more royal land grabs, making the king extraordinarily rich in land (Jaffee 1971: 593). It was rarely cited before Hale used it, perhaps because of the renowned corruption of the judges involved as well as the fact that objections to the practice it supported led to the Great Rebellion of 1642 (MacGrady 1975: 562). However, in 1667 Hale cited this case and two others—neither of which had anything to say about crown ownership of the foreshore[9]—as authority for crown ownership of the foreshore. The first reliable case in English common law about crown ownership of the foreshore was the 1795 case of *Attorney General v. Richards,* and that one relied almost entirely on the authority of Lord Hale!

On these slender grounds, enhanced by masterful and persuasive logic and narrative, Hale became the authority. He wrote that the foreshore "by prima facie and by common right belongs to the king, both in the shore of the sea and the shore of the arms of the sea" (cited in MacGrady 1975: 549–50). Hale framed this within notions of *jus privatum* and *jus publicum* and asserted the inalienability of the *jus publicum,* a major point adopted by American courts in their construction of the public trust doctrine (Johnson and Johnson 1975: 87). But Hale's position was not quite the same as that of the American lawyers, judges, and treatise writers who relied on him. Hale recognized that the foreshore may be part of a manor or belong to a subject; ownership is only *prima facie* in the king, referring to an evidentiary presumption rather than a rule of substantive law as many of the American writers would have it. In other words, in English common law, ownership was considered a question of fact, of evidence, and from there it was assumed that the king was owner unless someone had evidence otherwise (through grant, "presumption," or custom). But as the public trust doctrine developed in America, the state was owner of tidewater lands as a matter of principle, not just fact. Title from any source other than the state was contestable.

James Kent: In Law if Not in Fact

Another feature of the American version of the public trust doctrine, evident in the opinions of Kirkpatrick and Taney and contested by consultants to the Proprietors, is conflation of fishing rights with rights to submerged lands (MacGrady 1975). Strangely, James Kent, one of those who counseled the Proprietors of East New Jersey to contest the public trust doctrine ruling, paved the way for this aspect of it in one of his early cases. *Palmer v. Mulligan* (1805) brought up the possibility that if there were public rights of fishery, then crown ownership of subjacent soil was presumed. The case concerned a dispute between mill owners on the Hudson River about a dam constructed by one mill that disrupted the water flow used by the other. Kent used English fishing rights cases to deal with questions of ownership. In his analysis, sovereign rights to a fishery became sovereign ownership of the riverbeds. In chapter 6 I discuss a New Jersey case about shad-fishing rights, *Fitzgerald v. Faunce* (1884), where the same logic was applied to argue that if someone held exclusive fishing rights, he must therefore hold exclusive rights to the land used for that fishery, despite a long and well-documented history of property rights in aspects of fishing distinct from ownership of the land.

In *Palmer v. Mulligan,* Kent also set the framework for later nineteenth-century decisions by insisting on an association between navigability and tidality, a topic I have not addressed but that is central to the public trust doctrine. Legal confusion has long reigned over the question of whether tidality or navigability is the criterion for public rights of navigation and fishing or for sovereign rights in the soil underwater (MacGrady 1975: 579). If a waterway is navigable above the tidal reach, is it still public? If it is tidal but not navigable, does the sovereign / state own it? In America the question was most recently decided in 1988 (in favor of tidality) by the United States Supreme Court in the case of *Phillips Petroleum v. Mississippi,* where rights to oil-bearing wetlands were at stake.

Kent's opinion, which added to the confusion, was that a waterway is only navigable in law so far as it is tidal in fact. He observed that the Hudson River was not navigable at the locale of the disputing mills because it was not tidal there no matter what boats did. Therefore, exclusive use of areas of such a river could be granted to private persons.[10] MacGrady (1975) argues that Kent was wrong, that there was no precedent in English common law for linking tidality to navigability. How to account for the invention? One possibility is that Kent misread the cases he used; he made an error. The other is that "he made an intuitive leap" to resolve rhetorical confusion (MacGrady 1975: 584). His reading was intended to make sense out of both the law and the situation. "Whatever Kent's process of ratiocination, he not only settled the American understanding of English law, but, 63 years later, settled the English understanding of English law" (MacGrady 1975: 585). By 1868, Chancellor James Kent of New York was the authority for a conflict in Ireland, *Murphy v. Ryan,* where the court merged bed rights with fishing rights and navigability with tidality, holding that the river was not "technically" navigable if it was not tidal (MacGrady 1975: 586).

Kent was also one of the leaders in the effort to create an American tradition of full reports on cases and to encourage codification of the American version of the common law through the publication of learned treatises and commentaries. When Kent retired from the bench, he tried to do for America what Blackstone had done for England: compile the relevant common law in a set of *Commentaries on American Law* (Friedman 1973: 291). His commentaries were first published in four volumes between 1826 and 1830; there were fourteen subsequent editions, the last in 1896. This work was a law office "Bible," the nineteenth century's most influential general treatise on American law. Together with Joseph Angell's 1826 *Treatise on the Right of Property in Tide Waters and in the Soil and Shores Thereof,* Kent's commentaries more specifically played an important role in the development of the public trust doctrine. And therein he adopted Kirkpatrick's interpretation of the public trust, emphasizing the inalienability of common rights of navigability and fishing as well as the absolute nature of state ownership.

In Defense of Kirkpatrick and Taney

MacGrady, whose goal, it must be said, was to denigrate the authority of the American public trust doctrine, argued that "[n]onexistent at English common law, the doctrine was created by an obscure and unprepared state court judge [Kirkpatrick], adopted by the inventive Roger Taney, and repeated forever after in hundreds of American decisions, affecting title to millions of acres of submerged land" (1975: 591). He misread this history.

A Modern Traditionalist. It is true that in the fall term of 1821 Kirkpatrick apologized for not having been able to investigate the question as much as he would have liked, having been abroad since the spring session, when arguments were heard on the case (*Arnold v. Mundy* 1821: 69–70). But he was neither obscure nor unprepared. To the contrary, he was both accomplished and known for erudition, especially in property law:

> He was a very handsome man, with a white head of hair, still wearing a cue, but not requiring the powder. He spoke and wrote correct and idiomatic English; was a learned, and in the law of real estate, a profoundly learned lawyer; . . . His opinions . . . upon questions relating to the law of real estate, deserve the most careful study of every lawyer aspiring to understand this most difficult branch of the law. They will be found to exhibit a fullness and accuracy of knowledge, a clearness of comprehension and a justness of reasoning which secured him the confidence of the profession and entitle him to rank among the most eminent of American jurists. (Elmer 1872: 308; see also Wilson 1870; Keasbey 1912)

Elmer, who like others of his generation was ambivalent because Kirkpatrick was not always kind in court, added: "[he was] not well versed in modern innovations, which he regarded as blemishes and not as improvements, and did not care to study" (Elmer 1872: 308–9). He was more than a traditionalist, though. In his *Arnold v. Mundy* opinion, Kirkpatrick listed the many things that a legislature might do as inheritor of the sovereign's ownership of tidewater lands (chapter 4), but he took care to point to an important limitation: "[t]he sovereign power . . . cannot, consistently with the principles of the law of nature and the constitution of a well ordered society, make a direct and absolute grant of the waters of the state, divesting all the citizens of their common right. It would be a grievance which never could be long borne by a free people" (*Arnold v. Mundy* 1821: 78). This passage about the inalienability of public trust lands was treated as "mere" *obiter dicta* by other judges in New Jersey through the nineteenth century, but it was resurrected in other courts and other times as the foundation of the American public trust doctrine, remaining one of its tantalizing possibilities, as shown in the beach access cases of the 1970s and 1980s in New Jersey (chapter 13).

Moreover, the *Arnold v. Mundy* opinion reflected a modern conception of the common law. Well into the nineteenth century the "traditional" conception was that the law was there to be discovered, to be found, in the accumulated decisions of the past. In contrast was the notion, derived partly from Blackstone and partly from the Enlightenment political philosophers, that its basis was, *au fond,* the consent of the people (Horwitz 1971). "It would be a grievance which never could be long borne by a free people": that is quite different from the idea of natural laws or the common law legitimized by the wisdom of the ages.

Kirkpatrick understood that his work as a judge had social policy implications, that its relevance was not restricted to the case at hand. He was reluctant to decide the case because of the seeming impossibility of coming up with a solution that would protect both the peace and the oysters:

> However the case was decided, it had the potential of furthering decline in natural oysters and exacerbating conflict among oystermen by exciting false hopes or false fears, by encouraging those who claim a common right to make unlawful aggressions, or those who claim several [exclusive] rights to make unlawful defences, and in their conflict for superiority, for awhile, not only to disturb the peace of society but also to destroy the very subject matter of controversy. (*Arnold v. Mundy* 1821: 9)

Here too he was on the leading edge of his profession in his time and a budding modernist. Early-nineteenth-century judges were concerned about the potentially disruptive role their decisions could play. They recognized that legal doctrines served particular economic or social interests and that any change would affect power relations and upset a delicate balance in society (Friedman 1973: 19).

Kirkpatrick appears to have been engaged, however uneasily, in redefining the role of the courts in relation to broader social policy. His decision was remarkable in its legal and political context, coming at a time when state legislatures still granted exclusive privileges for riverain transportation, including bridges, ferries, and steamboat service. In the early years of the nineteenth century courts were not all that eager to defend public interests or common rights against monopolies that were viewed as promoting economic growth, although this would soon change (Horwitz 1977). Kirkpatrick's ruling fit into several developing trends of the early nineteenth century and was pivotal in the recognition of the inherent and inalienably public nature of some resources, namely, waterways. It was the most important case of his career (Elmer 1872: 308). As I have already noted, it may also have led to the end of his distinguished career as a state supreme court judge.

Clever Invention and States' Rights. MacGrady reduced Roger Taney's role to that of clever invention, but we can understand this invention better if we appreciate the context and Taney's background. The three decades of Taney's Court saw the rise of Jacksonian democracy and the corporation, economic and industrial growth, and the deepening conflicts over sectionalism and slavery that culminated tragically in the Civil War (Siegel 1987). Roger Taney is most remembered for his unfortunate decision in the Dred Scott case, that Negroes could never be citizens of the United States (Swisher 1974). Taney's three decades on the Court were also a time when the Supreme Court had great prestige and power (Siegel 1987). The public trust ruling was part of this Court's numerous considerations of and defense of property and vested interests. Taney's Supreme Court had to deal with several tidewater property cases. The stakes were high along the Atlantic Ocean and the shores of the Gulf of Mexico, where economic development increased the value of waterfront and intertidal land and encouraged landfilling. Several cases involving underwater tracts and newly created land came before the United States Supreme Court at or near the same time. There were legal battles over tidewater land in the rural interior, along the coasts, and in cities like Mobile, St. Louis, Chicago, and New Orleans (Swisher 1974: 749).

One of Taney's biographers noted that in the *Martin v. Waddell* decision, "Taney's lucid handling of the complex issues involved showed him at the top of his form" (Siegel 1987: 136), making a clear separation between rights of property and rights of sovereignty, although another is more reluctant to give Taney such credit: it was "one of the seminal cases affecting riparian rights, dealing with confusing and conflicting theories of sovereign jurisdiction and title to ownership, and leaving those theories in about the same state of confusion and conflict as it found them" (Swisher 1974: 749). Although Taney closely followed Kirkpatrick's arguments, he did not simply copy them. For one thing, in the courts of the time, heavily influenced by the judicial federalism developed by his famous predecessor, John Marshall, Taney had to justify paying any attention at all to a state court decision. Taney was an appointee of Andrew Jackson but did not, as many thought he would, go entirely over to states' rights (Siegel 1987: 241; see also Scheiber 1973). Yet he greatly strengthened the jural powers of the states in his argument in *Martin v. Waddell* (1842: 367) that while state rulings, such as that of Kirkpatrick of New Jersey, did not bind a federal court, they were entitled to great weight in federal courts (Siegel 1987: 22).

It is also misleading to criticize Taney and Kirkpatrick for misreading English common law. They gave the appearance of continuity with English common law in their decisions despite profound change in their interpretations partly because this is what good common law judges did. Their role was to uncover or "find" the law (Friedman 1973: 19). It was not to make the law or to tamper with it when found. The modern idea of the law as an essentially manmade tool or instrument was foreign to classic common law, so change had to be hidden and disguised. Blunt, overt reforms by judges were out of the question.

Finally, it should be noted that both Kirkpatrick and Taney were well-enough versed in the intricacies of riparian and tidewater law. Coincidental, perhaps, was the fact that in 1821, when Kirkpatrick ruled on state ownership and the public trust in *Arnold v. Mundy*, Roger Taney was a young Maryland lawyer arguing a related case in the court of appeals in Baltimore (Swisher 1974: 749). It was a terribly complicated dispute over rights to real estate in the city of Baltimore. Most of the issues of public trust doctrine were manifest in the case, and it is clear from the list of sources that Taney was well versed in the authorities, as were other American lawyers. The opinion, which held for Taney's side, reflected in part the idea of the restricted nature of sovereign ownership of tidewater resources that is so central to the public trust doctrine: "[t]he King of England had the right to grant land covered by navigable waters, subject to the right of the public to fish and navigate them" (*Browne v. Kennedy* 1821).

Epilogue: The Proprietors, Continued

The Proprietors did not give up. Late in the nineteenth century they were still active at the margins and plotting to challenge *Martin v. Waddell* as they had earlier schemed to orchestrate a test case to challenge *Arnold v. Mundy*. In 1881 the state legislature carried out a major investigation of the Board of General Proprietors of East New Jersey in an attempt to "get inside" their operations (New Jersey Riparian Committee 1882). In the same year, the Proprietors, anticipating that investigation, created yet another document that sought to justify their claims and actions (Anonymous 1881). I discovered the 1881 document more than a decade after doing the initial research for this book. It turns out that the Proprietors and I were on the same track, which is not entirely coincidental; some documents are available because the Proprietors had them printed or reprinted.

The 1881 hearings were about existing or pending claims through the Proprietors and their surveyors to beachfront land in the shoreside towns of Barnegat, Point Pleasant, and Ocean Beach; to entire lake beds and three hundred feet around them in central New Jersey (Lake Hopatcong, among others); to a large tidal river called Shark River; to waterfront and submerged islands in the Hudson River; and to much of the spit of land called Sandy Hook at the entrance to New York harbor. At issue in 1881 was the right of the Proprietors to grant these lands, as against a body known as the riparian commission (chapters 9 and 10), which claimed sole right to dispense lands beneath high-water mark as an agency of the state.

Also at issue were the role of such claims in harming common rights of navigation and fishing; the procedures and practices of the Proprietors, which included alleged unwillingness to allow others to review their records, deeds, and surveys; and a disinclination to tell adjoining landowners about intentions to claim land. In other words, it was suspected that the Proprietors found ways to ensure that only they and their friends would have a chance at the "gores," tidal lands, and other lands that they claimed. For instance, although there was a public sale on February 5, 1881, at the surveyor general's office in Perth Amboy, the news must not have gone very far. The person who bought between three and six thousand acres of Shark River, plus a quit-claim of three hundred feet of the banks, was H. H. Yard, a Proprietor and surveyor (it was not unusual for surveyors to become Proprietors) (New Jersey Riparian Committee 1882: 100, 29). The Proprietors would share the $975 he paid according to their holdings in the tenancy in common.

This transaction directly challenged the state's ownership claim, exercised through its riparian commission. It also challenged the rights of oystermen who leased lands in a tidal river called Shark River under an 1860 law, amended in 1871 and reenacted in 1880, authorizing county freeholders to lease oyster grounds there (New Jersey Riparian Committee 1882: 86). Finally, the transaction directly threatened the public trust dimension of the state's ownership, protecting common rights of the public to fishery and navigation. The following interchange between one of the legislators and Mr. Yard focused on the problem: "Q: 'Do you think you will acquire the clams and oysters?' A: 'I think I shall.' Q: 'Fishery and rights of fishery?' A: 'I think so' " (New Jersey Riparian Committee 1882: 86).

The Proprietors tried to defend their claims in yet another publication, *East Jersey Proprietary Rights: Abstract of Title and Opinions of Chancellor Kent and E. Van Arsdale, Esq. 1497–1881* (Anonymous 1881), in which they reprinted the opinions commissioned back in 1825. The documentation was put together in 1879, judging from the text, and the Council of Proprietors (formerly the Board of General Proprietors) approved it, including the recommendation "that the Council of Proprietors take such action as will bring the matter to trial and settlement" (Anonymous 1881: 11), and ordered it printed May 17, 1881, about a month before the legislative committee's investigations. It summarized the Proprietors' view of history and then raised the possibility of a challenge to *Martin v. Waddell:* "the opinion of the respectable minority of that court was so strongly in favor of the rights of the Proprietors [in lands underwater] that there seems good ground for a reexamination of the whole case, or, if not of the whole, at least of some peculiar parts included in it" (Anonymous 1881: 4). This time their argument rested more on the involvement of colonial Proprietors in Indian land sales, which, they argued, included purchase of the Indians' fishing rights, validating the Proprietors' claims to ownership of riparian lands (Anonymous 1881: 5–6; Grumet 1979).

The Proprietors' 1881 claims also rested on several stories that I tell in this book. The first was that of the "natural privileges" of Cape May (retold by the Proprietors to show that the Proprietors of *West* Jersey clearly owned rights of fishing, fowling, etc.; see the introduction). Second was the story of the private shad fisheries along the Delaware River, which the 1881 document claims were "all held under grants from the Proprietors, and they extend to the middle of the river," even though the case of *Fitzgerald v. Faunce* (1884), which was then awaiting trial, did not use the Proprietors to support claims to private property in haul seine fisheries (see chapter 6). The third is the Shark River leasing system, which was used to show that the rights of individual property in oyster beds were recognized by the legislature (see chapter 8). The fourth was another contentious subject of this study: "the common sense and practice of the people all along the sea shore, and the bays, creeks and sounds of salt water, [which] recognizes the rights of property in grounds planted with oysters, and such grounds are respected as individual property, and considered of great value" (Anonymous 1881: 10).

The Proprietors made reference to their own practice and policy. The fact that "in many instances [they had] made grants of land under water, and persons taking title from them still hold possession," supported their claim, they said. (The 1881 committee of the legislature did not get much evidence from them of these former grants, except statements that some were known to exist.) The Proprietors' policy was restated: going back to the original "grants and concessions" and quit-rent agreements, it was that "lands that have never been sold, or, if sold, have never been improved according to conditions of rent, still belong to the Proprietors" (Anonymous 1881: 10).

The reason for this effort was clear: "[s]uch lands are now coming to be in demand at considerable prices." One argument was that the oyster grounds had not been developed to their potential, and thus it was "just and equitable" that the Proprietors take over "as the successors of the original owners from whom they purchased them." In any case, "the demand for them for useful purposes is now so immediate that we think it is due to the Proprietors and to the State to have the titles fully investigated and the questions at issue settled" (Anonymous 1881: 10). They referred solely to oyster grounds, even though it is evident from the New Jersey Riparian Committee interviews that coastal resort use was very much involved.

"Local custom" played a major role in the claims of the Proprietors as well as deliberations of the courts. The next three chapters explore the meaning and use of the legal construct of local custom, showing above all how it helped justify an interpretation of the public trust doctrine that reduced the trust part and increased the power of private property owners.

Part III Local Custom and Enclosure of the Commons

Introduction

The third section of the book moves beyond oysters and oyster planting. It pertains to the shad fisheries of the Delaware Bay, the waterfront of the Hudson River, and, returning to oysters, how legal interpretations under the rubric of local custom evolved such that a court could agree to enclosure of oystering commons despite the public trust doctrine.

The anthropological endeavor has always emphasized custom as part of the rich complex of culture. Custom refers to practices, rules, and beliefs that gain their shape and authority less from written records and political and administrative bodies than from the practice and oral or local interpretation of ordinary folk. In nation-states with well-developed political and legal systems, the relationship between custom and "law" is problematic, as the social historian E. P. Thompson showed in his studies of conflicts over common and other rights in England (1975, 1978). Nonetheless, in English common law at least since the seventeenth century it has been possible to use the principle of custom to vest property rights in land for the benefit of a local community, as in easements for public passage over private lands or for fairs (Delo 1974). American courts, on the other hand, have always been leery of customary claims and were actively hostile to them by the end of the nineteenth century (Rose 1986: 141). It was not until 1969 that a court upheld the use of the principle of custom to establish public property rights (in that case, a public easement for recreation in dry sand areas of Oregon's beaches), and questions remain about whether any other court might rule the same (Havey 1994). Given the marginality of custom as a principle in American common law, it is therefore surprising to discover how important the concept of local custom was in the nineteenth-century public trust and fisheries cases and how thoroughly its use and form were shaped by the demands of industrial capitalism, albeit dressed in pastoral imagery.

Chapter 6 Local Custom in the Delaware Shad Fisheries

Recall that the lawyer for Robert Arnold, the landed oyster planter on the Raritan River, argued in 1821 that English common law came to America "purified of local dross" and was here developed with America's own "local customs." Chief Justice Kirkpatrick denied the argument, but it reappeared in later cases as a way to support private alienation of public trust lands. Local custom in American law is distinct from the principle of customary use, an old English way of creating property rights that was rarely used in American courts (Rose 1986: 141) until its recent use to protect public access to beaches in the state of Oregon (Havey 1994). In America, local custom was often used as the authority for changes in or exceptions to the common law, even though it might be a gloss for jural invention and special interests (Friedman 1973). Also known as local common law, it was a way for courts to grapple with discrepancies between American practice and the common law.

Several Fisheries

Arguments for local custom in New Jersey tidewater law commonly refer to the way the shad fisheries of the Delaware River were organized. Commercial and subsistence seine fisheries for shad and other species were almost completely privatized. In English common law terms, they were "several," or exclusive, fisheries. Recognized and supported by acts of the legislature concerning fisheries management, the system managed conflict and preserved rights of access to valuable fish resources to the propertied few.

Privatization made logistical sense. Haul seine fishing for shad, sturgeon, and other migratory fishes (but mostly shad) was highly sedentary and localized. The strategy was to capture the fish as they came by, not to search for and pursue them as they went. Reliable access to riverside land was thus critical for access to shad fishing, as was access to a good fishing site within seining distance with suitable water depth and flow. Together, the riverbank hauling site and the fishing pool were called a "fishery." The term "fishery" was also used to refer to the social unit involved, whether a group of shareholders who split the catch among themselves or one or more people who held the fishery rights plus the people they hired to work for them. In early times and in remote locations, communal systems of sharing ownership of seines and rights to the catch were found, but on the mainstream of the Delaware River and in the nineteenth century privatization took on more individualized and industrialist forms.

In 1871 there were about thirty shad fisheries from the head of Delaware Bay to Trenton, on the New Jersey side, and about eighty from Trenton north to the New York State line on the Jersey side. Today there is one still functioning, at Lewis' Island in Lambertville, north of Trenton; shad fishing is now almost entirely for sport and for celebration of the heritage of the river (Stutz 1992). The scale of some of the "shore fisheries," especially those below Trenton, was impressive. In 1837, before dams, pollution, and fishing effort had sharply reduced the size of river runs of shad, the Fancy Hill fishery six miles below Philadelphia supplied up to seventy wagons a day with salted shad and employed about a hundred men, including fifteen to twenty-five to manage a seine net as well as foremen, clerks, marketmen, tide watchers, and so on (MacDonald 1887: 656). Shad fishing fit into the local farming routines. Its seasonality focused on brief runs of fish in the spring and sometimes the fall, happily timed so that shad fishing could "give profitable employment to a great number of men at a season when their services are not particularly required in agricultural labor" (MacDonald 1887: 656). Even late in the nineteenth century, when shad runs were noticeably down, some of the fisheries were very large operations. In 1891 the Gloucester fishery hired fifty-three men to work a thousand-yard-long seine during a month's season in the late spring (Stevenson 1899: 237).

Turn and Turn About in Quarter Shares

The case of *Yard v. Carman* (1812) demonstrates intricate details of property in a shad fishery as well as early jural concern about whether such private fisheries were another manifestation of the social injustice represented by the Game Laws of England. Here is the situation as it came to the state supreme court from a lower court:

> the witnesses fully proved, that in the season of 1802, that is, the season next before the will was made, that Thompson fished at the lower or bar fishery, which was the fishery in controversy, under a lease from Carman; and that Joshua and Joseph

> Carman also fished at the same fishery the same season. . . . Thompson had one half, and Joshua and Joseph the other, fishing, turn and turn about; that after the death of Caleb Carman, Yard, under the lease of Benjamin, claimed one fourth of the fishery, and fished there, one season, taking the fourth haul, and commenced the same way in the spring of 1808, when the defendant disputed his right, and according to the phraseology of fishermen, underrun him, and actually cut the line of his net while he was making a haul. (*Yard v. Carman* 1812: 495)

Yard, the man whose net was undercut, also claimed exclusive fishing rights: he held one quarter of the "lower or bar fishery" at Duck Island, having leased it from another Carman, who had inherited it from his father and grandfather before him. The other three quarters of the fishery were held separately by two other Carman brothers and the lessee of one of them (Thompson in the section quoted above). They managed to work under these circumstances by doing something quite familiar to drift-net and seine fishermen: they took turns setting out and pulling in their seines when the tide was right. "Turn and turn about" they called it. The fragmented rights were called "hauls." Yard took the "fourth haul" when he bought into the fishery. They all had "their separate rights to fish, haul and haul about" (*Yard v. Carman* 1812: 497) and had to work out mutually acceptable ways of coordinating their uses of those rights. For some reason, they could not work them out, at least not well enough, and the case went to the courts as a dispute over the validity of claims through inheritance, purchase, and tenancies.

The facts of the case show that a fishery was treated as a partible estate. Partition was not only of fishing space but also of the right to make a sweep of a fishing spot with a haul seine. In other words, two persons could fish the same fishing pool "in halves," taking turns when the tide was right, turn and turn about. Rights could be divided further. In this instance fishing time was divided into quarters, four persons taking their separate rights to fish, haul, and haul about. Thus, the property system served the important management function of reducing conflict by regulating access to fishing space that was extremely valuable: as many as forty thousand shad had been taken at Duck Island in one short season.

The tenurial system of the Delaware River shad fisheries is remarkable less for its details than for the fact that those details were framed by wills, deeds, and laws. Taking turns at hauling large seines in a confined area is one thing. Having the exclusive, heritable, salable right to take a turn, say, the fourth haul or the third haul, is yet another. It is remarkable in light of what we know about local and informal systems of fisheries management today, where turn taking is almost always part of an informal and customary mode of regulation (but see Martin 1994 on Columbia River gill-netters). It was remarkable then, too, and one of the jurists who heard the case saw fit to remark upon it.

The case was decided on narrow grounds, on the issue of who had rights how to what, an issue that called for Solomon-like skills on the part of the court, given the entanglements of the property claims involved. The decision had little effect on what happened on the Delaware. Yard and the Carmans probably went back to Duck Island and renewed their competition for fish and fishing space and their disputes over rights. However, Associate Justice William Pennington, who wrote the opinion, raised a question about whether the exclusive rights they fought over could and should exist, a question emphasized in the published report of the case although apparently not part of the actual decision. Presaging *Arnold v. Mundy,* Pennington reviewed the "usual" English authorities on public trust fisheries law: Blackstone, Lord Coke, Sir Matthew Hale. Admitting some dissension among them, especially about the meaning of the term "free fishery,"[1] Pennington interpreted them and the common law to mean that without a specific grant, any fishery on "branches of the sea in which the tide ebbs and flows" is a "public common of fishery" (*Yard v. Carman* 1812). Pennington was disturbed that the court was asked to decide on competing rights "to haul and haul about" when the litigants should be asking whether the exclusive rights they were fighting over, and the original title from which their claims derived, ever existed or should exist: "I am not satisfied that two litigant parties are to be indulged in admitting rights, incompatible with the rights of the people, and thereby endangering the rights of every member of the community" (*Yard v. Carman* 1812: 500).

Pennington saw the common right to fish as a natural right, upheld in English law after the Magna Carta. Any curtailment of that right was analogous to the socially discriminatory Game Laws of England, the laws that for centuries reserved the right to hunt wild game to the nobility and the landed and even made poaching game a capital punishment (Thompson 1975). "The exercise of this exclusive right of fishing in the arms of the sea and great rivers, was thought by our English ancestors, a restraint on their natural rights, as odious or more injurious than the game laws" (*Yard v. Carman* 1812: 501).

Pennington's opinion is consistent with his biography. He was among the founders of a populist political movement that emphasized the "common man" (Elmer 1872: 163; Keasbey 1912; Fee 1933: 196). However, Pennington was in the minority in this case and was to remain marginal to the issue he broached.[2] But his social equity concerns were echoed in Kirkpatrick's much later enunciation of the inalienability of the public trust doctrine. It should be noted that Kirkpatrick was chief justice in *Yard v. Carman* too, although he spoke only to procedural issues in the published report.

Seiners versus Netters: *Bennett v. Boggs* (1831)

Exclusive rights of fishing for Delaware River shad remained solidly entrenched in custom and law despite concerns like Pennington's and despite the public trust ruling of Kirkpatrick in 1821. They were supported by fisheries management legislation. Indeed, like oystering, shad fishing shows how early and well developed fisheries management was in this region, contrary to the standard wisdom of the inability of people to halt "tragedies" of open access fishing. Very early on people with interests in the fishery tried to use the authority and power of the courts and the state to regulate and restrict access to it. Formal regulation of the Delaware River commons began in 1765, when the colonial assemblies of Pennsylvania and New Jersey, which disagreed about boundaries of jurisdiction,[3] passed acts that outlawed "wears [weirs], racks, baskets, fishing dams, [and] pounds" that obstructed fish migration (Bush 1986: 342–45). They also established minimum mesh sizes and enforcement measures. Further acts were passed in the eighteenth century. After 1793, the two new states agreed to concurrent jurisdiction up to the low-water mark on each side of the river, and their regulations were coordinated to protect the shore fisheries from ship traffic. They also cooperated to protect the fisheries from "persons fishing under claim of a common right" (New Jersey General Assembly 1799: 581). By 1808 regulations explicitly protected haul seiners from common-right fishermen by outlawing the use of all other kinds of fishing gear in areas defined as "fishing pools" or "fishing places," which in turn were defined as whatever water was encompassed in the sweep of the great seines from the riverbanks (New Jersey Laws 1808: 106).

The regulations and in particular the exclusive rights of the owners of the haul seine fisheries were persistently challenged. The phrase "fishing under claim of a common right" reappears in subsequent regulations; the claimants and the issue would not go away and were difficult to control. Hence *Bennett v. Boggs* (1831). It arose from one of many attempts by common-right fishermen to challenge the exclusivity of the "fishing pools." It was colored by the fact that the defendant, who claimed common rights of fishing, was a gill-netter from Philadelphia and the plaintiff, who claimed private rights, was a haul seiner from New Jersey. As an interstate matter, it went to the federal district court, meeting in Philadelphia, like *Keen v. Rice* in 1822 (chapter 2). Presiding was Henry Baldwin, who later participated in the 1837 case of *John Den ex dem. William C. H. Waddell v. Merrit Martin and Others* in favor of the Proprietors of East New Jersey. Like that case, it was immediately printed because of great public and special interest in both interstate matters and riparian property rights.

For eight days in late March 1829, during the height of the annual upriver migration of shad, Samuel Boggs of Philadelphia tried to take his gilling seine into the fishing pools used by riparian rights holders. The following description of Abraham Bennett's haul seine fishery, in Waterford Township, Gloucester County, New Jersey, shows how crowded the shore fisheries were and why Boggs's gilling seine was more than an annoyance:

> [Bennett's] haul is from the upper line of the lands of Benjamin Cooper, down to the mouth of Cooper's Creek. Petty's Island lies between this fishery and the Pennsylvania shore. On part of this island, on the Jersey side, is another fishery; so that the two seines sweep partly over the same pool when out, though hauled in on different sides of the river. These . . . seines . . . are usually about 50 or 60 fathoms in length; are extended across the channel, and drift with the tide. (*Bennett v. Boggs* 1831: 4–5)

Bennett sued Boggs. Boggs then tried to use the regulatory system to justify his action. He registered his gill net in a bond transaction in Philadelphia. Pennsylvania and New Jersey had "concurrent jurisdiction," and thus New Jersey was supposed to accept his Pennsylvania registration. He specified a fishing area just as the riparian owners did. He claimed that he fished inside this area and was careful not to fish above low-water mark and not to go on the shore; he "had always drifted in that part of the river which is covered by water at all times of the tide" (*Bennett v. Boggs* 1831: 6). Thus, he claimed that he too had a fishery, constituted by his own fifty-fathom net with a six-inch mesh. Samuel Boggs went too far, though. Not only did he dare to claim rights to a fishery without owning the adjacent land, but the fishing area he claimed was about five miles long, on each side of the river, and it happened to encompass the private claims of numerous riparian owners. Needless to say, none of them had given him permission to fish in the areas they claimed.

Boggs audaciously claimed a right to fish with his seine anywhere on the river within the bounds he had described in his bond. Echoing the Pennsylvanians in the earlier oyster cases (chapter 2), his other defense was that the act protecting the private rights of riparian owners was unconstitutional, "being in restriction of a right common to all the citizens of the United States" (*Bennett v. Boggs* 1831: 6). Attorneys for Bennett, on the other hand, defended the constitutionality of the act. They argued that restricting common rights was justified for conservation reasons, being a way to control the use of damaging fishing gear:

"the provisions therein [are] wise and salutary, and greatly beneficial to the community, in preserving a valuable species of fish, which the gilling seines have a tendency to destroy and frighten from our waters" (*Bennett v. Boggs* 1831: 6).

The law as interpreted by Justice Baldwin was clearly on the side of the riparian property holders and the right of the state to impose restrictions on common-right fishing for purposes of conservation. Boggs's claim to a fishing pool was impossible, by definition: "[t]he . . . law of 1808 . . . defines a pool or fishing place . . . to be, from the place where seines are usually thrown in, to the place where they have been usually taken out, or where they may hereafter be so thrown in or taken out" (*Bennett v. Boggs* 1831: 7). Baldwin also noted that Boggs's belated attempt to register his fishing place was a ruse, undertaken only "for the purpose of evading the laws of New Jersey" (*Bennett v. Boggs* 1831: 9).

Baldwin dismissed the relevance of the fact offered in Boggs's defense that the Proprietors of West New Jersey had granted a common right of fishing to all inhabitants in 1676. Baldwin's position in this 1831 case differs from the position he took in 1837 while attempting to overturn the *Arnold v. Mundy* public trust ruling (*Waddell's Lessee v. Martin et al.* 1837). Here he denigrated the claim of common rights through the Proprietors of West New Jersey: he interpreted political history such that the Proprietors had no property rights or jurisdiction over fishing and navigation. Those remained with the crown and after the American Revolution went to the states. Six years later he would argue in favor of private rights through the Proprietors of East New Jersey.

Whether the state was within its rights to make fishery laws had come up in the oystering conflict between Jerseyans and Philadelphians discussed in chapter 2. It was central to Baldwin's deliberation, and he fully supported the state's powers, declaring also that if anyone felt the laws passed conflicted "with our opinions of policy, expediency, or justice," the proper recourse was political, not judicial (*Bennett v. Boggs* 1831: 12–13).

Finally, he said that there was no question about the rights of riparian owners in front of their lands on the Delaware River: "[t]hey undoubtedly had rights of fishery to a certain extent under the colonial government, which were recognized by New Jersey and Pennsylvania, by the compact of 1783. It is admitted, that from a very early period of the history of the state, shore fisheries have been considered as private property, capable of being devised and alienated with, or separate from the land to which they were annexed, subject to taxation, and taxed as other real estate" (*Bennett v. Boggs* 1831: 14). The state legislature was within its right to support these fisheries and to prohibit other fisheries that might compete or conflict with them: "[i]n thus enlarging the private, and restraining the common right of fishery, they have infringed no constitutional injunction; their acts are the law of state" (*Bennett v. Boggs* 1831: 15).

Boggs lost and had to pay a fine for trying to catch shad in the riverside fishing pools. The federal district court upheld Bennett's property claims and the state laws protecting them. In later years, judges and attorneys trying to support the rights of the Proprietors against those of the state or to invoke the use of local custom as an exception to the public trust doctrine almost always turned to the local custom of the private shad fisheries of the Delaware, sometimes citing *Bennett v. Boggs,* sometimes citing the 1884 case to which I now turn.

Riparian versus Customary Rights: *Fitzgerald v. Faunce* (1884)

Fitzgerald v. Faunce adds a new source of property rights: a state agency. Supported by the public trust and fishery cases, the state legislature asserted its ownership of tidewater lands against common law or customary claims of riparian owners and then got into the business of selling off riparian lands to corporations and individuals by creating a separate agency more or less immune from legislative interference. In 1871 the legislature appointed a riparian commission that was to survey tidewater lands of the northern part of the state and the Delaware and to sell the underwater land for the purposes of land improvement and economic development. In 1891 its domain was extended to the rest of the state.[4] As will be discussed later, the commission was very controversial, particularly when the commissioners granted away natural beds of oysters (chapters 9 and 10). On the Delaware River and Bay one of the reasons for controversy was their use of their power as yet another way to claim exclusive rights in shad fishing.

Here is the problem. Wilson Fitzgerald claimed exclusive fishery rights through a riparian grant received from the new riparian commission. Christian Faunce's claim was one of title through purchase and inheritance dating back to the late eighteenth century. The major question was whether anyone held the property rights that Faunce claimed to have purchased, given public trust rulings about land below high-water mark and common rights for fishing and navigation.

The facts of the case are similar to those of *Yard v. Carman* in showing how precise and separable fishing rights could be. The deed granted by a Mr. Whitall to Christian Faunce in 1818 was for complete title to one small riverside lot that had a cabin on it. In addition, for two other lots (off a sluice in Little Mantua

Creek) Faunce purchased "the sole right, privilege, use and enjoyment at all times for all purposes of fishing whatsoever, and for no other purpose" (*Fitzgerald v. Faunce* 1884: 537). This was a right of fishery separable from other uses of the land and the subject of the case. In addition, the deed shows that fishing rights could be divided into lunar tide units. Whitall deeded to Faunce "the right and privilege of laying off the nets used on the said ground at the flood fishing" over a specified distance and reserved to himself the right of laying off the nets used in his lower fishing ground at the ebb fishing for shad and herring up to a certain point on the river (*Bennett v. Boggs* 1831: 537–38). Also specified in the deed was the right to dry the nets on a certain meadow of the Whitall farm, close to the place "where the soap-house now stands." The rights were clearly specified and delimited by place and function, and none of them were defined as exclusive ownership rights of the land itself.

Eventually Fitzgerald fenced off access to the tidal lands that he claimed through the riparian commission. Faunce and his "workmen" broke down that fence at the beginning of the spring shad season in April 1881. They fished from the disputed riverbank throughout the season of 1881, making hauls at high water near the foot of the bank and at low water just outside the flats. Then they went to court.

In the local circuit court Faunce claimed the "right of several fishery" against Fitzgerald's claim of proprietorship through the riparian commissioners. Faunce presented the original deed and other evidence to support his claim. In the instructions to the jury, the Gloucester County circuit court judge reviewed the various objections to Faunce's claim, including the public trust doctrine:

> By the common law the land-owner had no right beyond high-water mark, and therefore could not, under such law, derive title to a several fishery by deed from the Proprietors. It has been decided in this state by the court of last resort, that at common law the State of New Jersey is the absolute owner of land in all navigable waters where the tide ebbs and flows . . . , and that the state can grant such land to any one to be for his exclusive use. (*Fitzgerald v. Faunce* 1884: 544)

In response, the defendant, Faunce, brought up local custom: "there is a local custom, or local common law in New Jersey, applicable to shore fisheries along the river Delaware, which recognizes the right of property in several fishery, and that this right has been acknowledged and maintained by the legislature and the courts" (*Fitzgerald v. Faunce* 1884: 545).

The local jury upheld Faunce's claim to "several" rights of fishery. It then went on appeal to the state supreme court. Justice Depue delivered the court's unanimous opinion, which reviewed the entire history of the shad fisheries of

New Jersey and the common law of tidelands. The challenge was to reconcile the fact that Faunce and many other shad fishermen on the river claimed and enjoyed exclusive fishing rights with the public trust doctrine, which reserved all property below mean high-water mark to the state and protected common use rights for fishing and navigation.

The decision is a lesson in the persuasive power of narrative at law: the case report casts the exclusive fishery and fishing rights of the Delaware River as unbroken tradition. Fact upon fact is listed to show that several fishing rights have been accepted for the Delaware River region from time immemorial, as the legal phrase goes. From the eighteenth century on, the fisheries of the Delaware were acknowledged as private property in local practice, in interstate compacts concerning jurisdiction of the river, in numerous legislative acts and taxation practices, and in the courts. They were treated as real estate: "[s]ometimes they passed with the shore, at other times they were detached, but whether united or severed from the shore they were regarded and treated as real property" (*Fitzgerald v. Faunce* 1884: 546). They were the subject of inheritance, sale, and partition, as shown above, and were registered with local courts. They were even taxed as real estate.[5] They were treated as private property in the interstate compacts between New Jersey and Pennsylvania. Finally, they were recognized and protected through numerous legislative acts to regulate fishing on the Delaware River. Therefore, the court pointed out, the idea of a local custom or local common law appeared to have been derived from a "common understanding" among owners, the public, and the courts.

In his opinion, Justice Depue set aside—or dodged—the question of whether the property claimed by Faunce was superior or subordinate to title of the state in lands under tidewaters: "[t]here are other questions to be disposed of before that question can arise" (*Fitzgerald v. Faunce* 1884: 591). He did this by denying the separability of fishing rights from land rights, one of the "American inventions" (chapter 5). The court determined that Christian Faunce received not just a license or easement but a full estate in the property he received from Whitall in 1818, even though the deed was to "the sole right, privilege, use and enjoyment at all times for all purposes of fishing whatsoever, and for no other purpose" (*Fitzgerald v. Faunce* 1884: 596, 537). The argument, given authority by reference to English common law and the long catalog of New Jersey custom but ignoring English practice (see Hull 1924), was that any grant of exclusive use of lands that excludes the person granting it is, de facto, "a grant of the soil itself, and not a mere easement" (*Fitzgerald v. Faunce* 1884: 596).

The fishing rights were not separable after all. Faunce had more than fishing rights; he became, in the court's terms, "riparian owner" (*Fitzgerald v. Faunce*

1884: 598) of the land whose exclusive fishing rights were conveyed to him in 1818. This called into question Fitzgerald's claim to a riparian grant, because the terms of riparian law deriving from an act of 1871 restricted such grants to the owners of land upon which the tide flows: Faunce had inadvertently become that owner.

Given the intricacy of many of its deliberations and its recognition of the contingency of ownership claims on the good will of the legislature and particular courts, the court's conclusion was surprisingly confident and unequivocal. It was that Faunce had the exclusive shad-fishing rights because he was not just the holder of those rights but a riverain landowner as well, and "by the law of this state owners of lands upon the Delaware river have a right of fishery adjacent to the shore front in their ownership, which is the subject of exclusive enjoyment and capable of alienation" (*Fitzgerald v. Faunce* 1884: 599). By the end of the opinion, the question of whether there was a legitimate claim prior to the riparian grant given by the state was beyond question.

Conclusion

The privatized tenure system of the Delaware fisheries declined only as the shad diminished in number and as shad fishermen who could move up and down the river and into Delaware Bay to find fish and follow them through their migratory rounds gained competitive advantage (Stevenson 1899). Haul seining gave way to gill netting, especially after the 1850s, and private property rights in fisheries gradually became less salient as fishermen moved offshore and as dams and other artifacts of economic growth blocked the migratory paths and fouled the breeding grounds of shad. Although the private fisheries declined in importance, the local common law they embodied and came to symbolize did not, and courts consistently ignored or sidestepped the question raised in 1812 by Justice Pennington: whether the exclusive fishing rights on the Delaware River were as unjustly discriminatory as the Game Laws of England.

Chapter 7 Local Custom on the Banks of the Hudson

The geography of the local custom and legal disputes of this study shifts to the colonial province of East New Jersey, to the line between New York and New Jersey, on the Hudson River and New York Bay, a region of uplands and extensive tidal meadows and marshes that became increasingly valuable during the nineteenth century "because of its neighborhood to the great Emporium of the Continent," New York City (Parker 1864: 49). A series of very confusing cases about grass cutting, plus others on rights of waterfront property owners, dealt with aspects of tidewater law that led to a very solid appreciation of the power of a state legislature to alienate the public trust.

The Right to Cut Grass on a Riverbank

Sometime in the late 1830s, Mary Bell cut grass on a bank along the Hudson River in a place called Harsimus Cove. Edward Gough accused Mrs. Bell of trespassing; he was a tenant of the Coles family, which claimed to own the place where Mary cut the grass. Coles's land title was through a 1668 grant through one of the original proprietary grants to the town of Bergen. At issue was whether this included the right to fill adjacent land and claim that land as private property. Mary Bell, for her part, claimed that she owned that place and the right to cut the grass there because not long before it had been underwater, and she held title to the underwater land. Gough had reclaimed the land from the river, but it was not his to reclaim; it was hers.

The conflict perplexed the courts. The first hearing was in 1844 at the Hudson circuit of the courts (Zabriskie 1871: 38); it went to the state's highest court in 1847 and again in 1850 and 1852. It reemerged in federal district court as an ejectment case in 1853. The last was not reported as such; the chief justice's charge to the jury was reprinted in 1864 (Grier 1864). The first, third, and fourth decisions were on the side of Edward Gough and the Coles family; the second and the fifth were in favor of Mary Bell but clearly denied her claim to a structure known as the "Long Dock" that had been built out into Harsimus Cove.

Although the cases took up much court time and public attention, little information exists beyond the case reports themselves. Neither Bell nor Gough appears in New Jersey's published biographies. Some information appears in discussions of that case in the context of a dissenting opinion by Abraham Zabriskie, who was then chancellor in the state, in an 1870 case, *Stevens v. Paterson and Newark Railroad Company,* which also will be discussed below. His dissenting opinion in the *Stevens* case was published as part of a pamphlet (Anonymous 1871; cited hereafter as Zabriskie 1871), printed in Jersey City in 1871 and attributed to the Paterson and Newark Railroad Company. It was directed at all riparian landowners and urged them to support an attempt to have all of New Jersey's riparian laws repealed. Zabriskie had been counsel in the earliest version of the Bell/Gough dispute (Zabriskie 1871), and in 1851 he was instrumental in passing the Wharf Act (Robson 1877: 103–5), an attempt by the legislature to clarify what was still murky from the *Bell v. Gough* decisions.

The story goes back to the beginning of the nineteenth century, when Nathaniel Budd, Mary Bell's father, took up the ferry business at Harsimus Cove. He did not own any land; he built his house and the ferry dock on land that was claimed by another family but contested by the township. The dispute hurt his business, so he went to the legislature to get a franchise for his ferry and some land for his ferry house. This was in 1804 (Grier 1864: 82–83). To better secure his position, in the same year he also took title to fifty-three and a half acres of river bottom in Harsimus Cove itself. This he got in a roundabout way, through a notable lawyer and public figure, Elisha Boudinot, who had gone to the Board of General Proprietors of East New Jersey the year before, in 1803, to have the cove surveyed and deeded over. Boudinot's claim is the first record I have found of a Proprietor's grant to tidelands.

Budd abandoned the ferry soon after, in 1806. There is no information about what Nathaniel Budd did after giving up the ferry business. Nor do we know for sure why he went to the legislature thirty years later to get title to muddy bottom, although the fact that Edward Gough filled in part of that bottom and claimed it as his own must have played a role: this happened in 1836, just before Budd went to the legislature (Zabriskie 1871). The public trust ruling of *Arnold v. Mundy* created uncertainty about the validity of all titles to submarine land gained through the Proprietors, and thus an act of the legislature was required under the state ownership doctrine.

The Larger Picture

A woman cutting grass on the side of the river presents a pastoral image, but it is more appropriate to imagine steamboats and railway lines and canals, because this is likely what the participants in this case were imagining, beginning to see, and trying to construct at the time. Harsimus Cove is at the northern side of Jersey City, a new town that was the site of several other important cases, located as it was at the heart of the industrializing Northeast on the banks of the Hudson River across from Manhattan Island. Several groups of investors were trying to gain control of the area for development. For example, in 1837 the legislature gave rights to a corporation to purchase a thousand acres of land "under and above water" in Harsimus Cove and to reclaim and build bulkheads, locks, piers, wharves, and docks.[1] This development, like others, was stalled for many years, partly because of difficulty getting clear definition of property rights.

Accordingly, the actions of Nathaniel Budd and his grass-cutting daughter and others that shortly followed were closely watched and possibly part of a very high stakes game. Recall, this was only two years after the Board of General Proprietors of East New Jersey made the contentious lease to Waddell, and the federal district court case had not yet been held (see chapter 5). As one of the lawyers involved wrote in retrospect, "the conflicting claims of the State and the proprietors drew the attention of the public" (Zabriskie 1871: 37).

The context and hints here and there suggest that this too was a test case, designed for the purpose of determining property rights with the intent of gaining control of very valuable property for speculation or industrial development. Apart from Budd and his daughter, the people involved were clearly among the elite of the region. As I have said, little historical information is available, but we do know that very soon after the legislature granted Budd's title on November 8, 1836, there was a foreclosure sale on the property, and it was purchased by Budd's daughter, Mary Bell (Zabriskie 1871). However, one report states that she did not actually buy it herself. Willis Hall bought the property from Budd in October 1835, a year before the legislature confirmed Budd's title (*Gough v. Bell* 1850: 157). Willis Hall, a former attorney general of New York, became Mary Bell's lawyer. These facts—but no clue about how Mary Bell's property rights were derived from Hall's purchase—were mentioned by another one of her lawyers, Abraham Zabriskie, who like Hall was eminent in his profession. As noted above, Zabriskie was very active in New Jersey politics and law, including railroad politics and waterfront property law, and he became chancellor in New Jersey (Zabriskie 1871: 38). Also to the point, he engineered the 1851

Wharf Act, which built upon the legal plight of Mary Bell and Edward Gough (Robson 1877: 103–5). So we may suspect that Hall and Zabriskie took on Mary Bell's case for more than the lawyer's fee or the chance to express gallantry.

Local Custom: The Rights of Wharfing Out and Filling In

The 1844 circuit court decision about Mary Bell's grass-cutting rights was on behalf of Edward Gough, denying that Mary Bell had any title. The 1847 state supreme court supported Bell on the grounds that the state held title below high-water mark, and thus the legislature could grant the land to her father, as it did in the act of 1836. However, in 1850 the supreme court gave benefit to Gough on the grounds that "continued custom" or "local custom" gave the adjacent landowner the right to fill in the shore in front of his lands and to appropriate that land. Sitting as the court of errors and appeals in 1852, the court reaffirmed that decision (Zabriskie 1871: 38).

Local custom in this case was the practice of appropriating the foreshore for landfilling, docking, and other purposes. Two points were clear and contradictory: the state was the owner of land below high-water mark, and shore landowners held special rights or privileges in adjacent intertidal lands. Some justices, concerned to defend both the primacy of English common law *and* the position of waterfront property owners, acknowledged the latter as privileges of "adjacency." The waterfront landowner was better situated than most to enjoy uses of the tidewaters but otherwise had no rights against the state, following the American reading of English common law.[2] The majority, however, accepted the argument that in this case English common law did not apply. In the words of Cortlandt Parker, a lawyer generally opposed to this perspective who wrote at a later stage of debate about the same issue:

> In the application of this doctrine [public trust] a difference has been made in New Jersey according to circumstances, and the character of the property in question. A peculiar common law has been recognized by the highest Courts of the State. Common law comprises customs "whereof the memory of man runneth not to the contrary"—and the first year of King Richard I. is the established date of this memory. But it has been decided, first by our Supreme Court (2 Zab. 441), and then by the Court of Errors (3 Zab. 624) [two *Gough v. Bell* cases], that there was a *peculiar common law* in this State, applicable to this subject, deducible from ordinary usage, received opinions popularly and at the bar, and implied admissions in Legislative acts; and that by this, if a shore owner took possession and actually reclaimed land down to low-water mark, it became his, so that he could sue, if need be, for trespass, should any one enter thereon. (Parker 1864: 50, emphasis added)

Riparian landowners were the loudest in raising concerns about the policy implications of the court rulings. Although their rights to fill in and appropriate were acknowledged, so was the state's ownership up to high-water mark. Accordingly, in 1851 the legislature passed the Wharf Act, which was introduced and carried through to passage by Abraham Zabriskie in the state senate (he had been counsel in the 1844 case), plus another senator who was the leading counsel of *Gough v. Bell* (Zabriskie 1871: 42–43). The Wharf Act was supposed to clearly recognize the rights of riparian proprietors to wharf out as far as low-water mark and beyond that to do so with license from county boards of freeholders, which were required to provide the license unless so doing would hurt public rights of navigation. The Wharf Act codified local custom and supported local control.

According to Zabriskie, writing at a later phase of state assertion of its ownership powers, the Wharf Act "was intended to settle and quiet the rights of the shore owners in lands underwater in front of them. It had been the general impression in the state that the title to the shore to low water mark was vested absolutely in the shore owner. These decisions had disturbed them and left their rights somewhat vague and indefinite" (Zabriskie 1864: 59).

State Ownership and the Riparian Commissions

In the decade following the *Gough v. Bell* decisions and the Wharf Act, shoreside real estate business was brisk: "strips of land along the shore, themselves of no value, have been sold at large prices, for the right of reclaiming existing and confirmed and defined by this [wharf] act" (Zabriskie 1864: 60). In 1864 the state senate and house of assembly held an inquiry into the extent to which the state should be sharing in the profits from the situation, eliciting the opinions of eminent lawyers. Zabriskie (1864) continued his support of the "local common law" or "rights of adjacency" of the shoreside property owners. Others, Cortlandt Parker in particular, argued that wharfing out was a privilege, to be licensed by the state (Parker 1864). At particular issue was whether the state could take the rights/privileges of the riparian proprietors in order to raise money to support the state government. Zabriskie argued against it: "this is not the public purpose for which the power [of eminent domain] is reserved" (1864: 61).

Following the inquiry in 1864, the legislature created a riparian commission that was to identify the "rights of the state" in the northern, industrializing area of the Hudson River, in New York Bay, and in Kill van Kull, the waterway separating New Jersey from New York (Staten Island). Licenses continued to be issued by the county boards of chosen freeholders under the Wharf Act. The commissioners secured agreement on a line beyond which the tidal lands could not be filled in, in order to protect public interests in navigation in places like Harsimus Cove that were rapidly being filled in by railroads and other businesses.

The subsequent history of the state's attempt to define and gain from its public trust claims to foreshore and bay bottoms is one of a series of riparian commissions. They were highly politicized and often controversial bodies engaged in selling or giving away (it varied in both fact and interpretation) the state's claims to intertidal and tidal lands. In 1869 the legislature created a riparian commission that was intended to take from country freeholders the work of deciding on conveyances of state property to private firms and individuals through grants and leases. It was made up of four members, appointed for life; for any grant or lease, three of the four had to agree, as did the governor and the attorney general of the state. Due to concern about politicization and cronyism, the structural details and personnel were often changed. In the early 1880s the legislature limited the terms of the commissioners to four years; early in the 1890s the commissioners "were legislated out of office" (New Jersey Riparian Committee 1906–7: 255) and replaced by a new group that included the governor. Later in the 1890s they were "legislated out" yet again, and an attempt was made to balance the politics inherent in this land-granting commission by requiring that no more than two of the four commissioners (besides the governor) should belong to the same political party. The situation was reviewed several times in the twentieth century as well. The riparian commissioners were moved from one agency to another. In 1945, they moved from the Board of Commerce and Navigation, which was abolished, to the new Department of Conservation, which changed names several times and in 1970 was replaced by the Department of Environmental Protection. In the course of these changes, the riparian commission itself changed in name and form several times. In 1970 it became the Natural Resource Council, which continued the system of gubernatorial appointments of citizens to multiyear terms, with the mandate to demarcate and allocate public trust lands. It is now the Tidelands Management Office of DEP.

The Railroad Cases

But let us return to the latter nineteenth century, particularly the 1860s and 1870s, when the state legislature attempted to stake out a clear claim to tidelands while providing a mechanism for disbursing them to private uses. Railroads were among the key private users, and important legal cases reflected and supported this fact. The second group of riparian commissioners, the first to have a clear mandate from the legislature, met in Hoboken in April 1869. A survey done in 1865 was revisited, and the surveyor reported that Central Railroad Company of New Jersey and the New York and Erie Railroad Company were illegally developing the tidewater lands of the state, "making encroachments beyond the lines for solid filling in Harsimus Cove, and on the Hudson River" (New Jersey Riparian Commissioners 1870: 1018). The major and difficult task was to persuade corporations and individuals to apply for grants or leases from the state.

The situation was once again marked by legal controversy. Two major test cases delayed action. One was a suit in 1871 by the attorney general of New York against a railroad (*People of the State of New York v. Central Railroad of New Jersey*), once more asserting the jurisdiction of New York State up to the low-water mark on New Jersey's side of the Hudson River and New York Bay. Any structure beyond that mark was a nuisance, according to the suit. Fortunately for New Jersey, the New York Court of Appeals ruled in favor of New Jersey's own "right to claim, control and dispose of the water or shore-front privileges known as 'Riparian' " (Randolph 1871: 961).[3]

The second critical case holding up the work of the riparian commission was *Stevens v. Paterson and Newark Railroad Company,* heard in 1870 in the state's supreme court. It was based on a conflict between Frederick Stevens, a riparian landowner, and one of the large railroads to which the state had granted trust lands and which had prevented Stevens from access to the waterfront. The 1870 court determined that the state was free to grant land underwater to a private individual or corporation (the railroad company) even if this cut off the riparian owner (Stevens) from the benefits derived from his property's contiguity to the water. Moreover, the riparian owner had no legal right to compensation.

Zabriskie and others who participated in the *Stevens* case helped shape general understanding about the public trust: "[i]n all these decisions it was held by the courts that by the common law the State owned the fee of the shore, and that the right to reclaim and appropriate was based upon a change in the common law, made like many changes which have been made, to adapt it to the condition and circumstances of the people" (Zabriskie 1871: 38). The common law had changed, as it should, and it was "local common law, established in New Jersey" (Zabriskie 1871: 38). However, the law was still uncertain about the rights of riparian landowners to wharf out and fill in. The majority held that the rulings of *Gough v. Bell* were merely *dicta,* not necessarily precedent. Left open was the question of rights of adjacency, including whether even the expectation of being able to fill in and appropriate was a property right.

The case settled the question of whether state ownership was "merely" a matter of sovereignty or whether it was true proprietorship. According to Governor

Randolph, in his message of 1871, the result was "that the state is in no sense a mere trustee of a property, of value to some of her citizens, and of no interest to others." The state could grant absolute title to riparian lands without compensating the owner of adjacent lands.

However, the governor hedged on behalf of the riparian landowners, as opposed to the public at large: "[c]omplete and final as is this decision in favor of the state, I should deem it most unwise in policy, and unjust to a large class of our citizens, who have inherited or purchased these water-fronts—under the common impression of their superior value—to take advantage of the power the state has secured" (Randolph 1871: 10–11). He said they would continue to "prefer" the riparian owner in leases or sales. Indeed, in the first year of the riparian commission (1869–70), all of the grants made were to riparian landowners (New Jersey Riparian Commissioners 1870: 1019).

Conclusion: Local Custom and the Public Trust

The language of the law colored much of this debate with a pastoralism ill suited to the harsher realities of landfills, railroad bridges, and the other transforming activities of industrialism. For example, in the *Stevens* debate, the position of the railroad was represented as equivalent to the position of someone drawing a boat up to a riverbank or spreading nets out to dry. An example comes from a statement by Justice Beasley, arguing for the need to distinguish the specific rights of a riparian proprietor from those he holds as a member of the larger public. First, Beasley quoted Justice Potts, from *Gough v. Bell,* as enumerating the rights of the riparian landowner: "as appurtenant to the upland: a right of towing on the banks, of landing, lading and unlading; a right of way to the shore; a right to draw seines upon the upland, and of erecting fishing huts. He has the right of fishery, of ferry, and every other which is properly appendant to the owner of the soil; and he holds every one of these by as sacred a tenure as he holds the land from which they emanate" (Potts, in *Gough v. Bell,* cited by Beasley in *Stevens v. Paterson and Newark Railroad Company* 1870: 968). The pastoral imagery is retained in the important argument that follows:

> [Potts is wrong in] . . . overlooking the fact that some of the rights enumerated belong to the riparian proprietor as a member of the community, and that others of them belong to him in his character of owner of the soil. Not one of the privileges in the water which are ascribed to him, emanate from his ownership of the land. In common with every other citizen, he can fish in the water, and pass and repass to

> and from the water along the shore. But he has not these rights by virtue of his property; they attach to him as an individual, and he holds them in common with other citizens. They are part *rerum communium*. Then, again, it is true, it is lawful for him to land on the bank, and to dry his nets and to build fishing huts there. But the right to do these things . . . appertain to him, in the ordinary way, as the owner of the land. (*Stevens v. Paterson and Newark Railroad Company* 1870: 968–69)

The chief justice gave no clue that the *rerum communium* might include railroads and steamships, even though he argued for their rights as against the more rural pursuits of Mr. Stevens, who was no longer able to get to the water from his property.

In the rest of this passage Beasley redefined what local custom is all about and dismissed its relevance to the public trust issue in favor of a more pragmatic test: "[t]he case is merely this: the man who owns the land next to navigable water, is more conveniently situated for the enjoyment of the public easement than the rest of the community. But a mere enumeration of the advantages of that position falls far short of showing that such proprietor has, in the *jus publicum,* by the common law, more or higher rights than others" (*Stevens v. Paterson and Newark Railroad Company* 1870: 969). Beasley interpreted the earlier New Jersey court and legislative recognition of the local custom of riparian claims to tidelands as "privilege, by local custom" rather than as right by common law that might hold against the power of the legislature.

Local custom had played a major role protecting the rights of waterfront landowners as against the state and, by implication, the boating and fishing public, and it would retain that role. As Leonard Jaffee wrote in 1971, in the context of recent conflicts about public trust lands in New Jersey, the nineteenth-century courts in their use of local custom could allow property owners to translate the convenience of their situations into improvements such as building wharves and filling in lands. If the legislature did not intervene, then the public was held to have acquiesced, and local custom was established. By this means riparian owners could carve out private domain from the public commons (Jaffee 1971: 662). However, the courts were quite capable of changing their minds, particularly when more powerful interests were at stake, and this appears to be what Beasley was doing in *Stevens*.

Although local custom was often advanced to support the claims of riparian owners against the rights of the state (and those to whom the state wished to lease or give rights), the state gradually won out, at least in the courts. In a dispute between the state and the mayor of Jersey City (representing a corporation that had obtained waterfront rights from the legislature years before), the court recognized the state's right to grant riparian lands (*State v. Mayor of Jersey City* 1856; Keys 1986). In 1864 and 1869, as mentioned above, and in 1871, in response to the court cases discussed, the legislature passed other acts that eventually replaced the general right of the riparian owner with rights obtained only by application to agents of the state, the riparian commissioners. In 1891 the legislature clarified that the Wharf Act no longer applied. The rights of riparian landowners were derived only from the ownership rights of the state (see Goldschore 1979: 25, for a summary history).

That the state "won" does not mean that the notion of a public trust, in the sense of sovereign stewardship that Kirkpatrick talked about in *Arnold v. Mundy,* remained unscathed. On the contrary, the battle was between two classes of proprietors, and it was over who should reap the benefits of private property. The state's claims were represented and alienated through riparian commissions. The state was "fee simple" proprietor more than trustee for the public. In *Stevens v. Paterson and Newark Railroad Company,* Chief Justice Beasley compared the position of the state legislature to that of the English parliament, which, unlike the king, had the authority to take away public rights of navigation and fishing (1870: 977). So, too, "the American legislature has the authority to regulate or destroy at its pleasure, and for the common welfare, the public rights in navigable rivers" (*Stevens v. Paterson and Newark Railroad Company* 1870: 978).

Chapter 8 Alienation of the Public Trust

Common use rights are often thought of as reliant on local social systems and their customs and moral economies (Thompson 1991), but the opposite was true in nineteenth-century New Jersey, where the local was the private. The Delaware River shad fisheries became the basis of a local common law to justify riparian claims for industrial development, which in turn were used to support private claims to oyster fisheries. In this chapter I show the last through a case that moves to Shark River, on the northern part of New Jersey's Atlantic coast. The 1874 case was heard by the court that also dealt with *Stevens v. Paterson and Newark Railroad Company*. It shows the interpenetration of waterfront and oystering laws and further development of the notion that state ownership was more that of a fee simple proprietor than that of a public trustee. The chapter ends with a discussion of the landmark public trust case concerning a legislature's giveaway of a city's waterfront to a railroad company.

Local-Level Fisheries Management versus Local Custom

A policy supported by the legal construct of local custom could challenge and even destroy common rights, particularly where the local custom was that of private property. In *Wooley v. Campbell* (1874), a New Jersey Supreme Court case about rights to oysters, the long-standing rule supporting common rights to oysters that were found where oysters naturally grow, was overridden in favor of the private rights of lessees from the state. The case clearly shows change from the notions of inalienable stewardship implied by Kirkpatrick in *Arnold v. Mundy* to that of government as real estate agency. Ironically, it also provides a glimpse of a local-level system of fisheries management.

In 1861 the legislature authorized oyster leases and set up a management system for Shark River, a small embayment on the northern part of New Jersey's Atlantic coast (New Jersey Laws, March 14, 1861). The legislature gave ownership of part of Shark River to the board of chosen freeholders of Monmouth County for a twenty-year period so that the county officers would govern the oyster-leasing system.

The county board of freeholders was to appoint two or more commissioners whose job it was to survey the area and stake off subdivisions for oyster planting. The act's provisos were that the public right of navigation could not be obstructed and "that no person shall own more than two acres, and no company more than five." The commissioners then auctioned the lots to the highest bidders, who agreed to pay annual rents and received exclusive leaseholds for one to five years. The first offense for trespassing was an action of trespass; the second a misdemeanor that could be fined up to $100 or three months' imprisonment. Leaseholders had to be citizens and residents of the state. Revenues went to the state school fund (as would later be the case for revenues from riparian grants).

Going into effect in 1862, the Shark River oyster management system continued for many years thereafter as an unusual example of local-level management of the shellfisheries. Several legislative supplements to the act were passed by the legislature, mostly to extend it. In 1870 it was extended to 1881, and in 1881 it was extended to 1901. Sometime thereafter the state took over managing the leases of Shark River. I was introduced to Shark River in the early 1980s by William Jenks III, a bayman who took me "treading" for hard clams there. He remembered old-timers who still claimed oystering leases, although the oysters were long gone, and pollution had closed the waters to shellfishing of any kind except for state-run "relays" of clams from the river to cleaner waters in the bays.

Did the legislature have any right at all to create leases in Shark River or any other tidal, navigable body of water? This question was considered in a dispute over oysters in 1874. The case shows the policy shift from a view of the state as a trustee or public-minded sovereign expounded by Kirkpatrick and Taney, to a very different interpretation of sovereignty, where the state legislature functioned just as the Proprietors did, able to grant lands with little concern about public claims.

Campbell and his partner jointly used leaseholds in Shark River for oyster planting. Wooley took oysters from one of their leases, and they sued him. Wooley lost in the local municipal court and at the county court of pleas. The case went to the state supreme court *on certiorari* for review in 1874 as *Wooley v. Campbell*. Justice Depue gave the verdict of the court: Wooley, the commoner, lost again.

The first point raised to justify Wooley's right to take the oysters was that the lease in question was larger than the two acres allowed per person; it was four acres in size. However, the court made short shrift of this argument, noting that there was nothing wrong with two men combining the two-acre plots they each held and working them jointly. The second point was that there were natural oysters on the lease in question, and by law every citizen has the common right to take natural oysters. Wooley could not be expected to be able to distinguish between the oysters planted by the leaseholders and the natural ones. Therefore, he could take whatever he found. The legal narrative of "abandonment" appeared in many of the shellfish cases, highlighting this issue of how to discern natural from planted oysters. *Townsend v. Brown* (1853) included this issue in the commentary of Justice Elmer (one of Kirkpatrick's protégés), who helped acquit the common-right oysterman: when he entered the staked bed of the planter, how could he distinguish planted from natural oysters?[1] However, in *Wooley*, the fact that a lease had been given was enough, the court said, to protect the leaseholders' claim to all oysters found on the lease and to protect them from the conclusion that they had abandoned their property in the oysters they planted by putting them on a natural oyster bed. This ruling was an important buttress for holders of shellfish leases in New Jersey. Natural growth of clams or oysters might occur on their leaseholds even though, in principle, there was no natural growth when the leases were granted.

The main point of contention in *Wooley*, the reason the state supreme court agreed to hear it, was the nature of state ownership. Wooley's attorney argued that the legislature had no right to abridge or take away the public right of fishing in tidal waters. The state owned the waters as a public trust for all citizens.

The court went through much the same body of case law as had earlier courts. It agreed with the construction of English common law that holds that individuals could have exclusive rights in tidal waters only if they could prove a grant or prescription as early as the reign of Henry II, that is, before the Magna Carta went into effect. But then Justice Depue, who delivered the majority opinion of the court, added a twist not found in either *Arnold v. Mundy* or *Martin v. Waddell* but evident in the *Gough v. Bell* cases. He pointed out that the Magna Carta intended only to curb the sovereign power of the king; "it could not operate to abridge the power of Parliament over public and common rights. . . . Of necessity, the jurisdiction to regulate and dispose of those rights which are public and common, must reside in the legislative body, which is the representative of the people" (*Wooley v. Campbell* 1874: 165–66).

Depue admitted that he knew of no instance in which Parliament had actually granted an exclusive right of fishery. But it had certainly allowed the destruction of public rights of navigation and fishery in its role in approving the construction of railroads, wharves, and docks.

The Shark River dispute was deliberated in the context of the other riparian conflicts and the general trend toward laissez-faire interpretations of state ownership. A question that arose from these early cases was whether the state's title to lands under tidewaters was solely that of a trustee, to hold for the common benefit. If so, then such lands "could not be converted by the legislature to the private use of individuals, to the exclusion of the common right of the public, without a breach of trust" (*Wooley v. Campbell* 1874: 167). On the other hand, Justice Depue observed that in *Martin v. Waddell,* Chief Justice Taney appeared to have assumed the power of the legislature to make an exclusive grant of land underwater for oyster-planting purposes.

Depue finally bowed to his own earlier decision in *Stevens v. Paterson and Newark Railroad Company* (1870): "the title of the state is proprietary, an attribute of which is the unqualified right of disposition to public or private uses, either absolutely, or for a qualified estate, as in legislative discretion may be deemed most conducive to the public interest" (as quoted in *Wooley v. Campbell* 1874: 168).

The Illinois Central Case and Measured Alienability

The New Jersey decisions were part of a much larger trend toward state disposition of public lands. Legislatures were even pressured to convey navigable waterways into private hands, as in a New York attempt to grant exclusive navigation rights to the owner of a steamboat company. More often, as in New Jersey's riparian acts and in the Illinois case to be discussed, the property at stake was waterfront and the adjacent submerged beds were for purposes of industrial development.

In 1869 the legislature of Illinois granted virtually all of the Chicago commercial waterfront and submerged adjacent lands in Lake Michigan, over a thousand acres, to the Illinois Central Railroad Company. In 1873 the legislature repealed the grant after realizing its extent, and in 1892 the United States Supreme Court declared the 1869 grant invalid in language that is often quoted to support the idea of public trust and the existence of the doctrine in federal as well as state law:

> It is the settled law of this country that the ownership of and dominion and sovereignty over lands covered by tide waters, within the limits of the several states,

> belong to the respective States within which they are found, with the consequent right to use or dispose of any portion thereof, when that can be done without substantial impairment of the interest of the public in the waters, and subject always to the paramount right of Congress to control the regulation of commerce with foreign nations and among the States. (*Illinois Central Railway Company v. State of Illinois* 1892: 452)

The Supreme Court also repeated the common rights part of the doctrine. The state holds title in tidal lands "in trust for the people of the State that they may enjoy the navigation of the waters, carry on commerce over them, and have liberty of fishing therein freed from the obstruction or interference of private parties." It strengthened the status of the public trust: "[t]he State can no more abdicate its trust over property in which the whole people are interested . . . than it can abdicate its police powers" (*Illinois Central Railway Company v. State of Illinois* 1892: 452). This ruling was strongly influenced by the New Jersey public trust cases.

In *Illinois Central,* the inalienability emphasized by Kirkpatrick in the oystering conflict of 1821 was affirmed at last, but with a difference. It was measurable and tradable inalienability, subject to tests of comparative advantage and public and private interests. Inalienability was treated as a matter of degree and thus dependent on the calculi of special and short-term interests (Johnson and Johnson 1975: 90). However, as Kirkpatrick too said, the legislature can "improve" the public interest in navigation and commerce by erecting wharves, docks, and piers, for which purpose the state may grant parcels of land. Such granting can be "a valid exercise of legislative power consistently with the trust to the public upon which such lands are held by the State."

The 1892 court did not declare the Illinois riparian grant invalid on the grounds of the inalienability of the public trust (cf. Stevens 1980). It was, instead, a matter of degree, of weighing one interest against another. The 1869 Illinois legislature gave away *too much* of the Chicago waterfront, and did so to *not enough* public purpose to make up for the fact that the grant "impaired" the public interest in whatever waterfront and tidewater that remained. A court could determine how much was too much and whether public interests were served or, in the language of the case, were "substantially impaired." Accordingly, the *Illinois Central* case, while known as a landmark holding on behalf of the public trust, also recognized and helped realize the potential for allowing alienation of public trust to private uses.

The question that arises from the use of weighing scales is when public interests become private ones, and that has varied from court to court (Johnson and Johnson 1975: 91). *Illinois Central* could be used in courts as authority for an inalienable public trust, on the one hand, or as authority for a state's right to alienate both *jus privatum* and *jus publicum* for private purposes, on the other. Thus far, no state has gone so far as to explicitly abandon at least the language of public interest and some consideration of navigation rights (Johnson and Johnson 1975: 91), but in practice great tidewaters and tracts of submerged land have been granted and sold with little protection for common rights of navigation, fishing, and recreation (Jaffee 1971).

In New Jersey, the trade-offs were built into the Riparian Act of 1871 and subsequent acts. As noted earlier, the state legislature got into the business of selling off riparian lands to corporations and individuals by creating a separate agency more or less immune from legislative interference. The riparian commission implemented the philosophy of proprietorship by selling off tidewater lands. The public trust that attaches to state ownership of tidewater lands was preserved, first, by a general policy, not always honored, that public rights of navigation, if not fishing, were to be protected in the riparian grants, and second, by a policy of trading the loss of public lands against gains to public schools. The proceeds from riparian land sales went at first into liquidation of state debt and thereafter were invested, with interest paid, into a Fund for Support of Free Public Schools. The fund, established by the legislature in 1817, continues and was made perpetual in the revised state constitution of 1844 (New Jersey Department of Environmental Protection 1977; Keys 1986). The money in the fund is used to guarantee local school bond issues and thereby increases their rating (New Jersey Department of Environmental Protection 1982). The dedication of riparian funds to the school fund has played an important role in recent title controversies (Keys 1986). However, New Jersey courts have recognized that the public's right to use tidewater property is not eliminated by the fact that some compensation has been paid for grants and leases (see footnote 5 in the syllabus for *Matthews v. Bay Head Improvement Association, Inc.* 1987).

Conclusion: The Demise of Public Trust

The cases and legislation concerning riparian rights in the mid– and late nineteenth century are confusing and probably confused, but with time one of the outcomes became clear. This legal history created the message that the legislature "could dispose of public water resource interests as freely as it could exercise the power of eminent domain" (Jaffee 1971: 659). The irony is, from this distance, patent. *Martin v. Waddell* supported the public trust doctrine but was also available to support the state legislature's power to *alienate* erstwhile common rights and resources. In a New York case, and then a later New Jersey one, Taney's United States Supreme Court clearly confirmed the latter perspective. The New Jersey case, *Russell v. Jersey Company* (1854), again concerned title to waterfront land in Jersey City that had probably been filled in with New York City garbage. The court decided that the state had the right to give title to the filled-in land—previously submerged and hence state property—to the corporation originally formed to establish Jersey City instead of deciding that the previously submerged area had been held by the state in perpetuity for the benefit of its citizens.

In mid- and late-nineteenth-century cases, judges began to entertain the argument that local custom could justify exceptions to the common law of public rights to tidewater lands, especially when they coincided with the tendency of the legislature to "give away" more and more of the state's water commons by leasing and granting riparian rights to individuals and corporations. The courts did their part in adapting the law to local custom. "Local custom" could be little more than a gloss for exceptions that undercut the rule of the law but promoted other objectives.

When railroad companies, industrialists, and others tried to seek legal support for vast riparian claims in the state, they often brought up the Delaware shore fisheries as a precedent for the weight of local custom. By calling upon local custom they—or at least their lawyers—intended, in context, to give authority and legitimacy to the exceptions they claimed to certain broad principles of the law. If there could be local custom on the Delaware River, then the local custom of Jersey City that a riparian owner could extend landfill out beyond high-water mark and claim the high land created as his own is acceptable, too, irrespective of state and federal court rulings protecting common rights to tidewater lands.

The power of the railroads, and the industrialists depending on them, was far greater than the power of the law to safeguard other private or public interests in tidewaters. In the case of *Stevens v. Paterson and Newark Railroad Company* (1870), New Jersey's highest court continued to relax its doctrine on the state's obligation to safeguard tidal lands (Keys 1986), although it upheld *Arnold v. Mundy*. The state was free to grant land underwater to a private individual (or corporation) even if this cut off the riparian owner from the benefits derived from his property's contiguity to the water, and the riparian owner had no legal right to compensation. The decision was upheld in later cases. It is the basis of the modern-day doctrine that the state is free to lease or grant tidal land to private individuals (Keys 1986). However, the extent to which that can be used to deny public rights of fishing, navigation, swimming, bathing, and other activities is an issue that is still very much alive and arguable.

In England, the Magna Carta and other documents, events, and processes were part of struggles to delimit the power of the king. By the eighteenth century the common law understanding of limits to the king's right to alienate common property—especially navigable tidewaters—was the result of a struggle for power between the crown and Parliament (Sax 1970; Jaffee 1971). The majority decisions of *Arnold v. Mundy* and *Martin v. Waddell* were based on this notion of constraints on the rights of the sovereign to alienate marine and tidal lands from the public trust. They did not address American implications of the fact that the English Parliament could exercise "what we would call the police power, to enlarge or diminish the public rights for some legitimate public purpose" (Sax 1970: 476). However, the court of *Wooley v. Campbell* and other courts whose rulings it reviewed did. Like the English Parliament, American legislatures could do what kings and colonial Proprietors could not.

Part IV Riparian Rights and Oyster Wars

Introduction

Of particular interest in studying institutional change are "constitutional moments," or points where legal doctrine and the interpretation of situations are articulated in a way that preserves them for future use, reinterpretation, and revival. The landmark cases of high courts are such moments, including the Raritan Bay cases that led to the public trust doctrine rulings and later cases that underscored the validity of local common law protecting private property. However, in the following accounts of later oyster wars, in Delaware Bay and the Mullica River, the law was less important than responses by the state legislature, which carried out investigations and finally created a state agency for management of the shellfisheries. The constitutional moments followed the oyster wars and court conflicts, when the new Bureau of Shell Fisheries came out with strong policy directives supporting the rights of common fishing on natural shellfish beds.

Shellfishery conflicts were dominated by opposition between planters and tongers, but at the turn of the century and particularly in the Atlantic coast and northern bays, "clammers" entered the fray. Chapter 11 explores court cases arising from incidents where oyster-planting grounds in the Raritan Bay were raided by people who claimed that the oyster beds encroached upon natural clam beds. Decline in the natural seed beds of the region prompted investigations and attempts to privatize them as incentive to restore them. Objection to this, or to any restrictions on the natural beds, on the part of fishermen known as seeders is explored as a more nuanced view of the notion of "social costs." In 1917 the unthinkable—privatizing the natural shellfish beds—became fact; around the same time a familiar analysis of the causes of problems in the shellfish industry was repeated: failure to expand oyster-planting ground was blamed on "the people who want to depend on nature to furnish them a livelihood, and [a] more or less sympathetic public" (New Jersey Board of Shell Fisheries 1918: 8). The real villain, though, was unbridled industrialization, which polluted and destroyed the shellfish beds.

Chapter 9 Riparian Rights and Oyster Wars on the Delaware Bay

Two of the most dramatic episodes in the history of the shellfisheries in New Jersey arose from conflicts over the use of riparian grants for oystering. The first, the subject of this chapter, took place in the Delaware Bay, beginning in 1889 and escalating to armed conflict in 1893–94. The second, in the next chapter, happened in 1907 on the Mullica River, on the state's Atlantic coast. Accounts of these oyster wars show again how central property rights were to social relations of the bay fisheries. It is also evident and important that the wars took place in the context of a strong movement for "scientific management," to deal with the vexing and serious problem of declining production of natural oysters. The push for privatization was earnest. Violent resistance to some kinds of privatization resulted in policy changes that reflected the public trust notion of inalienability of certain kinds of common use rights.

Riparian Grants on Delaware Bay

Enterprising oystermen did not wait long to use the riparian commission's powers as a way to stake out private property within the marine commons, even for the natural beds of oysters. The commission was created in 1871; in 1879 oystermen began to obtain riparian grants to oyster beds. Although riparian grants were not supposed to be used to create exclusive access to oystering grounds,[1] the riparian commissioners were as difficult to monitor and control and as subject to the temptations of political favor and economic reward as the Proprietors. To some people, riparian grants meant an opportunity to privatize shellfish grounds. To others, they abrogated public rights.

The most controversial riparian grants, of course, were those that carved private property out of areas long known to be natural oyster beds. The region of Delaware Bay that lies north of the "southwest line" is one such, "recognized by custom and in law ever since the industry of oyster-planting began" (New Jersey Bureau of Statistics of Labor and Industries 1897: 5) (map 2). In 1879 oystermen in the Newport area north of Maurice River Cove "began to absorb those natural beds by acquiring grants from the State under riparian titles." Between 1879 and 1893 nearly six miles of the bay shore frontage, extending about half a mile into the bay in the area of Fortescue Cove, had been "taken from public use" through riparian grants (Hall 1894: 518). In particular, in 1886 Luther Bateman, James G. Gandy, and F. N. and L. N. Bradford—all oystermen—obtained riparian grants in Delaware Bay for sums ranging from $175 to $635 (New Jersey Riparian Commissioners 1890).

Soon thereafter Gabriel Holmes of Cape May County (not Cumberland County, the site of the oyster grounds) took oysters from the grounds of Gandy, one of the riparian grantees. In 1889 Holmes's lawyer tried to defend his client by arguing that Gandy had planted oysters upon a natural bed and therefore whatever oysters were found there were the property of the public. Nonetheless, Holmes was convicted of larceny, sent to jail, and forced to pay a large fine (Anonymous 1894: 155).

The Gandy/Holmes incident was the first of the "frequent collisions and arrests between oystermen and [riparian] owners" that occurred on Delaware Bay in the late 1880s and the 1890s (New Jersey Bureau of Statistics of Labor and Industries 1897: 5). The matter was clearly serious to everyone. More was involved than just the incursion on nature and natural rights. In the state's report, the issue was seen as central to social relations of the industry. If the courts upheld the riparian owners,

> it is claimed that it will work a complete revolution in the oyster industry in Delaware Bay, because it will give to owners of the beds advantages amounting to a practical monopoly of the business. Being relieved from the restriction of the law relating to working the beds except at certain seasons of the year, they would have an advantage over others in marketing their products, and ultimately absorb the whole business. (New Jersey Bureau of Statistics of Labor and Industries 1897: 6)

This anonymous observer went on to explain how the larger operators were already favored, and how ownership and control were becoming centralized in a few people and companies due to the risky nature of oystering: "those who can afford to have more than one bed in different localities, are the only ones who can rely on having a certain income every year; so that like other industries the business is gradually becoming centralized by larger capitalists" (New Jersey Bureau of Statistics of Labor and Industries 1897: 6–7). Thus, he suggested, much of the strength of the opposition to riparian grants "up the bay," above the sacred southwest line, derived from broader concerns about the concentration of capital in the industry. This problem seemed all the more real because of "the great depression existing in the oyster industry" (report of a special investigating committee, cited in Hall 1894: 521), which tied up boats and put many men out of work.

Although it might be conjectured that Holmes's greed only became part of a larger cause when it went to court, the next major incident, of 1893–94, was clearly orchestrated by lawyers and industry groups to "try the right." The first stage of a full-fledged "war" on Delaware Bay took place in the spring of 1893, when a dredge boat run by a Captain Chew went onto one of the disputed riparian grounds in Fortescue Cove and took a few oysters. Chew took the oysters under advice from the lawyer of the Maurice River Cove Oyster Association and on notice to the riparian owners (Hall 1894: 519). He was arrested under a section of the 1892 Oyster Act for the area that made it a misdemeanor to dredge or catch oysters upon a bed duly staked out or belonging to any other person (one of several attempts by the legislature to secure planters' rights). The point was to challenge the owner of the ground, Peter Crosier, to bring civil action so that the court could "settle the right" (*Bateman v. Hollinger et al.* 1894: 1108). But Crosier insisted on criminal action. It did not come to trial. Crosier and other owners of the "private oyster fisheries" seemed to be purposely avoiding any legal settlement of the matter. At the annual meeting of the Maurice River Cove Oyster Association on March 19, 1894, the association's lawyer advised another test case: "the best way to settle the matter was for the men to peaceably take the oysters, from the natural bed, and for those who claim them under riparian grants to resist and bring action at law" (Hall 1894: 520). An executive committee was elected and charged to come up with a way to tax the oyster boats to cover the legal expenses of those who had the courage to carry out the "raid." The plans were publicly announced, and everyone was invited to join in the effort with some financial protection (*Bateman v. Hollinger et al.* 1894: 1109).

One of the riparian grantees, Luther Bateman, filed an equity suit against members of the executive committee—*Bateman v. Hollinger et al.* (1894)—in a vain attempt to prevent the association from using its powers to create the defense fund. Colonel William E. Potter, who served as attorney for Bateman and the other riparian grantees, said that this tax merely served "to encourage the spoliation of the grounds of my clients by a concerted raid, and of protecting those engaged in such a raid" (Anonymous 1894: 156). The equity court, on the other hand, felt that it was entirely within the powers of the association to do this.

Once word was out that a larger-scale raid on the riparian grants was imminent, preparations were made on all sides. Colonel Potter wrote a long and eloquent piece for a local newspaper to try to convince the public of the rights of the riparian grantees and the dangers of the raid. He also had his article reprinted immediately in the *New Jersey Law Journal* (Anonymous 1894: 155–56):

> The gathering of a fleet such as is now proposed to forcibly seize upon the property of the riparian grantees will constitute a riot. . . . The riparian grantees cannot be expected to stand idly by, and see their property violently taken by a large numbers [*sic*] of people, without using all lawful means of resistance. The proposed raid, therefore, may, and in the ordinary course of human events, will, naturally lead to serious breaches of the peace, and perhaps even to graver results.

Potter warned that the county would be held liable for damages to property or men. Accordingly, the county sheriff obtained a steam vessel and organized a *posse comitatus* (Hall 1894: 520). The sheriff and his posse warned several boats off, and then, after several days of no action, the sheriff discharged the posse and returned to his office in Bridgeton. Sheriff and posse gone, the war began on April 12, 1894: "in order that there might be a final settlement of the question in dispute and the rights of both parties defined, by advice of counsel various oystermen on a certain day in April, 1894, went upon these grounds and took oysters" (New Jersey Bureau of Statistics of Labor and Industries 1897: 6). "Soon after [the sheriff's] departure many vessels appeared and began dredging. One of the riparian owners shot at the invaders for the purpose of frightening them off. Over thirty persons were subsequently arrested and held for court" (Hall 1894: 520).

The Trenton correspondent of a Philadelphia newspaper wrote in May 1894 of "the liveliest kind of war on in south Jersey among the 3,000 oystermen. In consequence, from Camden to Cape May there is a general disturbance of commercial and social relations because of the row" (cited in Hall 1894: 518). The state assemblyman from the area introduced a joint resolution that created a special committee "to go to the oyster war and get the facts for the legislature." By May 1894 this committee had already filed its report and made its recommendations, which included finding a way to purchase the riparian grants and return the natural beds to the state.

Two other cases that arose from this conflict and surfaced at higher and thus retrievable levels of New Jersey's legal system are *Polhemus v. State of New Jersey* (1894) and *Polhemus v. Bateman* (1897). Zebulon Polhemus was among the men who raided the riparian grant of Luther Bateman. The judicial outcome, based on a very literal reading of the riparian statutes, was that Luther Bateman did not have exclusive rights to the riparian grant he claimed. The deed given to him in

1886 by the state riparian commissioners gave him the land underwater adjacent to his seventy acres of shore property plus "the right, liberty, privilege and franchise" to build dikes to drain the lands, to fill the lands, to otherwise improve them, and "to appropriate the lands above described to his exclusive private uses" (*Polhemus v. Bateman* 1897: 164). Since Bateman had used those underwater lands only to plant oysters or oyster shells (and perhaps take natural oysters), he did not qualify for the privilege of "exclusive appropriation." The privilege was contingent upon making improvements, which he had not pretended to do: "[t]he grant was only for the purpose of reclamation" (*Polhemus v. Bateman* 1897: 168). Thus Zebulon Polhemus and the other oystermen could take oysters there under common right.

Neither this decision nor the general outrage and specific acts of defiance extinguished riparian grants on Delaware Bay. As late as 1904 some of those that were the focus of contention in the 1880s and 1890s still existed. But the contentious grants were on the way out. One outcome of the conflict was a special legislative appropriation to the New Jersey Oyster Commission in 1902 to buy the disputed riparian grants from the owners (New Jersey Bureau of Shell Fisheries 1903: 29). By this time the state itself had emerged as a major actor in the oyster fisheries; legislative appropriations financed local and state bodies for managing the oyster fisheries, and the state had a Bureau of Shell Fisheries. Although the commission had trouble getting all of the owners to cooperate, in 1904, with the help of another appropriation, the last of the outstanding riparian grants had been purchased (New Jersey Bureau of Shell Fisheries 1904: 40).

The conflicts played a major role in institutionalizing the public trust principle as state shellfisheries policy. On page 40 of its 1904 report, the Bureau of Shell Fisheries wrote:

> We sincerely trust that never again will there be a private ownership of the natural oyster beds in the bay. . . . We are opposed to either selling or leasing any of the natural beds above the southwest line. These oyster beds are the natural heritage of all the people of the State, and should be forever preserved and kept sacred to the free public use of the inhabitants of the State, except in so far as their use may be reasonably regulated to prevent destruction.

Just so was the public trust revived through the actions of outraged oystermen and the responses of government officials and institutionalized as state policy. The process was incomplete, though, because very shortly a similar attempt to use the riparian commission to appropriate natural oyster beds took place in Atlantic County, as will be seen in the next chapter.

Oyster Science and Enclosure of the Commons

The oyster wars, although with a social dynamic of their own (cf. Wennersten 1981), were caused in part by great interest in privatization as a way to restore and enhance the productivity of nature:

> The area of bottom in Delaware Bay and Maurice River Cove at present entirely barren of oyster life, but naturally capable of sustaining it in teeming abundance, is at least six times greater in extent than that under cultivation. If the State would lease, or better still, sell plots outright in this immense field, hundreds of intelligent planters stand ready to put their capital and labor into it, and within a few years New Jersey would lead all other States in oyster production. (Stainsby 1902: 52)

In the nineteenth century many areas once known as productive natural beds became barren or nearly so. Beginning in 1846 attempts were made to control the use of the domestic seed beds by imposing closed seasons and by requiring tongers or dredgers to cull their catch while on the natural beds, returning undersized and dead oysters, empty shells, and other "refuse" back to the grounds to provide cultch. Both closed seasons and "rough cull" laws were difficult to enforce, and neither were universal. The question became more compelling at the turn of the century, when the legislature of Virginia, to protect the interests of Chesapeake Bay planters, outlawed the sale of seed oysters. Although this law did not completely cut off New Jersey's supply of oysters from the York River and other Virginia sites, the possibility that such would happen redirected attention to the task of protecting and enhancing New Jersey's own seed supply.

Another way to ensure that enough shell remained on the natural oyster beds to furnish the right amount and kind of cultch for oyster setting was to return shells to the natural beds. This came to be known as "shelling." Near the end of the nineteenth century, following upon the creation of a state fisheries agency in 1871, shelling programs were instituted and run by local shell commissioners. Although an excellent idea and the basis of oyster management in many areas, at the turn of the century in New Jersey the shelling programs faltered for reasons that included poaching, poor or uncertain results, and irregular financial support. Another problem was the fact that most oysters were sold in the shell rather than shucked, so that the shell went to market with the oysters; shucking houses did not appear in the Delaware Bay industry until the 1920s (Ford 1997). Meanwhile, pressure on the declining natural beds worsened because the increasing cost of imports from Virginia, Maryland, and Connecticut made the "natives" even more attractive. The situation appeared dire enough to enable actors and observers to propose what was otherwise unthinkable: the creation of private property in the sacred commons of the natural beds.

The discourse and debate began in the 1880s, part of the enthusiasm about the prospects of bringing science to fisheries management, largely through aquaculture. In 1883 Samuel Lockwood reviewed scientific experiments in oyster propagation with excitement about their prospects for New Jersey. He noted that on City Island, in the East River next to Manhattan, enterprising oystermen were "truly propagating oysters from seed caught upon artificial beds" by 1843 (Lockwood 1883: 290; see also Ingersoll 1887, who relied heavily on Lockwood's work and vice versa; also Lockwood 1882). Numerous scientists chopped and ground up "parent oysters," trying to combine eggs and sperm and get these to produce a "set" on the bottom. Francis Winslow of the United States Commission of Fish and Fisheries had done this with the cooperation of the owners of "true oyster farms" in the Long Island Sound waters off Connecticut (at that time, the only state that allowed individuals to buy oystering lands outright). Lockwood reviewed well-known European methods of oyster propagation—reeds and brush to capture oyster spat, propagating ponds, and so forth. Finally, he advocated "oyster parks" for New Jersey, in which "local nurserymen" could raise and sell oyster seed and also raise oysters for market (Lockwood 1883: 302).

Lockwood argued that the oyster park business would favor rich and poor alike: "[h]ere, then, would arise enterprise both among those of limited means as well as the expanded industry which fostering capital would evolve" (1883: 303). The tendency toward monopoly would be checked, in New Jersey, by the geographical fact that the best places for oyster parks were the numerous large and small coves and many small rivers and inlets that so strikingly characterize the state's marine topography (Lockwood 1883: 302). In other words, since the areas suitable for oyster propagation were small, so would be the scale of the enterprise.

The theme was picked up by Ansley Hall, the field agent in the Division of Statistics and Methods of the Fisheries of the United States Commission of Fish and Fisheries, who wrote "Notes on the Oyster Industry of New Jersey" for the commission in 1892, an important source for this study (Hall 1894). Hall observed the problem of depleted oyster beds in New Jersey (as elsewhere on the Atlantic seaboard) and recommended the Connecticut practice of planting shells or other suitable materials on oyster grounds to attract seed oysters that would then grow there. However, he noted that whereas in Connecticut the method was used on private grounds, in New Jersey it would have to be on public grounds for a reason that should be familiar by now:

> In New Jersey the natural oyster grounds have always been carefully exempted from private ownership, and any system of oyster cultivation involving proprietary rights in them has been unfavorably regarded. The planters have succeeded in acquiring a legal right to hold non-producing areas, for the purpose of planting oysters, as against the individual citizens, but not as against the State; and even this advantage has, in some sections, been gained in the face of strenuous opposition. (Hall 1894: 465–66)

Changes in Shellfish Management and Shelling Programs

In 1893 the state legislature created an oyster commission whose job was to survey and inspect the natural oyster beds and see that a supply of shells was spread upon them to enhance natural growth. The state was divided into seven districts, each with its own shell commission made up of local oystermen who used state appropriations to return shell to depleted natural beds. This system, barraged by criticism, ended with the advent of more direct state involvement in oyster management.

As noted above, the legislative committee that investigated the oyster war of 1893–94 in Delaware Bay advised the state to acquire title to the riparian lands to restore them to public property (Hall 1894: 524). This committee also sanctioned an entirely new policy for the oystering industry: explicit state control and regulation, rather than implicit and indirect involvement through various laws and local commissions. In 1899 the policy went into effect for the Maurice River Cove and Delaware Bay oystering industry, in 1902 for Ocean County, in 1905 for Atlantic County, and thereafter the entire state.

For the first time the state was engaged in shellfish management as a bureaucratic and administrative, not just legislative, institution. The legislature created a state agency, the Bureau of Shell Fisheries, whose appointed, salaried, full-time chief (at first and for many years Charles Bacon, also a journalist for a Philadelphia newspaper) oversaw the appointed local oyster commissions and superintendents. The bureau also oversaw, and depended on, the oyster biology research of Dr. Julius Nelson, a biologist with the state college of agriculture's agricultural experiment station. The new system was part of the larger development of the science of natural resource management. It was within the framework of this system that the concept of alienating oystering lands from the areas once known as natural beds received most attention.

Privatizing natural oyster beds was taken seriously when it seemed that nothing else would work. The local shelling programs appeared to have failed. In 1902 another legislative commission was appointed to decide whether the state should finally take control of the entire industry. The testimony it collected indicates that appropriations for the purpose of shelling the beds were too meager or were improperly used.[2]

Nature was not always cooperative, and people took unfair advantage of the state's largess. The shell commissions were not always able to enforce the closures they imposed on the shelled ground to protect natural growth upon the cultch. Planters found it only too tempting to transfer shells to their planting beds, a practice made easier by the tendency for the shell commissions to dump shells in heaps rather than scatter them about. The $12,000 a year appropriated to one of the shell commissions failed to permanently increase natural productivity, but it did help a few of the planters: "[i]t has undoubtedly produced a few thousand bushels of oysters, which have been presented as a free gift to the oystermen of the immediate vicinity of the planting of the shells" (New Jersey Bureau of Shell Fisheries 1908: 40).

The few benefited, but so did the many for a short, wonderful time when successful oyster beds were reopened for harvest. When the shell commissions declared the shelled natural seed beds open for harvest, one and all descended upon them in a mad rush to be first with the most. In one of the Atlantic coast areas, for example, the opening at sunrise on September 1 was signaled by a pistol shot, after which there was a "mad rush to secure a share of the 'crop' offered them by the state." Everyone in the region participated, "regular oystermen, the clam men, the farmer, his boy; in fact, everyone who can procure a boat and a pair of tongs." After a few days of high catch, production tapered off. "In from a week to three weeks the bed has been swept as clean of oysters and shells as though none ever existed on it" (New Jersey Bureau of Shell Fisheries 1908: 41). The bonanza was quickly depleted, and the beds were barer than ever. This was a classically competitive tragedy of the commons, and there was much pressure to find an alternative (New Jersey Bureau of Shell Fisheries 1908: 42) and, for the time being, to stop shelling the natural beds.

The shell commissions went out of business. The state took over regulation and control of the state's oystering lands through the legislative acts of 1899 (for Delaware Bay and Maurice River Cove), 1902 (for Ocean County), and 1905 (for Atlantic County), each of which set up an oyster commission under the auspices of the Bureau of Shell Fisheries. The Raritan Bay oystering industry was subsumed under the administration of that of Delaware Bay; Shark River's old management system was resurrected as a separate district in 1901. Cape May County, on the Atlantic coast side, had no "Oyster Act" into the early part of this

Figure 3. Oystering at the opening of the public oyster beds, the "Graveling." Mullica River, New Jersey, ca. 1906. (Based on a photograph from New Jersey Bureau of Shell Fisheries 1906: facing p. 104.)

century, because conflicts among oystermen and between them and clammers prevented agreement. But there, too, the shell commission (or "propagating commission") disappeared, leaving that section of the coast entirely without formal management. The Shrewsbury and Navesink Rivers oystering district was also without any formal management, but there was little oystering left to manage by 1902 (New Jersey Oyster Commission 1902; see chapter 3).

Although there were special legislative appropriations for shelling under the new commissions, the situation was cast as dire: "[w]ith the abolition of the old Shell Commission the State abandoned its policy of shelling these beds; since that they have been absolutely unproductive and are now practically swept bare" (New Jersey Bureau of Shell Fisheries 1907: 15).

Enclosure above the Southwest Line, Delaware Bay

The idea of leasing the barren grounds above the southwest line in Delaware Bay (map 2) came up in 1901, just after the state of Virginia passed its law prohibiting the export of seed oysters, placing the New Jersey planters in a difficult situation. Attention was focused on an area above the line of "now unproductive fifty thousand acres of bottom, suitable to be made first-class breeding grounds" (New Jersey Bureau of Shell Fisheries 1901: 21).

The local oyster commissioners, who were industry members, argued for change in the law that would allow the leasing of lands above the line so that private enterprise could manage the resource by shelling and improving the barren lands. State shelling was deemed inappropriate, given both the scale of the problem and the dubious social philosophy involved: "it would be as reasonable to ask the State to clear and improve all the unimproved farm lands in the State." Just as it is up to private farmers to clear and improve lands for farming, so should it be up to private oystermen to improve lands for oystering. However, "the private individual will not do it, unless he is made secure by a lease of the bottom which he literally makes" (New Jersey Bureau of Shell Fisheries 1901: 21).

Compelling as the argument was at the time, it created a dilemma in the face of the hard-won agreement that the area of Delaware Bay above the southwest line should remain forever public. One approach was semantic and had been tried earlier. The legislature's committee formed in response to the oyster war of 1893–94 in Delaware Bay recognized that there were good arguments for reconsidering the notion that all of the oystering lands north of the southwest line in Delaware Bay were encompassed by the term "natural bed," since spots where oysters naturally grow in large numbers are scattered, well defined, and well known. In a bit of verbal legerdemain, probably designed to appease the "many members of the Oyster Association" who "strongly" and "vigorously" argued that everything above the southwest line was "natural" and hence should remain common property, the committee suggested calling that area a "natural oyster *ground*," within which are found numerous but scattered "natural oyster *beds*" (New Jersey Bureau of Shell Fisheries 1901: 21). In oystering, the term "ground" is used in reference to oyster-planting lands as opposed to the term "bed," which is usually reserved for natural oyster habitat.

In 1901 the oyster commissioners of the Maurice River Cove and Delaware Bay area returned to arguments that were more solidly based on economic rationality: "[t]he average man will . . . ask . . . : 'Well, why not give him a lease at a yearly rental, which would bring a large revenue to the State? It produces nothing now to any one; nor, so far as can be foreseen, ever will; so, why not lease it to those who may wish to acquire and improve it; for it is certain that no one would care to acquire it at a considerable cost, unless he meant to improve it' " (New Jersey Bureau of Shell Fisheries 1901: 21). They noted that this had been done in Connecticut, Virginia, and other states, but they also acknowledged that it had so far failed in New Jersey because of the strength of political opposition to it: "[a]ny proposition to move in the matter would cause such a howl of wrath from a portion of the oystermen as might well cause its proposers to hesitate" (New Jersey Bureau of Shell Fisheries 1901: 21).

Trying to drum up support for direct state control of the shellfisheries as had been accomplished in the Delaware Bay in 1899, a legislative commission toured the state to investigate problems in the oyster industry, including the linked issues of rights to natural seed beds, the shelling of beds, and the development of leases for propagation purposes (New Jersey Oyster Commission 1902). The commission's sense of urgency came from the fact that the Maryland and Virginia legislatures had just passed laws against the export of oysters less than three inches long: "[t]he question now arises where shall our planters secure needed seeds, there being no longer any great source of supply open except the sound, and that liable to be closed at any time" (Stainsby 1902: 47). Moreover, although the oyster commission had recommended shelling to supply cultch to the seed-producing area of Delaware Bay and Maurice River Cove, there was doubt that this would work any better than it had in the past. Instead, the special incentives of private ownership were required:

> Private enterprise must do the work if it is done at all, and the individuals who undertake it should be given leases of plots to be cultivated by them, and also protected in their exclusive right to the product of the same, just as the planter's ownership of his beds during the term of his lease [is] now recognized and secured to him by law [a law of 1899]. . . . Such a policy could by no possible means injure anyone, but on the contrary, if adopted, the entire industry would be benefited. In a few years we should have a growth of seed on these vast areas of now unproductive bottom, sufficient to supply all the oyster planting grounds of the State. (Stainsby 1902: 47)

The people interviewed felt that it was only a matter of time before these would be leased, despite opposition (New Jersey Oyster Commission 1902: 25). However, within a couple of years the oyster commissioners had changed their tune, apparently having underestimated the opposition: "we desire to record ourselves as being opposed to either selling or leasing any of the natural oyster beds north of the southwest line. These oyster beds are the natural heritage of all the people of the State, and should be forever preserved and kept sacred to the free public use of the inhabitants of the State, except in so far as their use may be reasonably regulated to prevent destruction" (New Jersey Bureau of Shell Fisheries 1904: 40).

In 1905 the local oyster commission concluded that "private ownership of natural spawning beds has proven impracticable and unpopular" (New Jersey Bureau of Shell Fisheries 1905: 20) and returned to the old tactic of asking for state help in shelling the natural beds, including "old abandoned" ones.[3] The commons up the bay was secured.

Social Bases of Opposition to Privatization

What happened to the proposal to use the incentive structure of private property to restore natural oyster productivity? In 1901, when the oyster commissioners were trying to persuade others and the legislature to allow leasing of now-barren oystering lands above the southwest line in Delaware Bay, they wrote an analysis of opposition to the measure that provides insight into their perceptions of human nature and the situation on the Delaware as well as clues about the social relations of production in this highly developed sector of the state's oyster industry. Their analysis is also helpful in understanding opposition to leasing and other measures in other parts of the state then and now.

As shown in earlier chapters, social relations of production were structured by "two distinct classes of oystermen—designated by the oystermen themselves in discussing the matter as the 'big fellows' and the 'little fellows' " (New Jersey Bureau of Shell Fisheries 1901: 22). This was not the same as the distinction between planters and tongers, for tongers comprised yet a third class, so marginalized in the Delaware Bay that the oystermen themselves did not see them as involved in such important issues. The "big fellows" and the "little fellows" were two classes of planters, distinguished by different amounts of capital, technology, labor, "land," and hence profits.

The worldview of the reports is the familiar, modern, American one of industrial capitalism and pluralist politics, based upon an appreciation of human nature as innately selfish and fickle in ideology. From this perspective, combined with the assumption that the major process in the Delaware oyster industry was one of increase in the number of "big fellows" (reflecting actual increase in the scale of technology and capital in the industry), it was indeed only a matter of time before most people recognized the sense of using private enterprise to manage the oyster seed beds.

The commissioners, pressed as they were to argue for leasing, gave short shrift to the arguments of the "little fellows," but in the document we can find some clues as to what they were. One concern was that the creation of leaseholds up the bay would indeed reduce access to natural seed beds. The system is dynamic, and over time oyster beds that were barren in 1901 might naturally become productive later but would have been taken up by private enterprise (New Jersey Bureau of Shell Fisheries 1901: 24). Another was grounded on the old problem of how to define "natural beds." If a bed responds to the planting of cultch or shells by producing live oysters, then is it natural? If it is, then it properly belongs to the commons. The commissioners used a farming analogy to point up the illogic of this: "[i]t would be as sensible to say that when a pioneer has cleared a field from the forest, and planted and cultivated thereon a crop of corn, this proves that it is a *natural corn-field*." However, from the perspective of a forester or hunter-gatherer the pioneer's clearing and farming activities are real threats, even if the trees are no longer of value or the game or wild plants have been depleted. Once the land has been cleared and cultivated, the chances are that the remaining forests, wild game, or wild plants will be the provenance of no one but the farmers.

The Cape Shore

Another case from the Delaware Bay area reflects this concern with access and allocation that led to debates about areas once thought of as natural beds but now bereft of oysters. On the Cape Shore of the bay, in a region in which there was no leasing, a Baltimore firm, Mallory and Company, experimentally planted several thousand bushels of shells from the Chesapeake Bay sometime in the 1890s. They abandoned the grounds, thinking their experiment a failure. However, in 1901 local oystermen found a good growth in the area and staked up their claims to apply for leases on several hundred acres. Their act provoked tremendous protest from people who claimed that the grounds were in fact natural beds: some "quite old men" averred that their fathers had caught oysters there. If they were once natural, they could be again. In response to the complaints, the oyster commission dredged the beds and discovered that the shells found were all Chesapeake Bay shells, not Delaware Bay shells. On that basis they granted the leases. However, the matter went to the courts, and eventually much of the Cape Shore region came to be treated as natural oyster beds, reserved as a commons.[4]

Conclusion

Although many observers had hoped that the industry would move in the direction of tightly controlled aquaculture, the irony is that whatever has survived of it is primarily a common property enterprise: today, because of devastating oyster diseases, the only place where oystering can take place is on the natural beds (see chapter 12). In retrospect, the riparian "wars" of the 1890s helped ensure that that possibility remained.

The southwest line in Delaware Bay remained firm and is so today. It separates the public seed beds up the bay from the leased grounds in Maurice River Cove. This outcome, which was echoed in Maryland around the same time

(Power 1970), owed much to the strength of sentiments and success of the commoners in getting laws and policies that preserved certain areas as natural and thus as common property. Evidence that many areas were barren and arguments that private property and private enterprise are the best ways to manage declining oyster resources were outweighed by concerns about monopolistic takeover by big firms of resources that were important to the livelihoods of the many. We might add the notion that the productivity of nature *should* belong to everyone; another, more widespread value, often expressed in fishing, is that the American way is one of open competition. In chapter 12 I bring this account into recent decades of the twentieth century, focusing on comanagement and responses to shellfish disease. There I include excerpts of interviews with oystermen of Maurice River Cove that emphasize such "free enterprise" in the context of a recent decision to restrict the fishery to existing vessels. Such a limited entry system shifts the object of privatization from places and oyster beds to rights of access.

But first, I turn to Atlantic and Ocean Counties and then to the Raritan Bay, where similar contests over public and private rights to natural oyster beds occurred. The outcome was different, at least for a while: in both regions, "propagation leases" were created in areas once naturally productive of oysters.

Chapter 10 Riparian Rights and Oyster Wars on the Mullica River

The 1902 legislative commission on oystering focused even more on the vast shellfishing area of the bays, inlets, and tidal rivers of the Atlantic coast. In 1902 Ocean County gained an oyster commission and state-sanctioned leasing system; in 1905 so did Atlantic County. The systems supported private leaseholds for oyster planting. Both were controversial in inception and outcome. The biggest controversy was about the private "propagating grounds," or private leaseholds for the purpose of shelling and attracting natural growth of oysters.

The Tragedy of the Gravelings

In the context of debates about shelling the natural oyster beds, the state biologist, Julius Nelson, gave a graphic sketch of opening day on the Mullica River seed beds, the focus of much of this controversy. These beds, called "gravelings" or "gravlings," are among the richest natural oyster beds on the Atlantic coast. They were heavily utilized for years but seemed resilient because of the deep accumulations of oyster shells "from the unnumbered years of the past before man came to grab for this golden harvest" (New Jersey Bureau of Shell Fisheries 1906: 67). The beds were closed to harvest for much of the year and opened to one and all on October 1. The ensuing scenario strongly reminded Nelson "of the opening to the public of government lands in the west" (New Jersey Bureau of Shell Fisheries 1906: 66):

> These beds are two in number, the upper one is off Turtle Island, the lower bed a mile nearer the Bay. So limited is the area covered by natural seed in sufficient abundance to pay for tonging, that the water is crowded with boats of all descriptions that have come into position during the day preceding the opening. Here are

> sloops, schooners, yachts, smacks, sail crafts and naphtha launches, scows, garveys, rowboats, and dinkeys, almost wedged together. Just enough space is left to allow the tonger to push his load to the nearest "buying" boat.
>
> In this limited area, at sunrise October 1st, nearly a thousand persons set vigorously to work to tong up the oyster seed which is scarcely larger than a nickel. As fast as the load was secured it was sold, unloaded, and the tonger fell to work again. So it was all that day, and the next, and the next, but soon such tonging cleaned off the upper layer rich in spat and subsequent grabs became poorer in oysters until the buyer refused to catch at the price; meanwhile the crowd daily grows smaller and relatively few remain to work on these beds longer than a week. It was estimated that these beds yielded this season 200,000 bushels of seed that sold for $40,000. (New Jersey Bureau of Shell Fisheries 1906: 67)

Like the oyster commissioners, the biologist was worried about depletion of the natural seed beds and failure to replace shells as cultch for the spat of the next generation: "[t]he beds are much less productive than they were many years ago, and are surely, if slowly, destined to disappear yet the broad expanses of this river are suitable spatting grounds if only shells are placed there as cultch for the young oysters" (New Jersey Bureau of Shell Fisheries 1906: 67). State shelling was one way "to exploit this health," but Nelson seemed pessimistic about getting funds to do the work. At that time the tongers were licensed, and the license fees could be used for such a program, but it seemed doubtful that the fees would cover the costs to the state (and it proved difficult to get tongers to pay their fees, especially when the success of shelling was erratic). Nelson thus favored leasing the grounds to private persons as, he noted, was done effectively in Holland (New Jersey Bureau of Shell Fisheries 1906: 68; see van Ginkel 1988, 1989 for comparable social issues and resistance surrounding the practice in Holland).

Atlantic and Ocean County Debates about Privatizing the Natural Beds

Atlantic County was the site of the first and only experiment in leasing natural beds for propagating oysters. Here the problem of declining seed production was being addressed independently by many oyster planters, who were shelling grounds that they claimed by "law, custom, or usage." By 1902 the practice was reflected in the existence of four distinct classes of shellfishermen: planters, tongers, clammers, and "propagators" or "growers" (New Jersey Oyster Commission 1902: 18). The major point of controversy was the allegation that some of these propagators who put shells in the bay to attract natural oyster growth were in fact using areas that had been naturally productive in the past and that, according to many opponents, were still natural beds and thus by law open to the commoners.

The guiding vision of the Atlantic County oystermen and other entrepreneurs who favored propagation was the transformation of vast submarine acreage into "veritable gold mines" (New Jersey Oyster Commission 1902: 19). At the Tuckerton meeting of the legislative commission, a spokesman for many of the planters, John F. Hall, saw the whole area between the Mullica River and Great Egg Harbor as two thousand acres of potential seed-producing beds or propagating grounds (New Jersey Oyster Commission 1902: 19–20). Local planters had found themselves forced to "go to Connecticut for plants or retire from business" because of declining productivity of native beds and difficulty getting seed and "plants" from the Chesapeake. Connecticut plants were available but expensive and not as suitable as native ones.

George Mott, secretary of the state shell commission (which was still functioning in Atlantic County to place empty shells on natural seed beds), expressed a "general opinion" that the state should lease *all* of the shellfish grounds, clam and oyster, and thereby "give protection to those who lease them and propagate oysters or clams" (New Jersey Oyster Commission 1902: 14). The shell commission's efforts had not been very effective. Something had to be done. If they had leases, individuals might be motivated to enhance the seed stocks themselves. Incidentally, within a year Mott himself became a controversial entrepreneur in oystering. He joined a local judge and Joseph Wharton, a wealthy Philadelphian who owned a fish-processing factory on Crab Island in Tuckerton Bay, to plant oysters in a saltwater creek. The rub, and the subject of yet another court case (*State v. Mott* 1906, the so-called Mott case), was that the creek was within an area designated as natural oyster seed beds, according to the 1902 Ocean County oyster law, and indeed had been staked as such by Mott himself (New Jersey Bureau of Shell Fisheries 1906: 128).[1] Public uproar over this contributed to the creation of yet another investigatory committee.

The prevailing opinion in the 1902 recorded testimonies, which were dominated by planters, was that the state should provide greater protection for planters who already owned or claimed naturally productive ground and shelled it at their own expense. These planters and propagators were being unfairly pressured by others "to throw their natural grounds open to the public after all their work and expense." Even without so doing, planters had little incentive to improve the oyster stock, since "almost as fast as they planted, their beds were invaded by those who claimed the right to them" (New Jersey Oyster Commission 1902: 21).

One "owner of much natural ground" proposed clear demarcation of the following types of shellfish territory: propagating grounds (leased), natural seed beds (public), planting grounds (leased), and clamming grounds (public). The rub was that the new propagating grounds would go beyond those already "owned" and used by planters to include areas then "in the wilds" (New Jersey Oyster Commission 1902: 21).

But others who spoke to the commission voiced their fear that areas once known to be natural but now barren would be leased out for propagating and never returned to public access. Even planters spoke out against the leasing of erstwhile "natural" beds for propagation purposes. John Hall, for example, recommended that the shell commission simply change its practice of depositing shells in bunches to one of scattering them about on the public grounds to reduce the chances of nocturnal theft of the shells and the oysters that might result from them (New Jersey Oyster Commission 1902: 21). Other planters, such as Isaac Collins of Pleasantville (a shipper too), referred to "disputes between the growers and the planters" (New Jersey Oyster Commission 1902: 18) as reasons for not staking off natural beds. Planters and shippers also seemed wary of creating another level of specialization and hence increased cost in the industry: direct harvest of seed from natural beds or buying from independent baymen was cheaper than buying from propagators.

Baymen had already created a test case to challenge the local practice of using naturally productive shellfish beds as propagating grounds: two men went onto an area "owned" by planters who used them for propagating and took oysters. A local jury divided on the matter, and thus "this long controversy" was still not settled by 1902 (New Jersey Oyster Commission 1902: 22).

The legislative commission traveled north to Ocean County to the shellfishing town of Tuckerton. There, the issue was as much about clams as about oysters. The mayor of Tuckerton Borough, who was also a shipper of clams and oysters, argued for the recently enacted leasing system and referred to opposition, including "the mistaken notion among a certain class that clams and oysters, no matter where found, belong to any man with a rake." He also referred to claims "that some of the clammers had leased and staked up more land than they could take care of" (New Jersey Oyster Commission 1902: 22). Clam "culture" had begun and, like oyster culture, called for the protection of private property. In Tuckerton Bay several men were engaged in planting seed clams in response to gradual depletion of the clam beds. A Captain Stiles had gone as far as Nova Scotia to buy seed clams (New Jersey Oyster Commission 1902: 12, 14). This added a new wrinkle to the more widespread conflict between clammers and oystermen, the former the most vehement of the commoners and the latter personifying the propertied. Even some clammers were becoming propertied.

Despite opposition to the leasing of more ground in Atlantic County and Ocean County for propagating oysters and clams, the legislative commission was generally in favor of it. It was particularly impressed by what had happened in Connecticut, where the state had taken control of all of the deep-water oystering lands and then sold them outright to oyster propagators and planters (New Jersey Oyster Commission 1902: 25; Ingersoll 1881). The commission recognized that New Jersey law did not allow outright sale, only leases, but it pointed out that there was really no difference between outright sale and leasing. Reference was also made to the leasing of natural oyster grounds in Virginia. In addition, the commission noted that in Delaware Bay, where the most important natural oyster beds, above the southwest line, were preserved as a commons, it was only a matter of time before these would be leased, despite opposition.

The opposition was, however, vehement enough to influence the commission. In its final report, the 1902 legislative commission simply recommended that the state lease all but the natural beds (New Jersey Oyster Commission 1902: 50).

The Mullica River Oyster Wars

Interest in the privatization solution continued, and some oystermen used the riparian commission to implement it. Others objected. The dramatic climax of a complex sequence of events was another oyster war. On October 1, 1907, hundreds of oystermen went up the Mullica River and tonged for oysters on a spot of ground claimed as a riparian grant by E. T. and Watson C. Sooy. "The result was a violent clash between the opposing elements. Some two hundred oystermen were practically placed under arrest upon the charge of trespassing upon this ground. There was considerable personal violence, and at one time great fear of serious consequences" (New Jersey Bureau of Shell Fisheries 1907: 16).

Atlantic and Ocean County oystermen began to use riparian grants to secure private property rights in 1903. By 1906 there were at least three grants: two in the Mullica River (one of the Sooy cousins plus one claimed by the partners Chew and Gale) and one in Tuckerton Bay on a site that had been used for oyster planting by the Parker brothers. The first two were the most controversial. They challenged the local rule of the commons since they were within the area designated by the legislature as natural oystering ground: "[a]ll those lands lying under the tidal waters of Great Bay and Mullica River, north of a line running from Graveling Point in a southwesterly course to the Atlantic County line." Public outcries against this encroachment of the commons, as well as the Mott case, led to more inquiries and court cases. The importance of the Mott case and the riparian claims on the Mullica River in their time is shown by the fact that the Bureau of Shell Fisheries included in its annual report for 1906 the entire transcript of *State v. Mott,* held in Toms River on September 18, 1906, and of a meeting between baymen and a special investigating committee on the riparian grants that was held in the same place on December 15, 1906 (New Jersey Bureau of Shell Fisheries 1906: 19–37, 90–136).

The December 1906 meeting in Toms River was followed by the "war" of October 1907, and then the New Jersey Supreme Court case of *Attorney-General v. Sooy Oyster Company* in 1909. The events took place within the context of critical review of the state's riparian policy and its administration for alleged abuses of the riparian public trust. The December 1906 meeting was of a special committee of the legislature on that matter and is fully reported by that committee as well (New Jersey Riparian Committee 1906–7). It is a rich source of firsthand reports on the effects of privatization in the Mullica River oystering grounds.

The meeting was run by Edward A. Horner, Jr., the oyster superintendent for Ocean County, and a small committee of state legislators, as part of the larger investigation of the doings of the riparian commission. The baymen who gave sworn testimony in response to questions asked by Horner and one of the assemblymen were from towns such as New Gretna and Tuckerton, important sites of oystering and clamming, and, more generically, from Atlantic County.

The baymen testified that the grounds taken by Sooy and Company and by Chew and Gale were formerly used by themselves and had been seeded by the state as natural grounds. The grants were in the shallower waters of the river, so the baymen complained that "[t]hese grants drove [us] off on deeper water where [we] could not work" (New Jersey Bureau of Shell Fisheries 1906: 21). The disputed beds were of particular value because they provided shelter from the winds.

The committee had trouble getting a consistent estimate of how many men were employed oystering in the vicinity: one said "two or three hundred," another said "quite a lot," but when pressed further, "I think last season there must have been at least four hundred" (New Jersey Bureau of Shell Fisheries 1906: 22). Elsewhere in the bureau's report, Professor Julius Nelson described opening day on the natural beds of the Mullica River as involving "nearly a thousand persons" (New Jersey Bureau of Shell Fisheries 1906: 67). It was difficult for anyone to really know, since people using these oystering grounds came for opening day from up and down the Atlantic coast, and not all were professional oystermen: "[s]ome clam, some work on land around. They expect to make something to keep them through the winter" (New Jersey Bureau of Shell Fisheries 1906: 23).

The Sooys were remarkable men. Testimony confirmed general knowledge that Watson C. Sooy had been one of the shell commissioners in the ancien régime and hinted that he had abused this role. A later Bureau of Shell Fisheries report also hinted at this (1907: 14).[2] The major crime was that the Sooys, like others, had tried to take over the public oyster lands in what was called "one of the most scandalous cases of wrongdoing in the dark history of the State Riparian Commission," in which the commission "sold out both the State and the neighborhood oystermen for a paltry consideration of one thousand dollars" (New Jersey Bureau of Shell Fisheries 1907: 14).

The Sooys obtained their riparian grant in 1903, having managed to keep almost everyone in the dark about the transaction until it was completed. Then they began to oust the tongers: "I paid a license to go on natural ground. Mr. Sooy, who I think is interested, came and told me they had a grant for that. I had no right to work there. So went on that fall, but none since. Did not want to take any chance on that" (Charles C. Cranmer, New Gretna, in New Jersey Bureau of Shell Fisheries 1906: 28).

Among the scandalous features of the grant was that the usual riparian commission requirement that the grantee would make certain improvements (reclaiming the land, building docks and wharves) or forfeit the grant was not written into the deed (New Jersey Bureau of Shell Fisheries 1907: 14). Like the Delaware Bay riparian grantees, the Sooys made little or no pretense at reclamation or "improvement" besides digging some ditches up into the marshes for the purpose of planting oysters there. Moreover, although some of the Delaware Bay riparian grantees had received their deeds prior to an 1888 state law that explicitly forbade riparian grants on natural oyster beds, this law was clearly in effect in 1903 and had been blatantly ignored by both the Sooys and the riparian commission.

The Sooy riparian grant challenged the entire body of custom and law. Many people also saw it as a threat to the economics and social relations of the oyster business. At the December meeting, Assemblyman Minturn asked E. W. Giberson, who planted oysters near Absecon,

Q. If the State was to make a grant of all this land how many men would go out of business?
A. It would put hundreds out.
Q. What would be the effect of a grant of that kind by the State on the price of oysters at large? Would it tend to create a trust in the price?
A. Yes, sir.
Q. You would have to work for them or not at all?
A. That is the way it looks. (New Jersey Bureau of Shell Fisheries 1906: 23)

Attorney-General v. Sooy Oyster Company

Enough has been said to indicate what lay behind the oyster war of October 1, 1907, on the Mullica River oyster beds claimed by the Sooys. Published accounts of that raid are terse. Oral tradition claims that it did indeed involve hundreds of men and a great deal of violence.[3] In addition, Arnold Cranmer, one of the witnesses at the December 1906 meeting, was a leader of the raid, but, it is said, he was one of the first to try to find other means of gaining private property in the Mullica River oyster beds, that is, getting the state to lease private rights to propagating grounds. Accordingly, motivations were mixed. Some raiders were fighting for their natural rights and the social order of the commons, while others may have been merely jealous.

The court case that arose from this conflict reached the state supreme court in 1909 as *Attorney-General v. Sooy Oyster Company*. The text shows that judges and lawyers were as capable of scandalous behavior as were the Sooys and the state riparian commission. The case was a morass of technicalities. At the lower court, no testimony was allowed on the key issue, whether the riparian grants were made on natural oyster beds. The higher court honored that procedural point, resulting in a split decision on the issue. Consequently, the Sooys kept their right to the riparian grant.

The thick web of procedural and jurisdictional questions only partly masked an enduring power struggle between the riparian commissioners and the shellfish management bodies of New Jersey. The court considered whether the riparian commission had general jurisdiction over the state's tidelands or whether the commission's jurisdiction stopped wherever natural shellfish beds occurred. In 1888 the legislature had specifically excluded natural oyster beds from the domain of the riparian commission, logically following the long history of public and legislative sentiment that had resulted in a clear and important separation of tidal lands into two classes: "those which are natural beds and those which are not natural oyster beds" (*Attorney-General v. Sooy Oyster Company* 1909: 429).

The Sooys' riparian grant was within an area long known as natural oystering ground and recognized as such in the 1902 shellfish law. Accordingly, there should be no doubt about the impropriety of the grant. However, the arcane workings of the law led to the opposite conclusion. The state attorney general and the baymen were not allowed to present testimony in court about whether or not the disputed territory was the home of natural oysters. The technical problem was the dismal state of surveying in the state's tidal waters. Since no proper survey existed, the only evidence was oral testimony. In an "action of ejectment" of a "collateral attack," oral testimony was not allowable. Thus, neither the court nor any jury was allowed to hear testimony concerning natural oyster beds in the Mullica River.

An Alice in Wonderland argument also appeared: the disputed area could not be the site of natural oyster beds because the riparian commissioners had granted it to the Sooys. The commissioners were supposed to check into whether a grant application broke the rule about natural oyster beds before making the grant. Therefore, the fact that the grant was made was sufficient evidence that no natural oysters existed there! The perversity of the argument is similar to the one reportedly made by the river pirates of the Shrewsbury around the same time that if one could not lease areas that were naturally productive, then, if no lease existed, the area must be deemed naturally productive and therefore open to everyone (chapter 3).

Underlying these legal maneuvers was concern on the part of some judges that a challenge to an existing riparian claim would open the door to suits against riparian owners throughout the state. If such insecurity of tenure were created, state revenue from riparian grants would be reduced. "If our riparian grants are to be subject to such indirect attacks it is difficult to believe that any prudent man would purchase so insecure a tenure" (*Attorney-General v. Sooy Oyster Company* 1909: 404).

The supreme court was sharply divided on both technical and policy matters. Justice Swayze, who opposed the above arguments, noted the importance of the case to the interests of the state, "since it affects not only valuable lands under tidewater which the state for many years has been sedulous to improve and preserve for the benefit of the public in the supply of an important article of food, but it affects the power of the legislature to control its own agents by its public statutes. The decision goes much deeper than the mere question of procedure" (*Attorney-General v. Sooy Oyster Company* 1909: 409). He later said, "I am aware of the importance of sustaining the validity of riparian grants when legally made, but it is equally important to maintain the rights of the state as against individuals who seek to acquire lands contrary to law" (*Attorney-General v. Sooy Oyster Company* 1909: 411).

The issue of state rights to public lands was very much in the forefront of riparian and public lands law at the time. The United States Supreme Court only recently had made its landmark decision in the case of *Illinois Central Railway Company v. State of Illinois* (1892) that reiterated and affirmed the *Arnold v. Mundy* public trust and state ownership doctrine concerning tidewater lands. The tendency in New Jersey for the trusteeship over such property to be translated into fee simple absolute ownership or proprietorship was, therefore, checked by public interests in navigation, fishing, and other common rights. Indeed, the state of New Jersey had reflected this in its reservation of natural oyster beds from the domain of the riparian commissioners in 1888.

The riparian commissioners were accused of ignoring both public interests and the shellfish commissioners' mandate to manage and improve public shellfish beds. A related issue was the power of government agencies versus state legislatures in the management of public lands. Swayze argued that the fact that the riparian commissioners operate as an administrative arm does not mean that they can ignore the limits to their power created by the legislature (*Attorney-General v. Sooy Oyster Company* 1909: 415). This was a matter affecting the administration of all public lands and mining claims in the United States. He also argued that a review of similar cases showed that "parole" or oral evidence could be used when grants made by government agencies contravened public laws.

In an ultimately futile attempt to overturn the riparian grants on the Mullica River, the dissenting opinions also dealt with the question of knowledge, part of the debate over the use of oral evidence in the case. Swayze reviewed New Jersey's legislative history concerning natural and unnatural shellfish grounds and insisted that the legislature had always recognized the existence of local knowledge and general consensus concerning the location of natural oyster beds. Another judge, Minturn, who had been one of the assemblymen present at the 1906 hearing on the riparian issue at the Toms River courthouse, pointed out that the riparian claim was within an area for which the legislature had appropriated money for placing oyster shells to enhance natural growth (*Attorney-General v. Sooy Oyster Company* 1909: 431–32), specifically designating it as a natural oyster bed. For these matters, oral testimony (and allowing a trial jury to hear and weigh it) must and should have been allowed: "[h]ad the proffered testimony been allowed it might have been shown that for generations a hardy race of seafaring men had made an independent existence from these beds, and the existence of the beds was as notorious as was the beacon light at Barnegat" (*Attorney-General v. Sooy Oyster Company* 1909: 433). So, also, it would have shown that the state had spent thousands of dollars to place shells on the beds and improve them for the benefit of the industry.

Minturn tried to make the case for common rights by evoking an image of dispossessed commoners. He made a direct analogy between the riparian legislation and other enclosure processes in history:

> In the light of history it requires no exuberance of fancy to picture the dire results to the state if the public policy inspired by this grant be adopted, as a result of which

> this great natural industry, the prolific toiling-place of generations of independent self-supporting citizens shall be aliened forever, and they themselves evicted as completely and as effectually, . . . as were the thrifty Highland crofters of Scotland under the great "Sutherland clearance" at Lochaber, when a whole people were swept into exile, to make way for sheep walks and pasture lands. (*Attorney-General v. Sooy Oyster Company* 1909: 438)

If the court allowed such riparian forms of enclosure to proceed, they would not only displace many baymen but would also go against tendencies in other domains to recognize and ameliorate the evils of enclosure. The English House of Commons had struggled for many years "to regain and retrieve from class ownership the lost privileges of the people" (*Attorney-General v. Sooy Oyster Company* 1909: 438, referring to changes in the Game Laws as well as the numerous Commons Acts of the late nineteenth and early twentieth centuries that sought to preserve the remaining common lands of England and Scotland against the effects of prior Enclosure Acts). Similarly, he said, two recent federal administrations in the United States had tried to recover "lost forest, mineral and swamp lands, the common heritage of the nation" (*Attorney-General v. Sooy Oyster Company* 1909: 438).

Minturn might have referred also to the hard-won and recently enunciated policy in New Jersey that the oyster beds "are the natural heritage of all the people of the State" (New Jersey Bureau of Shell Fisheries 1904: 40), as well as the sentiment expressed many years before by Chief Justice Green of the state supreme court that the courts should lean on the side of public rights when forced to interpret disputing claims, given that "public rights are yielded to private interests with sufficient alacrity" (*Townsend v. Brown* 1853: 87).

Ultimately, *Attorney-General v. Sooy* was a nondecision due to a divided court. By default it supported the Sooys' riparian claims to productive oyster beds on the Mullica River. The law did not serve the interests of the larger group of baymen. However, by this time the legislature had acted. In 1906, in response to the complaints of the oystermen about the riparian grants, the legislature ordered the riparian commission to stop the practice of granting riparian tracts in shellfish-bearing grounds at least for the time being (New Jersey Bureau of Shell Fisheries 1906). The predations of pirates and the costs of further legal cases may have been obstacles enough to grants after the 1909 court case.

It is not clear what happened to the disputed grants. At least one remains, having been sold and inherited over the generations. It is still in murky legal waters (Thomas McCloy, personal communication, April 18, 1984). One can still see a series of ditches dug across narrow necks of marshland at bends in the

Mullica River that were created by the Sooys in an apparent attempt to create oyster bottom from the high grounds part of their grant (Ford 1997). This property was sold to the Cranmers, descendants of whom maintain exclusive oystering rights until their death, at which time rights revert to the Forsythe National Wildlife Refuge (Stephen Potter, personal communication, December 1988). The public trust is now protected by federal law, but most of the oysters have succumbed to MSX, a disease that obeys no law.

Return to Propagating Leases

The riparian oyster wars in the Mullica River area captured most of the energies and attention of Atlantic coast shellfish politics from 1903 to 1909. However, some of the leaders of the opposition to the Sooys' riparian claim on natural oyster beds in the Mullica River are remembered in oral tradition as turncoats. Soon after their raid against the Sooys' riparian grants they resurrected the issue of leases for propagating purposes.

The oyster superintendent of Ocean County, Mr. Horner, wrote eloquently in his 1908 report of the need to do something about the problem of declining native seed stock (New Jersey Bureau of Shell Fisheries 1908: 39–42). He linked the need to enhance local seed to the plight of the small-scale oysterman. Oyster planting was uneconomical for the majority because of the high cost of importing plants from Virginia and New York. The small planter could not afford to import plants: they cost about seventy-five cents per bushel, to which should be added the two years required to wait for the development of the marketable oyster, interest on invested capital, cost of handling, and loss from various causes (injury in handling, damage by ice, depredations by drum fish and snails, the smothering of plants, and, according to other observers, piracy). The price was "simply prohibitive to the small planter; certainly very restrictive to the larger, well-established planters" (New Jersey Bureau of Shell Fisheries 1908: 40).

The cost of domestic seed, transplanted at from thirty-five to forty cents per bushel, was also considerable. Horner depicted a bleak situation:

> Is it cause for wonder then that everywhere one hears complaints of the decline of oyster planting brought about by restrictive conditions, incident hard times for the baymen, and gradual failure of the bays, under the present system, as a means of livelihood? . . . there are thousands of acres of bay bottom . . . that must go unworked on account of lack of seed within the reach of the planter. There are also areas that were once productive natural seed beds—Cedar Creek, Tuckerton Cove, Parker's Cove—that are now depleted; only the Graveling at the mouth of the Mullica River remains, and that is laid bare after two or three days after the opening of the season.

A remedy was in sight: "[i]n Ocean county we have the natural resources to help ourselves once they are properly developed under the wise administration of the State."[4] How? Privatization:

> The unanimous opinion is that the State should take under direct control the large but now unproductive areas described, and by appropriate legislation make it possible to lease to individuals lands for the propagation of oyster seed. There is little doubt but that such lands would be quickly taken up and sufficient seed raised thereon to supply, at a reasonable price, planters, or would-be planters, who now clamor in vain for seed they cannot buy. (New Jersey Bureau of Shell Fisheries 1908: 41)

Areas still productive "might still be left open to the public at certain seasons, but greater care should be exercised over them by the State."

Again, the issue generated strenuous and often violent opposition on the part of many of the smaller planters as well as tongers and clammers, who feared "that persons with large capital and influence would be able practically to monopolize these seed bearing areas by taking out a lease for nearly all the acreage" (New Jersey Board of Shell Fisheries 1909: 8). Accordingly, a bill introduced into the legislature in 1909 to enable leasing was withdrawn at the request of politicians from Ocean County and Atlantic County (New Jersey Bureau of Shell Fisheries 1908: 8–9).

Finally, in 1910 the state legislature passed a bill sponsored by Senator Walter E. Edge of Atlantic County that allowed propagation leases in a relatively small area, three hundred "barren" acres of Atlantic County, specifically in the Tuckahoe, Middle, and Great Egg Harbor Rivers. A compromise provision to help get the bill passed, responsive to the demands of smaller planters, restricted the amount of acreage that could be leased to no more than five acres and agreed to make the price of a lease low enough "to come within the reach of the poorest oystermen." The annual rental fee was three dollars an acre—more than the one dollar an acre charged for other leases in Atlantic County (by then in effect) but still affordable.

There was also a provision that propagating lands not leased within three years could be auctioned to the highest bidders in pieces up to ten acres each (New Jersey Board of Shell Fisheries 1910). This provision never came into effect. My examination of the lease records shows that until the demise of the system by 1917, no propagating lease was more than five acres in size. Larger holdings could, of course, be gained through the common tactic of applying for several leases in the names of females and children in a family—in 1912 seven out of the fifty lessees were women with the same surname as one or more male lessees (New Jersey Board of Shell Fisheries 1912: 128)—as well as by combining the leases of close male kin. However, the lease records of 1910–16 suggest that the more egalitarian sentiments of those who had initially opposed propagating leases were implemented.[5]

The statistical reality provided in the Board of Shell Fisheries records of propagating bed leases was affected by the political reality of continued opposition and the emergence of new problems. In 1910, at the outset of the new system, it was challenged in court and taken to the state supreme court for review. In 1911 political ferment resulted in the removal of the old members of the Atlantic County oyster commission and the installation of new ones, partly in response to accusations of favoritism in granting propagation leases (New Jersey Board of Shell Fisheries 1911: 18).

The propagating lease system was not given much of a chance to show whether shelling and seeding natural beds would help restore their productivity. Within a year, the new commission resolved to repeal the 1910 law, claiming that it had removed the means of obtaining a livelihood and had allowed the leasing of grounds that were not, in fact, barren. Oyster catches were low, and baymen resented being excluded from natural beds. Some of the grounds leased for propagation were in the Great Egg Harbor River, where the catch for the year was dismal: "there was no catch on the public beds and on the leased grounds the catch was very small" (New Jersey Board of Shell Fisheries 1911: 45). The commissioner asked for repeal of the 1910 act, giving the leased propagating grounds in the river back to the "public . . . in as much as they are the only grounds in this river on which there are any oysters for the public to catch" (New Jersey Board of Shell Fisheries 1911: 45).

Between 1912 and 1916, however, the situation was more hopeful. In 1913 the Atlantic County oyster commissioners reported that "the feeling of a few baymen who fear that they might be deprived of a slender income by this change . . . has practically disappeared" (New Jersey Board of Shell Fisheries 1913: 8). The propagating leases seemed to work. In 1913 the leased propagating grounds in Great Egg Harbor River had an abundant catch. This was used to support the practice: "[a]s this is the first time there had been a catch in this district since the law to lease private individuals has been in effect the lessees feel very much encouraged" (New Jersey Board of Shell Fisheries 1913: 39). As three years had passed, the rental went up from three to five dollars an acre.

Nonetheless, the state's legitimacy as a benthic landlord was in question, and leaseholders found their rights as tenuous as ever. "A certain class of people" totally disregarded the state leasing system and planted grounds without a lease and hence without paying money to the state. Most of all, the leaseholders were upset at the lack of enforcement provided them in holding exclusive rights to the fruits of their labors and shells, a problem that continues to this day. In this case, the county shellfish commission argued that it had no legal backing to hire guards. The state attorney general pointed out that it was the law and the commission's duty to do so and that it had appropriations that could be used for the purpose (New Jersey Board of Shell Fisheries 1912: 24). However, the commission and the leaseholders experienced "difficulty in securing proper safeguards for the grounds set apart for leasing," both propagation and planting grounds. Some of the leaseholders had refused to renew their leases for this reason, and the state attorney general's office had to issue a letter advising the commissioners that not only did they have the power and funds but also the duty to provide safeguards.

Without strong popular sentiment for the program it was, as usual, extremely difficult to enforce private property in the marine commons. Although later reports are silent on the question of the productivity of the propagating leases, we may reasonably assume that this was disappointing as well. One bit of circumstantial evidence is that none of the leading planters, shippers, or members of the local oyster commission held propagating leases by 1915–16; surely they would have if such leases were clearly shown to be worthwhile. This, in combination with the enforcement problem, contributed to the disappearance of an experiment in managing the oystering commons.

Conclusion

Privatizing natural shellfish beds struck at the core of the property rights system that had evolved through conflict, conciliation, and legal action, giving rise to large-scale and violent oyster wars. The wars of the Delaware Bay and the Mullica River took place at a time when shellfishermen, state legislators, and scientists were debating the wisdom of extending private property tenure in oystering to the natural oyster beds in order to let private enterprise do what the state and the commoners seemingly could not: properly manage the state's natural oyster resources. The oyster wars checked the impulse and reestablished, once and for all, that the natural oyster beds must remain the natural heritage of the people. Privatization was viewed by baymen and state representatives alike as potentially very harmful to the majority of people, especially the poor, and this eventually was articulated as a legitimate concern of state policy: "[i]f it is the policy of the State to dispose of these lands it should be done in a manner that would give the oystermen a square deal and not allow four or five men to be made wealthy at the expense of eight or twelve hundred poor oystermen" (New Jersey Bureau of Shell Fisheries 1906: 50).

The oyster wars took place within the context of widespread concern about declining oyster stocks, which intensified as sources of seed and plants from other states became harder to obtain. At the peak of the New Jersey oyster industry, from about 1870 to 1930, the Atlantic coast region, from Barnegat Bay to Cape May, produced about 20 percent of all market oysters harvested in the state (Ford 1997). By 1930, it produced less than 5 percent, and by the 1950s its production was insignificant, clamming having risen to much greater importance. Was the policy protecting common rights to natural beds the cause? Surely it contributed to overharvesting, but the larger, longer picture focuses more on other things. In Barnegat Bay, oystering gradually declined due to overfishing of the relatively small natural beds and changes in salinity that came about because of changes in inlets to the bay, particularly a canal at the northern end of the bay (Nelson 1933).

The graveling and other seed beds of the Mullica River and the private leases on Great Bay remain the sites of small-scale oystering. Many of the seed beds were maintained as a public resource by the state until 1982, when a lack of funds forced discontinuance of active state involvement, including transplanting seed oysters from the public beds to tongers' private beds in Great Bay. Oyster diseases have sharply limited production here as elsewhere (Ford 1997).

The next chapter returns to Raritan Bay, the site of the original public trust cases and, as we shall see, a last-ditch effort to save the natural oysters through privatization while avoiding the larger problems of habitat destruction and pollution, which were even more devastating there.

Chapter 11 Commoners and Other Nuisances on the Raritan Bay

In 1894, Ansley Hall, reporting on the shellfish industries for the Department of Labor and Industries, had this to say about the Raritan Bay shellfisheries: "[t]here has been considerable friction . . . between the oyster-planters and the clam fishermen relative to the acquirement and holding of grounds for planting purposes. The clam fishermen, refusing to recognize the right of the planters to the possession of bottom for private enterprise, have at various times trespassed upon the cultivated beds under the pretext of taking clams, and numerous cases of litigation have ensued" (1894: 470).[1]

The situation reflected a larger shift from the "age old contest between planters and [oyster] tongers" to a "very general contest between the oystermen and the clammers" (*De Graff v. Truesdale* 1887: 90). Contributing to it was the fact that independent, common-right oyster tongers were fewer in number with the rise of planting, and many had turned to clamming instead. Clamming, always important for subsistence and local trade, emerged as a major commercial fishery in New Jersey in the late nineteenth century.

The contest between oystermen and clammers was yet another one over property rights and hence class and control. Control over oystering, and to some extent oystering lands, had become concentrated in a merchant class of buyers, shippers, and vessel owners and an incipient industry organized around planting, practices such as "floating" oysters prior to marketing, and oyster shucking and canning factories. Clamming, on the other hand, stayed much more egalitarian, part of the bayman way of life. The most important and abundant clam species was and is the hard clam, or quahog, sold in the shell and consumed raw or cooked.

More specifically, conflicts between oystermen and clammers arose because oystering grounds—especially the "barren" ones approved for planting—can be good places to catch clams. What is barren for one species may be rich and "natural" for another (clams have a range of salinity, temperature, and other natural requirements that differs from that of oysters). Raritan Bay, in particular, was and is highly productive in hard clams, a species that has shown itself remarkably resilient in the face of pollution. The resilience of the clammers, however, was checked by the extension of oyster-planting leases, and they turned to the law for assistance.

Nature and Nuisance: The Legal Issues

The technical question in the late-nineteenth-century Raritan Bay cases was the old one about whether oysters had been planted on natural beds. Courts and custom upheld the idea that oysters planted in clearly staked areas that were not natural oyster beds could be claimed as private property by the planters. Conversely, oysters planted where shellfish naturally grow were very difficult to defend as private property. But it was often hard to prove that a particular shellfish bed was or was not "naturally" productive of oysters or clams. Accordingly, staking off oyster grounds might constitute "encroachment upon the public right" (*Metzger v. Post* 1882: 77) and hence a public nuisance. What shellfishermen could do about this public nuisance was yet another question.

A problem was how to distinguish between true test cases and ones in which baymen were defending theft and trespass by after-the-fact recourse to the law. The question of authenticity came up in an earlier Cape May oystering conflict (*State v. Taylor* 1858), where the state supreme court observed that just because something might be a nuisance by encroaching on public rights does not mean that an individual has the right to steal it. A person might have a right to remove or destroy but not to steal or appropriate to his own use planted oysters that interfered with his right to fish, the right of navigation, or any other public right in the waters.

The case gave common law recognition to the private property rights of oyster planters. It also was a threat to people who used theft to show their objections to enclosure as well as to gain a few oysters on the side. On the other hand, its use of the public nuisance argument opened up more possibilities for "trying the right" action, although the court sharply restricted how that was done. It was often very difficult for defendants to show that they had taken the oysters with anything other than intent to steal. By the 1880s it was apparently even more difficult. Thus, in a Delaware Bay oystering conflict (*Grace v. Willetts* 1888), decided about the same time as the Raritan Bay cases to be described, the court slapped down the defendants for taking oysters from planted beds being claimed as natural ones even though an 1882 legislative statute pertaining to the Delaware Bay industry called for forfeiture of oysters planted on natural beds. Forfeiture was one thing; letting someone else take the oysters was quite another.

Metzger v. Post (1882) was the first of the Raritan Bay cases in this context and probably one of those to which Ansley Hall referred. Caleb Post and George Russell "dredged, raked, and tonged over, upon, and through a certain large bed . . . of oysters" off the town of Keyport in Raritan Bay. The oyster bed was used for planting by Peter Metzger and Benjamin Carhart, who sued for trespass, claiming the loss of $2,000 worth of oysters, or fifteen hundred bushels, a goodly amount. The case is scantily reported, but it is clear that the baymen were unable to make their case *in re* the natural bed rule. The case was thus considered only in terms of public nuisance problems, and although the court apparently accepted that oyster-planting claims to private property were a public nuisance, it ruled that private persons did not have the right to abate a public nuisance.

The New Jersey Supreme Court's decision was simple: Post and Russell should not have taken the oysters found on the planting grounds of Metzger and Carhart. It decided in favor of the two Raritan Bay oyster planters but directed the defendants, Caleb Post and George Russell, to try again, making a more specific case for their rights under the natural bed rule. No direct evidence can be found about whether they did this, but they likely were involved in the cases that soon followed: *De Graff v. Truesdale* (1887) and *Brown v. De Groff* [*sic*] (1888). The record shows that these incidents were part of larger collective attempts to protect the common property interests of clammers against oyster planting: "[o]ysters were planted and the ground staked off. The clammers believed the beds encroached upon their natural clamming grounds. After a great deal of controversy and litigation, a plan to test the rights of the parties was devised" (*De Graff v. Truesdale* 1887: 90).

The baymen raided De Graff's oyster bed in April 1886: "a number of clammers went deliberately upon the oyster-bed and found and brought up natural clams." One thing the baymen and their lawyers had learned from previous court cases was not to take or damage planted oysters in their raids: "[t]hey found oysters also, but did not take them away." Even so, the lower court reproached the baymen for taking matters into their own hands: "[i]f the men who take clams for a living think that the oystermen are staking off grounds that they have no right to, they have the courts to fall back on for redress, and must not use personal force" (*De Graff v. Truesdale* 1887: 90). It found for the planter. However, upon appeal to the state supreme court (*Brown v. De Groff* 1888), the Raritan baymen succeeded in establishing their common right to clam, even within the staked and planted oyster beds of Raritan Bay. The higher court decided in favor of the baymen, as against the planter, taking the position that the baymen each held the private right to clam in the "public highways" of the state's navigable water. Thus the public nuisance of oyster-planting grounds in Raritan Bay became a private one, and the private individual was within his rights to try to abate it in very direct ways.

In his 1894 report, Ansley Hall added that most of the legal cases "terminated in favor of the oystermen" rather than the clammers. A review of the cases shows that the situation was closer to a draw. Hall may have been unaware of the decision on the 1893 New Jersey Supreme Court case, *State v. Abraham Post,* where the court once more upheld the rights of commoners. In 1890, in yet another attempt to give more security to the oyster planters, the legislature had passed an act making it a misdemeanor to take oysters without permission from beds that had been used and occupied since January 1, 1880, for oyster planting. Abraham Post, perhaps related to the Caleb Post of *Metzger v. Post,* apparently broke the law by taking oysters from a ground claimed thereby.

Post's defense was a new one, enabled by recent amendments to the state's constitution that constrained the legislature's ability to make grants to individuals and corporations through "special, local or private laws" (*State v. Post* 1893: 265). His defense was that the law was invalid in selecting certain individuals or corporations—in this instance, those planting oysters from 1880 to 1890—for special privileges and making no provisions for any other classes of persons. The indictment of Abraham Post was quashed and the legal status of the planting grounds of Raritan Bay and elsewhere in the state thrown again into question.

Insecurity of Tenure

It is a puzzle why the tenure of oyster planters in the Raritan Bay was insecure at the end of the nineteenth century, given the long history of conflict and legislation and court rulings on the matter, but so it was, in part because of challenges such as those reviewed above. As late as 1892 only a small percentage of the Raritan Bay bottom believed to be suitable for oyster planting was in fact leased and used for that purpose (Hall 1894: 469), and insecurity of tenure in planted beds was the major reason given.[2] Neither the court rulings nor other, mostly unrecorded acts of resistance to the planting system that have given the baymen of this region the reputation of pirates were able to check the social processes at play in Raritan Bay oystering that led to both economic concentration and environmental destruction.

A possible explanation for why insecurity of tenure seemed so much worse for the planters of the Raritan Bay than for those of the Delaware Bay to the south concerns the importance of clamming in the Raritan Bay and hence the persistence of claims to the shellfish commons. The commoners of the Delaware—the oyster tongers—had nothing as suitable and abundant as an alternative to oystering as the hard clams found elsewhere in the state. Where there were hard clams in abundance, as in Raritan Bay and the Atlantic coast shellfish regions, the baymen remained in numbers and continued to fight for their common property interests. At the turn of the century these were further institutionalized through the demarcation of public clam grounds in many parts of the state.

Raritan Bay planters sought protection. Whether test cases or outright theft, the baymen's activities increased the expenses of the oyster planters, who in 1882 formed an oyster planters association at Keyport to coordinate patrolling and defending the planted beds against the depredations of the baymen (Anonymous 1940). In 1902, following the example of the Delaware Bay planters, they gained state support in leasing and protecting private property in the planted beds, as the state defined and accepted responsibility to manage all shellfish waters and industries of the state (New Jersey Oyster Commission 1902).

In this region, state management did not pretend to maintain shellfishing for the majority. Very quickly the best planting grounds were taken by men of prominence and wealth. By 1907, five years after the state took over leasing and protection of oyster-planting beds in the Raritan Bay, the oyster beds off Keyport were divided into eighteen leases, of which only five were under ten acres in size. The rest were extremely large: oyster "farms" of 182.75 acres, 91.75 acres, and 51.5 acres were held in the names of individuals; a bank held 18 acres; a group of men with the same surname plus their partners held several leases totaling 328 acres (New Jersey Bureau of Shell Fisheries 1907). As we have seen for South Jersey and as has been shown for other regions, like Great South Bay, Long Island (Gabriel 1921: 97), and the Maryland waters of Chesapeake Bay (Kennedy and Breisch 1983), small-scale oystermen, the "little fellows," tried to counter the monopolistic trend widely believed to follow oyster planting. They sought and gained legislation that limited the size of each leased "farm" in order to make them unprofitable for large businesses but sufficient to supplement the other activities of baymen. This had happened in Raritan Bay in 1824 but not in 1902.

Although the concentration of property in the oyster leaseholds of Raritan Bay kept most baymen from oyster planting, the baymen had their effect on the industry. The incidents and claims of the clammers shown in the court cases reviewed above were blamed (or credited) for keeping oyster-planting acreage small. At Keyport, oyster shippers told a 1902 commission that only about one twentieth of the beds that were suitable for oyster planting were actually set aside for that purpose "largely because of the claims of clammers" (New Jersey Oyster Commission 1902: 6). Later, in a plea for more protection from the state, they argued that the clammers, though equal in numbers to those employed in the Keyport oyster industry (about 230 in the oyster industry, about 250 in clamming), were less deserving of help from the state because they had "scarcely any capital invested," their output was unknown, and the state got no tax or other money from them (New Jersey Bureau of Shell Fisheries 1907: 7). Public policy was not then—nor has it been since—structured to favor the small-scale, independent clammer as opposed to the more capitalized and better organized oyster planters.

Public and Private Nuisances

Nuisance law has a long and special history in the common law, one that may outdo the public trust doctrine for confusion, as between private and public nuisances. Abrams and Washington (1990) note the tendency in modern times to conflate the two, with the possible result that a defendant who seriously damaged a public resource—say, a river—by action or inaction—say, allowing pollution—might be acquitted because it was not possible to show intention or negligence, a private nuisance cause for action, even when the problem affected public rights. The recent "takings" cases, such as *Lucas v. South Carolina Coastal Council* (1992), have raised other concerns about nuisance law (Humbach 1993; Government Law Center 1993).

The long-standing rule in nuisance law is that a private person could have legal standing in a public nuisance case only if that person suffered "special damages," as opposed to the same damages suffered by the rest of the public, in which case action should be taken by the attorney general of the state (Abrams and Washington 1990). Among other matters, there is debate about what constitutes interference with public rights, versus interference with the private rights of large numbers of people, and the New Jersey courts discussed some of these matters in the cases reviewed.

In *Brown v. De Groff* (1888) this issue was handled by interpreting common fishing rights as private ones. The state supreme court took the position that the baymen each held the private right to clam in the public highways of the state's navigable waters. Thus the public nuisance of oyster-planting grounds in Raritan Bay became a private one, and the private individual was within his rights to try to abate it in very direct ways.

Tragedies of the Commons, Specified

An important contribution of the ethnographic and comparative approaches of anthropology to natural resource management is in more accurately specifying the conditions, culture, and social relations surrounding the use and management of common resources (McCay and Acheson 1987b). From this perspective, constructs such as "the public" or "open access" or the bio-economic and other models represented by the phrase "tragedy of the commons" may be too broad or misleading to be useful in understanding and explaining particular situations and events (McCay and Vayda 1992; Vayda 1996).

Even terms such as "social" are not necessarily helpful unless further specified and linked to particular cases. For instance, in the neoclassical economics approach to commons dilemmas, the problem is defined as "social": the reason for overexploitation is that the short-term returns from overusing or abusing the commons are greater than their costs, because the costs are shared with others, known as "social costs" (Coase 1960). A different meaning of "social," tinted by the colors of class analysis, is raised when questioning the effects of privatization, highlighted by the phrase "tragedy of the commoners" (Ciriacy-Wantrup and Bishop 1975).

To underscore the need for specificity and a contextual approach, one that recognizes the fact that individuals interact with other individuals and environments while embedded in larger worlds of structure, significance, and change, I offer yet another New Jersey oystering story. This story, based on interviews done by a legislative commission in 1895, gives a more nuanced view of what a "social dilemma" can be.

The Dilemma of the Seedmen

Common property theory assumes that everyone has roughly equal access to a common resource and equivalent reasons for using it beyond its capacity. However, an 1895 interview with oyster planters and tongers, by then known as "seeders," who worked the declining seed beds of Newark and Raritan Bays (New Jersey Bureau of Statistics of Labor and Industries 1897) shows how wrong this theory is and reveals a more complex dynamic surrounding depletion of natural resources. Many erstwhile commoners worked within the planting industry as wage-laboring tongers or shoremen. Others were seedmen who raked natural oyster beds for the seed oysters that would be transplanted. The seedmen sold what they caught to oyster planters, and they often worked for planters, tonging more mature oysters from the planted beds. Their participation in oystering diminished as Raritan Bay planters reduced their labor requirements by using powerful technology, such as steamers, to dredge oysters from the planted beds: "[b]y operating in this manner but few steamers and men are needed to do the work which formerly required a much larger number of sailing vessels and men to perform" (United States Commissioner of Fish and Fisheries 1901: 458).

The Raritan Bay planters surveyed in 1895 wanted a long closed season or, better from their vantage point, a change in the law enabling the creation of private property in the natural beds to allow private enterprise to manage the resource. They cast the seeders as rapacious abusers of the commons: "[m]any of the men engaged in taking seed do not care whether they destroy the beds or not, so long as they get a skiff full of oysters to sell to planters" (New Jersey Bureau of Statistics of Labor and Industries 1897: 8). This view was echoed by scientists and legislative commissions sent out to survey the problems of the oystering industry.

Passionate in their defense of common property rights to natural beds, the poor seeders of Newark and Raritan Bays had mixed feelings about state regulation of the natural beds. Questioned in 1895, a Raritan Bay seeder stated, "I am not in favor of any law that prevents us from taking seed in any month of the year" (New Jersey Bureau of Statistics of Labor and Industries 1897: 7). By itself, this reads like an assertion of right against reason. However, he had a reason, grounded in his understanding of social relations and economic power in the industry: "if we stopped for any length of time the planters would send men and large boats and in a few days would obtain all they needed, and we would have to quit the business." Another Newark Bay seedman, somewhat more inclined toward state regulation of the natural beds, also worried about a long closed season for the same reason: "[o]ysters grow very fast, and if the time were longer the planters would take advantage of it and send men with large boats, and in a few days obtain all the seed they need, and leave us with nothing to do."

The tragedy of this commons was that the seedmen were forced to work year-round (despite an old law imposing a closed season on the natural beds, a law routinely ignored) *and* to keep the beds depleted in order to maintain the value of their labor. Their tragic choice lay between eventually destroying the resource upon which they depended or giving it all up to the planters. Like Long Island oystermen studied by Gabriel, they "stood between Scylla and Charybdis" (1921: 95), forced to fight for their right to destroy the resource.

The account suggests the value of a more complicated view of what tragedies of the commons can be about: in this case, a certain social relationship to production meant an important, and understandable, stake in maintaining relatively unimpeded access to depleted natural beds of oysters. The tragedy of *that* commons (it is important to be specific) was that the seedmen were forced to work year-round and keep the beds virtually depleted in order to maintain the value of their labor.

The social dilemma of the seedmen highlights the value of exploring the social contexts of abusers of the commons in their historical specificity. Another methodological point is the danger of focusing on the wrong thing or using too narrow or too wide a lens. Certainly in fisheries, and perhaps in other sectors, common pool resource users are often blamed for abuses that are caused or whose effects are intensified by others. Many more people used the waters of Newark Bay and Raritan Bay than the shellfishermen. The tragic choice of the seedmen of the Raritan area was much too narrowly defined. The tragedy of the northern oystering commons was also a tragedy of the side effects, Coase's "social costs," of urbanization and industrialization. As will be shown in the next section of this chapter, testimony to the human capacity to wear blinders and blame the victim is the fact that even as the oyster-planting firms in the Raritan Bay region were using private rights to drag refuse and polluted silt off the once productive oyster beds, their representatives continued to blame the "pirates" for the scarcity of oysters.

The Tragedy of the Polluted Commons

In Northern New Jersey (the Raritan Bay and the Shrewsbury and Navesink Rivers), oyster planting was in serious trouble by the latter half of the nineteenth century. This was partly because of overharvesting of the natural beds and conflicting claims to property in the tidal lands. But these problems were intensified and ultimately swamped by the fact that this was the region of heaviest shipping, industrialization, and population growth in the nation. The deleterious effects of industrial and municipal pollution on oyster beds and quality were apparent by 1885 (Blackford 1885: 156–63) and even more obvious by 1902 (Stainsby 1902: 23). Among the environmental problems were suffocation of oyster beds by dredge spoils and river-borne silt; predation by oyster drills, mussels, and starfish; the taking of good oystering bottom by eelgrass and other vegetation; oyster destruction and pollution by factory sewerage and coal-oil residues; and bed destruction through careless mooring of ships and channel dredging (Stainsby 1902). The recognition of public health hazards became preeminent around the turn of the century and resulted in the absolute shutdown of all oystering in the region by the 1920s. But the state of the industry was dismal long before that: "[t]he Amboy bay oyster is scarcely heard of today; the luscious Shrewsbury oyster, which fifteen years ago was the delight of epicures, is left to fatten and rot in the bed of the river; that king of bi-valves, the Shark river oyster, is only a memory" (New Jersey Board of Health 1908: 266–67).

The natural seed oyster beds of Newark Bay, Staten Island, and elsewhere were damaged as early as the 1880s by "the pouring of sludge, acid, and oily refuse into the waters" (Blackford 1885). Factory sewerage and the dumping of old bricks and other refuse along the riverbanks of Raritan Bay diminished the public seed beds there, while the old problems of siltation and predation, especially by mussels, continued to damage natural and planted beds (Stainsby 1902: 23, 24). Use of the natural seed beds was not regulated; oyster shells were burned for lime, and as of 1902 there was no attempt to put shells back into Newark Bay or to implement a rough cull law (New Jersey Oyster Commission 1902: 8, testimony from Keyport shippers William E. Wooley and William E. Maurer). Harvesting pressure on the natural seed beds was tremendous, but this was not because of the greed or freedoms of the seedmen. The planting industry created the demands for their product. Most of the oyster seed used in the local planting industry came from Newark Bay and the lower Passaic River, and great quantities of seed from both places were being shipped by the carload to be grown in Sacramento Bay, California, by J. and J. W. Elsworth (New Jersey Oyster Commission 1902: 10; the commission was told that 110 carloads were shipped by rail in 1901). But production in Newark Bay and Staten Island Sound had declined, some thought, from pollutants carried down the Passaic River as well as the state's failure to force people to leave shell on the beds or replant shells. Still, the local seed oysters, usually one or two years old, were in great demand, going for twenty to twenty-five cents a bushel more than Connecticut seed because they were hardier and developed more readily in planted ground than other oysters. Indeed, as one of the few remaining tongers told the 1902 commission, "They have to be hardy and strong to live in the waters of the bay."

These factors contributed to a marked decline in oyster production (United States Commissioner of Fish and Fisheries 1904) and to attrition of the oystering commons. Despite disappearance of natural sets of oysters in the Raritan Bay area after 1916 or 1917, oyster planting limped along a while longer. Another form of pollution threatened it and finally led to its demise: shellfish-borne disease. Local and distant epidemics of typhoid fever and cholera forced the state of New York to close the Staten Island oyster-planting beds in 1915; the city of New York then forbade the sale of oysters taken from the New Jersey side of Raritan Bay, too. The planters enlisted the help of the state Board of Health and the federal Public Health Service in defining the bacterial purity of New Jersey–

side waters of Raritan Bay (cf. New Jersey Board of Health 1916), but in 1921, and especially between 1924 and 1927, when an outbreak of typhoid fever linked to oysters took place in Chicago and other cities, pressure mounted, and all oyster beds in the New York Bays were "condemned."

Raritan Bay Propagation Leases: Too Much Too Late

In 1917 the unthinkable—privatizing the natural shellfish beds—became fact in the Raritan Bay in response to environmental problems. The recently formed New Jersey Board of Shell Fisheries leased "several large plots of ground in Newark Bay and Staten Island Sound for the propagation of seed oysters" to private firms in Raritan Bay (New Jersey Board of Shell Fisheries 1917: 6–8). Among them were the J. and J. W. Elsworth Company, the major firm in Keyport. The lessees were to use dredges and other equipment to remove stone ballast, cinder, ashes, and other debris, especially mud, from former oystering lands in order to "thoroughly clean these old beds and then spread clean shells over them hoping in this way to bring [them] back to a state of productiveness" (New Jersey Board of Shell Fisheries 1917: 7).

The idea of private leaseholds in natural oyster beds for the purpose of spreading shell for cultch in the hope of recreating natural growth was politically acceptable in the Raritan Bay region only because of horrible damage to shellfish habitat. The large planters were willing to bear the costs of this experiment because they were desperate. The natural supply of seed oysters from the area was severely depleted, now believed due to "the flow of trade waste into the streams, sound, and bays" (New Jersey Board of Shell Fisheries 1917: 7).

As soon as the leases were made, baymen protested that the lessees were abusing the intent of the leases by "removing thousands of bushels of the finest seed oysters from the grounds." The Board of Shell Fisheries investigated the matter and affirmed the necessity of the leases because of damage to the natural beds. The experiment was to no avail: as of 1919 there had been no "sets" in the Raritan Bay region since 1916, as in other industrialized regions of New York, Connecticut, and Rhode Island, due to "the dumping of trade waste into our streams" (New Jersey Board of Shell Fisheries 1919: 5). The entire oyster industry of Raritan Bay had been pushed almost to extinction by industrial development and unchecked waste disposal.

It is testimony to human optimism and the habit of blaming the wrong person, especially if a victim is at hand, that as late as 1918 some people were still expressing the old notions that parts of Raritan and Sandy Hook Bays were "the most valuable shell fish producing grounds in our State" and that development of the industry was constrained only by the fact that "the sentiment of that element of the people who want to depend on nature to furnish them a livelihood, and more or less sympathetic public" had led to much of the area finally being classified as a public clam ground (New Jersey Board of Shell Fisheries 1918: 8). The Board of Shell Fisheries recommended opening the public clam ground to leasing for oyster planting.

Meanwhile, the acreage used by the planters actually declined: it was estimated at over two thousand acres in 1895; in 1918, according to a manuscript note by the biologist Thurlow C. Nelson on page 8 of the Rutgers University library copy of the Board of Shell Fisheries report, the residents of Perth Amboy, Keyport, "and the Elsworths" (a large oyster-planting and -shucking firm, always treated as separate in state reports) leased only 904 acres, including the large "propagating grounds" up in Staten Island Sound and Newark Bay. In 1921 there were only 592 acres leased, and the number of lessees had declined from thirty in 1903 to nine in 1921. In that year all oystering was stopped to protect public health. Sentiment about common rights had little to do with this decline.

The proposal to lease "propagating grounds," or once productive oyster beds, for the purpose of laying shell in hopes of catching oyster spat is propounded to this day by biologists and economists. In a leasing or private rights system, the oystermen rather than the state pay the costs of shelling. In turn, the lessees retain rights to the resulting shellfish. The idea is that private owners or lessees will have the incentive to do what the state is so reluctant to do, if they have secure title to the grounds and the oysters.

To those who favored the system for the Raritan Bay, it posed a direct solution to the ancient tragedy of the commons. To those who opposed it, it represented yet another tragedy of the commoners. The fact that leasing natural grounds would diminish the scope of "the wilds"—the local term for public shellfishing areas—was patent and controversial enough to severely limit the range and time period of New Jersey's experiments in propagating grounds. Once again, a combination of forces, mainly the political and piratical opposition of the commoners, tidewater law, and the reluctance of nature to play the game, spelled the demise of a short-lived experiment in managing the shellfisheries through privatization.

Part V Past to Present

Introduction

The last part brings the account closer to the present and to current issues in ecosystem and natural resources management. Chapter 12 describes elements of "comanagement" in the Delaware Bay oyster fisheries, when oystermen, state officials, and university scientists collaborated in the face of ultimately devastating epidemics of oyster disease. The effects of those epidemics also sorely tried the long-standing rules reserving natural oyster beds from private claims. The rules have mostly remained, but crisis precipitated another fundamental change: the right to fish has been privatized. This happened first in the oyster industry and then in the offshore clam fishery, which in 1990 became subject to an even larger step toward privatization of the very right to fish: individual transferable quotas.

Although the public trust doctrine has not been explicitly brought into the courts with regard to privatizing fishing rights, it remains in the background. In chapter 13 I argue that it was kept alive, so to speak, in the shellfisheries not only in the constitutional moments forced by test cases but also in the panoply of regulations that make shellfishing appear most inefficient. And it has moved into other realms, including environmental law and public advocacy, as I show in the context of a review of three interpretations of the public trust doctrine: inalienable public rights; state fee simple ownership; and state responsibility for environmental stewardship and public rights. Since the 1970s, New Jersey's courts have revived Kirkpatrick's version of the public trust doctrine to support public rights of access to the state's beaches. However, the future of the doctrine is clouded by "takings" issues.

In the conclusion I return to the original question of why privatization was so limited. In that framework, I position the study within the multidisciplinary effort known as institutional analysis. In its broader form, including but not restricted to rational choice and rules and regulations, it has great potential for understanding environmental problems and dovetails neatly with what many people mean by political ecology. I also point to the dangers of overreliance on theoretical models and metaphors. Finally, in response to issues brought up in some of the cases reviewed as well as my own ethnographic research,

I consider the policy question of rights versus privileges in fisheries and raise the challenge of finding ways to capture the benefits of a rights-based approach without sacrificing the kinds of equity and other community concerns raised so often in the struggles over oystering lands, the main subject of the book.

Chapter 12 Comanaging and Enclosing the Commons

This chapter brings the account of the Delaware Bay oyster fishery up to date and introduces a fishery for offshore clams. One goal is to show comanagement at work in shellfishing, as well as the ways that oyster diseases affected and were met by participants in this system. Among their responses was "limited entry." The second goal of this chapter is to address this form of enclosing the commons, especially through individual transferable quotas, which commodify access to natural resources very much as privatizing oystering lands does, and to show the problematic nature of rights versus privileges and the disinclination of contemporary courts to address public trust issues.

Comanagement, Science, and Oysters in the Delaware Bay

Government involvement in natural resource management did not really take hold until the end of the nineteenth century and the beginning of the twentieth century in most Euramerican nations. Where it did, local and community-based management was mostly relegated to the "informal" domain. The interests and perspectives of resource users and other members of resource-dependent communities had to work within the structures of bureaucratized management systems. A recent survey of these systems shows that they vary greatly in the extent, degrees, and quality of user participation (Jentoft and McCay 1995; McCay and Jentoft 1996).

Of particular interest is a form of democracy in resource management known as "comanagement," or the sharing of powers of decision making with government agencies (Pinkerton 1989; Jentoft 1989). The oyster fisheries of this account have provided many and diverse cases in point. From the outset, members of the oyster industry have taken the lead in management, focusing on issues such as the need to return shell to the grounds to provide substrate for spat as well as property issues. They sought state support for their efforts where they could, in the courts and in the legislature. Around the turn of this century most of New Jersey's shellfish areas received support. What gradually evolved was a comanagement regime that involved shellfish industry representatives, officials of state agencies, and scientists, all working together at a local level. This collaborative venture began in the late nineteenth century. As is shown below, it crystallized into a formal, working system after World War II and was tested by a series of oyster disease epidemics that nearly destroyed the industry.

Congress created the United States Commission of Fish and Fisheries in 1871 (Goode 1881), and New Jersey, like many states, created a similar body to strengthen government involvement in fisheries matters. Numerous legislative inquiries and commissions deliberated on the problems of shad, oysters, menhaden, trout, and other fish. The regimes that resulted had many comanagement features, where industry, scientists, and state shellfish or "fish and game" agencies shared powers and responsibilities.

One reason for this cooperative effort was that the state itself had few resources and powers; in fisheries, these were primarily devoted to work in stocking freshwater and saltwater areas with cultured shad, trout, oysters, and even salmon. Increasingly, however, the state offered its police powers for monitoring and enforcement and provided bureaus, boards, and other forums for policy making and implementation, always, of course, closely responsive to the legislature, on the one hand, and individual and organized members of the industry, on the other.

The Delaware Bay oyster fishery was essentially self-regulating by the early 1870s (Ingersoll 1881). Authorized by the state legislature, oyster planters imposed closed seasons, tonnage taxes, and rough cull laws upon themselves through their local association, and they paid for watchmen and legal expenses by levying tonnage taxes. Small-scale tongers had their own representatives and license fees, and sections of the bay were set aside to accommodate tongers who continued marketing wild oysters from creeks, rivers, and river mouths. Dredging was prohibited on the "Tonger's Beds" (see map 2) and still is, although many of these have silted over (Ford 1997). Although Hall (1894) reported that the system worked very well, some of the larger oyster planters were unhappy. Their ability to defend their interests was limited and expensive. Accordingly, they petitioned the state to assume the responsibilities of their association.

In 1899 the state took control of managing the leased grounds in Maurice River Cove and all of the natural oyster beds in Delaware Bay. A three-member oyster commission, appointed by the governor from leading members of the industry, carried out much the same regulations as before but had more state resources available to enforce them. This commission was eventually replaced by a Board of Shell Fisheries, and then a bureaucratic state agency. Industry participation continued via regional advisory councils, the powers of which varied with tasks and time.[1]

Debates about privatizing natural beds and using riparian grants to secure them took place within the above context. The decision to maintain the natural oyster beds as the common property of the citizenry did not stop growth of the industry. The Delaware Bay oyster industry boomed. It replaced the Raritan Bay oyster industry as the largest in the state, at one point exceeding the value of the state's wheat crop (Ford 1997). The total leased acreage increased from twelve thousand acres in 1900 to nearly thirty thousand acres by 1914. Harvests in the Delaware Bay (including a smaller industry on the Delaware side) ranged between one and two million bushels from 1880 to 1930. Large schooners, outfitted for dredging natural oysters during the spring "bay season," when the public seed beds were opened for harvest, increased in size and number, their tonnage peaking in 1929, when the dredgers averaged 31 gross tons and numbered 247 vessels (Ford 1997).

Dredging on the natural seed beds was done under sail, by law, but on the leased beds the planters were allowed to use motorized power. The practice of "floating" oysters in fresh water to improve their market value came under scrutiny because of the public health hazards of keeping oysters close to population centers, and shucking houses gradually came into place, adding to the labor needs of the industry, which were largely filled by African Americans moving between the Chesapeake Bay and the Delaware Bay and between oystering and farm work. Self-imposed controls on technology played an important role in the sustainability of the system, and changes in that technology posed new challenges for management, which were met, with some success, in a new system of comanagement that centered on interactions between scientists, industry, and the state.

The role of science was evident at the beginning of this century, when the Rutgers University biologist Julius Nelson began to receive state appropriations for oyster science research. He and his sons, especially Thurlow Nelson, worked closely with the industry to improve scientific understanding and give advice about matters such as when to plant "cultch" for new oyster growth.

Even so, scientists did not play an explicit role in oyster management until after World War II. After the war, servicemen and officers returned with new ideas. In some areas of New Jersey's fisheries, they resulted in cooperatives (McCay 1980), but in the Delaware Bay, they resulted in a resolve to allow the use of fossil fuel–powered engines rather than sails on the dredge boats that worked the natural oyster beds up the bay. The result was disaster: natural oyster abundance reached historic lows (Haskin, personal communication, 1996).

Accordingly, research began in earnest on the factors limiting oyster abundance on the seed beds (Fegley et al. n.d.: 6). At the same time, a Rutgers University biologist, Harold ("Hal") Haskin (with the support of his mentor, Thurlow Nelson), tried to persuade oystermen of the need for "sanctuaries," or closed areas among the oyster beds to reduce the length of the harvest.

Helped by an official from the state who had experience with the local shellfishing industry, the effort led to a then-unusual system of science-based and collaborative fisheries management. Haskin and his associates at the Rutgers Department of Oyster Culture at Bivalve, New Jersey (now the Haskin Shellfish Research Laboratory), provided the science. Research on the behavior, location, and numbers of oyster larvae, spat, yearlings, older oysters, and transplantable seed oysters would provide information for making management decisions. Another tradition was created of collecting the data required and providing them as the basis for management (Fegley et al. n.d.: 6–7). This came to be known as the "seed bed rehabilitation program." It had two components: research and policy. The policy part involved attempts by Haskin to convince the state agency and, more importantly, the oystermen of the need for additional restrictions on seed transplants and the usefulness of scientifically collected data in decision making. This succeeded, in that by the mid-1950s it was accepted that the Rutgers Department of Oyster Culture should provide the information used by the industry shellfish council and the state regulatory agency. The system remains in effect for the Delaware Bay; there and for the Mullica River it is now coordinated with state agency biological expertise.

One of the comanagement features of the new regime was that the industry agreed to return a proportion of the oyster shell it harvested to the natural seed beds at its own expense (Ford 1997). It began doing this in 1946, in early recognition of the dangers of fuel-powered dredging as well as the dismal track record of reliance on state appropriations. It later involved per-bushel and per-gallon fees to cover costs of planting oyster shells, including a percentage given to the state for planting in the seed beds. The program ended in 1979. By then there were worse problems.

Predators like the oyster drill and, beginning in 1957, a protozoan parasite called MSX (now *Haplosporidum nelsoni*), devastated oysters on the leased grounds. MSX spread rapidly, and to the coastal bays as well. The disease settled into an endemic state, with very high levels of mortality, although there was some resistance through natural selection (Haskin and Ford 1979). Growers learned to minimize losses by practices such as shortening the period of transplantation to only one growing season (Ford 1997). Concern that the practice of importing oysters may have brought the disease and fear about spreading it farther resulted in a law against import and export; consequently, the industry relied exclusively on natural seed oysters, which further diminished production.

Although at a much smaller scale than before, the industry did fairly well from 1973 through 1985, aided by nature and the scientific and cooperative management system. A tremendous set on the natural beds in 1972, supplemented by fairly good sets in following years, attracted many small watermen into the business. Fifty to one hundred vessels, mostly former schooners, were used during an intensive four-week "bay season," which was regulated in cooperation with the university laboratory, the industry, and the state's shellfish agency.

The system seemed manageable, and in retrospect, scientists see what was accomplished up to 1985 as significant (Ford 1997). Moreover, they had begun to develop MSX-resistant strains of oysters that could be cultured. There were institutional, technological, and economic adjustments too. Among the long-standing rules of the Delaware Bay oyster fishery were prescriptions against marketing oysters directly from the natural beds, as opposed to the planted grounds, and against marketing them in July and August. In 1975 the shellfish council agreed to allow year-round marketing because of the MSX problem: oysters left for considerable periods on the planting grounds of Maurice River Cove are in greater jeopardy of perishing from the disease due to the higher salinity of those waters compared with waters of the natural beds up the bay.[2] Technology also changed: an automated culling machine was created in 1975, reducing labor requirements from ten to fourteen men per crew to one or two deckhands per crew. The leased area planted declined too: the thirty thousand acres planted in 1914 were reduced to about two thousand acres in the 1970s and 1980s, concentrated at the "up bay" edge of the leased area, where salinity is lower and, therefore, the incidence of MSX is also lower (Ford 1997). (Leases were kept, however, for speculation and to use for crab dredging.) Finally, in 1980 the state and industry agreed to a moratorium on new vessels in the fishery.

The 1972–85 miniboom ended. In 1987 the scientists presented data on low oyster abundance on the natural beds to the Delaware Bay shellfish council, and the council agreed to have no "bay season" that year. No one was allowed to take seed oysters from the natural beds up the bay. With the blessing of the council, the Rutgers scientists tried to identify and breed strains of MSX-resistant oysters and the conditions under which they might reproduce themselves. Working closely with the Maurice River Oyster Culture Foundation (a local consortium of industry, science, and government), they also sought ways to grow cultured, disease-resistant oysters economically in Delaware Bay.

Bay season reopened with large harvests in 1990, but in that year a new parasitic shellfish disease appeared. Dermo (*Perkinsus marinus*) soon spread throughout the region. The seed beds were closed again. The prospects of hatchery production of resistant oysters that would be put in the bay to grow out were dashed.

In the meantime, through the shellfish council, two of the sacred rules of the region's oyster business were challenged. First was the southwest line, or line separating the planting grounds in Maurice River Cove from the natural oyster beds up the bay, based on the principle that all natural oyster beds must be common property of the public. In the late 1970s, the council and state agency agreed to create some leaseholds above the southwest line, hoping that the planted oysters would have a greater chance of survival there. However, because of strong resistance to privatization of the natural beds, the new leasehold area ("E") was situated in parts of the bay with muddy bottom and other conditions unsuitable to oyster survival and growth (Ford, personal communication, July 10, 1996). The ancient principle of reserving natural beds for the commons remained. Of course, with limited entry and the harsher selective pressures of severe decline in the industry, few commoners remained.

The next desperate step was to change a second, more localized, but equally tenacious rule: that no oysters could be taken from the public seed beds for direct marketing. They had to be planted in leased beds and left on the planting grounds at least over a summer before marketing. In 1991 nearly 375,000 bushels of young seed oysters were transplanted, and most of them died from Dermo before harvest. Oyster growers and the shellfish council deliberated on allowing direct marketing. They could not agree until 1995, when the rule was temporarily lifted, allowing some direct sale of the small oysters, rather than forcing them to deal with the parasites and other risks of being shifted down the bay.

In 1997, proposals to "privatize" areas above the southwest line in Delaware Bay for pilot trials by oyster growers appeared in early drafts of a task force on revitalizing the oyster industry, controversial as ever. Nonetheless, the area remains sacred: all but area E is still public. Ironically, the public beds are the only sources of oyster production. Given the epidemiological problems, the higher-salinity waters of the private grounds below the line are more deadly than productive.

Privatizing the Right to Harvest Shellfish

As noted above, in 1980 the shellfish council for Delaware Bay agreed that no new boats could enter the fishery; replacements had to be the exact tonnage of the old vessels; anyone who wanted to enter the fishery had to purchase one of the existing boats. The "moratorium" closely followed a similar measure taken a few years earlier for the offshore surf clam fishery in both New Jersey waters (zero to three miles) and federal waters (three to two hundred miles, under the new international law of the sea).[3] Some of the oystermen and shucking houses participated in both fisheries, as did the shellfish scientists at Bivalve, who carried out surf clam surveys on behalf of the state shellfish agency.

At the time limited entry was widely advocated by economists and others as the only rational way to reduce the problem of overcapacity, following the same logic used to support privatizing oyster beds. Adam Smith's "invisible hand" of the marketplace cannot work without private property. But this argument had little to do with the immediate reasons for limiting entry in either oystering or surf clamming. Disease in oysters and a die-off of surf clams, combined with industry protectionism, were direct causes. The context of limited entry for surf clams was declining surf clam production throughout the region due to heavy harvesting pressure, a clear open-access problem, but more specifically a devastating "anoxic event," or fish kill, in the summer of 1976 off the northern coast of New Jersey. It killed most of the benthic creatures, including surf clams. The inshore waters of New Jersey had become newly attractive to the regional industry as clams elsewhere were scarce, leading New Jersey clammers and the state agency to close the fishery in state waters to new entrants. Soon thereafter the fishery in federal waters was also closed.

Limited entry creates a commodity out of access: the only way an outsider can engage in the fishery is to purchase a license or a boat with a license (depending on how it is designed). In the bay shellfisheries, the social issue had been private versus common rights to particular shellfish beds. Now the issue was private versus common rights to fish at all. For oystering, the question was almost immaterial: MSX and Dermo and the measures taken to protect the remaining seed beds left few opportunities for anyone.

However, with limited entry, as those in the fishery observed, only the larger firms and those with more diversified bases would remain, and so it was. Ironically, the dying oyster industry also has become an ever more concentrated corporate one: with declining production and shorter, sometimes closed bay seasons, smaller oyster planters sold out to larger companies, which continue to control large numbers of boats and leased acreage (one has thirteen vessels; several lease 2,500–3,500 acres) (Ford 1997). As of 1993 the ten shucking/packing houses with over four hundred employees that existed in 1977 were reduced to four, with about seventy-five people, in the town of Bivalve (there were even fewer in 1996). But they process mostly conchs, surf clams, and out-of-state oysters. Only one oyster-shucking house remains.

Limited Entry and the American Way

Debates about limited entry capture many of the social concerns and cultural metaphors and images found in debates about privatizing natural oyster beds, including ambivalence about economic and social goals. This can be seen in a short sample of interviews carried out in 1983 in Bivalve, New Jersey, the center of the Delaware Bay oyster industry, by anthropologist Lawrence Taylor as part of our Sea Grant research project on New Jersey fisheries (Taylor 1983). These conflicts speak to a value of common use rights or open access that is often brought up in discussions about privatizing fishing rights: the merits of open competition, cast as the "American way." Limiting entry can be viewed as "anti-American" and, in some discourse, as "socialist," despite the intention of the economists who advocate it to bring the rationality of capitalist markets to the fisheries.

One oysterman who objected to the new limited entry system and hoped (against hope, it turned out) that the system would be temporary said, "Well, I'm strictly a free enterprise man. Now, I don't know, I think economics sorts the weak from the strong, and maybe it's good and maybe it's not. . . . I would say the whole concept [of limited entry] is anti-everything I believe in, because I think an industry thrives with competition, and what limited entry does, it eliminates competition." An advocate, a well-known spokesman for the industry who called himself "probably the father of limited entry," acknowledged the anti–American way argument but pointed out that

> we've got a natural resource here. It may be a renewable natural resource, but there's a limit to what it can do, and by law we can go up the bay for seed oyster for eight weeks a year—we have done that for twenty some years—so that any time that the fleet is only workin' at 50 percent of its capability it must be twice too big, and if we allow it to happen we have the capability to totally wipe out that natural resource, in just a few years. Like I say, it's not the American way—but it's the way we got to do it. . . . We have to discourage people from going into this industry; we have to let attrition take over and actually reduce it. (Taylor 1983)

Some Bivalve oystermen dwelt on the equity or distributional consequences of limiting entry. Most of the grousing predictably came from smaller-scale oystermen, who owned only one boat and had hoped to increase its size or acquire more boats, as well as from others who saw oystering as something to enter in the future. However, even some of the "big fellows" who stood to benefit from the new system because of the number of vessels they owned showed some ambivalence. This may be because in the small coastal communities of South Jersey, the fishery is still to some extent embedded in the social structure of those communities. Thus, the owner of a large fleet of oyster dredge schooners acknowledged ambivalence, even though with five boats and vertical integration he could not be easily hurt by limited entry:

> I think the Lord put them oysters out there for everybody if anybody got the ambition and wants to go out there and get 'em. But they said, well, the bay's getting run down and you got to put a limit to what boats. Well, I can see part of that. But then my company's got five boats, other companies got six or seven boats. So these people could say, well, if the bay is getting done in, why do you let [himself] have five boats to go up that bay? Why don't you cut him out and only allow him to take two boats up the bay? . . . I mean because you got to have younger people coming into to take a hold of it. (Taylor 1983)

On the other hand, he mused, someone like himself has the bigger investment and should be protected: "[t]he guy with the little boat can tie it up. And of course if it gets bad he can go get a job, and then if it come back he can jump back in it. Well, I can see that point. . . . But when it is good, the guy with the four or five boats and the shucking house, he's still going to get the big end of the stick. Rather than the guy with the little boat." He then shifted back to the other perspective and in his comment about the community revealed a source of his ambivalence: "I know when I first started if they'd had something like [limited entry] I probably would be mad as a hornet because they wouldn't let me in it. And being here and living in this community, and they say, 'Oh no, you're not going to get in it.' I would have felt a little hurt, I think." In this awareness of the forces and morality of a small community, what social scientists might call "embeddedness" comes to the fore (see McCay and Jentoft 1996), and someone who is behaving rationally, as assumed in the tragedy of the commons model, is at least uneasy, knowing that there are other perspectives and other rationalities.

Individual Transferable Quotas

Competing rationalities and perspectives, grounded in the social structure of fisheries and the communities in which they are embedded, have played a strong role in the pace, form, and outcomes of management regimes based on individual transferable quotas, or ITQs, just as they have in contests over property rights in oyster beds or limits on entry into a fishery. They are all special tools of an old and general process: the expansion of market relations of monetary exchange to new areas.

By the late 1970s economists who had argued for limited entry to combat problems of overcapitalization and overexploitation were beginning to advocate the next step toward privatization: ITQs, whereby participants hold individual shares in an allowable harvest of fish or shellfish (e.g., Christy 1973; Moloney and Pearse 1979; see Squires, Kirkley, and Tisdell 1995). In an ITQ system with full transferability, such as the surf clam and ocean quahog management regime that began in 1990, shareholders are free to buy, sell, lease, or trade their shares. Then the market takes over allocation.

ITQs can reduce the overcapitalization and safety hazards of competitive quotas, which encourage investment in ways to get as much as possible before the quota is reached. They are also claimed to foster more responsible stewardship for management of natural resources. Consequently, ITQs are advocated by economists, environmentalists, and others (for overviews, see Neher, Arnason, and Mollett 1989; Young and McCay 1995; McCay 1995b; Anderson 1995). "Stock certificates" were considered for the offshore surf clam fishery as early as 1979 in the regional fishery management system established by the Magnuson Fishery Conservation and Management Act (1976), the same law of Congress that extended the U.S. claim of exclusive economic rights to two hundred miles. However, the Mid-Atlantic Fishery Management Council did not agree on ITQs for the surf clam and ocean quahog fishery for another decade; the new system, the first in U.S. waters, did not come into effect until 1990. The same social conditions that contributed to limits on the spread of privatized oyster-planting grounds in the past delayed the decision (see McCay and Creed 1990). Major structural differences between "little fellows" and "big fellows," particularly between independent owner-operators of clam vessels and vertically integrated firms that own and operate vessels, processing plants, and sometimes marketing, paralleled the structural differences between small-scale tongers and planters and the planters tied with shucking and shipping houses in the oyster business. Such differences translated into very different positions, the small-scale operators voicing concerns about equity and distributional effects of the change in property rights, the larger actors in the business worrying about the effects of the new system on their freedoms to maneuver, and both worrying about freedom and the American way, reminiscent of the debates in the old public trust cases.

In a survey done before a decision was made (McCay and Creed 1990: 214–22), we found that most owners shared an understanding that the larger firms would be the "winners," because they would be allocated the largest share of the quota, given their past advantages in the market. The losers would be the small vessels, small fleets, and independents, always vulnerable in the industry. It was also evident that the widespread resistance to the plan was based on concern about fairness and equitability, and that more than legal standards were at issue.

Fairness and equitability concerns devolved on the decision to use historical performance as the basis for making the initial allocations. We noted that

> [r]easons for dislike of the use of historical landings as the criterion for allocating shares of a quota to individual vessels are various. . . . They are not entirely explicable by the situations or self interests of the individuals who hold them. At times, people who would do comparatively well from . . . "history" have expressed their opposition. It may be that "history" has become a powerful symbol that condenses multiple, sometimes contradictory, meanings. (McCay and Creed 1990: 221)

One of the issues collapsed into "history" was the extent to which ITQs would trigger greater concentration of capital and power. No matter what their position on ITQs, everyone advocated a cautious approach because of uncertainty about the outcome of further concentration (McCay and Creed 1990: 222). The process had long been under way but was checked by the inefficiencies and regulations of the management system of the time, a moratorium combined with very onerous restrictions on the time spent fishing.

Agreement took a decade, partly because of the major social issues involved. The story has been eloquently told by David Keifer, a member of the Mid-Atlantic Fishery Management Council staff at the time. One of the problems was that the key issue of skewed distribution could not really be addressed in public. Summing up the problems noted above (the fact that the distribution of capital, wealth, and power in the industry was highly skewed, although changing over time, and that many people, particularly the "independents," were afraid that they would be unfairly short-changed in the allocation), Keifer put the situation this way:

> The Magnuson Act stipulates that no allocation system may allow individuals to accumulate excessive shares of a fishery. However, it is silent on the points of what is excessive and what to do if excessive shares exist before you do the allocation system. Without getting into the sacred field of NMFS [National Marine Fisheries Service] confidential data, one vertically integrated operation had a fleet approximating the navies of some small nations while most people had one boat. Because of the confidential data rules, the scope of "excessive" could never be debated publicly, a major obstacle in a process that can only work with open public debate. (Keifer n.d.: 7–8)

For other reasons, including the skewed representation of owners in the advisory process set up by the council, there was also little public discussion of the broader social implications of ITQs, including the loss of jobs for captain, crew, and dockside workers that would accompany the expected decline in the number of boats used as a result of ITQs (McCay, Gatewood, and Creed 1990). The decline occurred as expected: the fleet was slashed to about one quarter of its original size, and the number of crew was reduced to about one third (McCay and Creed 1994; Menzo 1996).

Creed and I surveyed a random sample of twenty-four quota holders a year after the system had begun, in the fall of 1991, and found a variety of cautious strategies and expected and unexpected effects (McCay and Creed 1994: 44ff.). Two strikingly different but familiar perspectives on the ITQ system emerged from the interviews. Some, like the oystermen interviewed by Taylor in 1983, interpreted the American way as free and open competition: even within quotas and time restrictions, vessel operators were free to catch as many surf clams as they could. They saw ITQs as interfering with that as well as needlessly putting many people out of work. Others accepted the economists' view of the way things should be. ITQs would create a welcome opportunity to run their businesses more efficiently, to expand them, and to make more money. By the end of the first year, owners had come to appreciate the meaning of the new property they had been given. As one owner said, explaining why he had not sold his ITQ allocation even though he had stopped clamming (he was leasing it to someone else): "[y]ou never sell what brings income. I'm going to hang in there because this ITQ is forever." ITQs were seen as real property, with the potential of generating income and carrying expectations of long-term security (McCay and Creed 1994: 44–45), even though they are officially described as revocable privileges, not property rights.

ITQs and Comanagement

The surf clam ITQ decision-making process had the surface attributes of comanagement, in that industry advisory committees and other groups were given considerable autonomy and responsibility for coming up with alternative measures and for gaining consensus for them (McCay et al. 1995). However, as Creed (1991) has shown, there was little opportunity for open and informed deliberation on critical matters, and several meetings where such might have occurred were manipulated by various interested persons to remain less than the "ideal speech situation" posited by the political philosopher Jürgen Habermas (1984). Truly participatory and effective (i.e., legitimate) management, particularly for complex and uncertain ecological systems so characteristic of the fisheries, requires situations where people can openly discuss matters and try to understand and persuade each other (Dryzek 1987, 1990; McCay and Jentoft 1996). However, during council meetings on ITQs that we observed, such deliberations typically devolved into jockeying for position after each owner at the meeting was provided with a computer printout of his or her vessel's probable allocation under a particular alternative. There were other ways that open deliberation and comanagement were undercut that are beyond the scope of this chapter. Moreover, critical decisions, including the very notion of using ITQs rather than nontransferable shares granted to individual vessels, which had been the focus of discussion from 1980 to 1987, were evidently made outside of the formal comanagement structure, albeit ratified by the council.

Property Rights or Privileges

Earlier I noted that quota owners in the privatized surf clam and ocean quahog fishery have begun to appreciate the values, virtuous and otherwise, of holding real property in a fishery. Whether ITQs are "property" is as contestable now as was the notion given shape by a federal district court in 1825 that the citizens of the state hold exclusive, albeit common, property rights in fishing (chapter 4). The U.S. government (like the governments of Canada and Iceland) insists that these are not property rights but revocable privileges, and the administrative regulations were written accordingly, making it impossible, for example, to use ITQs as collateral for loans. However, owners and bankers have worked around the system in a variety of ways, including having banks "own" the ITQs in exchange for financing their acquisition. Moreover, divorce courts and the Internal Revenue Service see ITQs as the kind of property that can be divided or from which taxes can be extracted, and they therefore have at least the several fishery status of the old shad fisheries of the Delaware River (chapter 9).

ITQs and Public Trust. The move to privatize fisheries in the United States has been extremely slow and halting in large part because of concern and conflict over the distributional questions, as shown in the surf clam case. Standing in the wings is the public trust issue of whether the government should be allowed to hand public trust property rights over to private citizens, particularly in a manner that looks like a gift to present participants, at the expense of future participants, who must buy in. Legal challenges to the system have focused on procedural questions as well as the requirements of the managing legislative act and agency, with predictable emphasis on antitrust problems (Milliken 1994). But neither in this situation nor in the situation of the evolving ITQ systems of the North Pacific fisheries off Alaska have the rights of commoners under the public trust doctrine been an important legal issue (Macinko 1993).[4]

Nonetheless, some of the sentiments that lie behind the public trust doctrine, particularly the notions of equity and fairness in protecting common use rights, have been very important to the politics of privatization in the fisheries and have made minor appearances in court. When ITQs were promulgated for the surf clam and ocean quahog fisheries, a group of New Jersey fishermen and dealers filed a lawsuit against the secretary of commerce (then Robert A. Mosbacher) (*Pearson v. Mosbacher* 1991). They claimed that the agencies had acted improperly, "in excess of statutory authority," in "privatizing" the fisheries, which were defined as "national" fisheries in ways that would harm the plaintiffs. The plaintiffs cast themselves as "small, independent fishermen with only a few vessels." They claimed that they would be hurt in competition with large fleet owners and eventually forced to sell out, resulting in consolidation of ownership with monopoly effects. One of the plaintiffs was a clam-processing firm that claimed the risk of being forced to buy clams at a much higher price as ownership of vessels consolidated. Another suit, *Sea Watch Int'l v. Mosbacher* (1991), was filed by a large clam buyer, small clam-processing firms, and an assortment of relatively small, independent fishers, each of which was able to demonstrate a drastic decline in allowable harvest under the new system. Although neither case referred to public trust directly, the idea appears in the concern about privatizing national fisheries as well as the general concern about equity. They were tried as civil cases, in reference to statutory law (the Magnuson Act of 1976). All that the courts took seriously was whether the agencies acted in accordance with that law and did not act arbitrarily and capriciously. The decisions were in favor of the agencies (the Department of Commerce and the Mid-Atlantic Fishery Management Council) (see Milliken 1994).

A recent case heard by the United States Court of Appeals for the Ninth Circuit in Alaska, *Alliance against IFQs v. Brown* (1996), followed other courts in upholding the agencies' actions, this time for the new ITQ system for sablefish and Pacific halibut in federal waters of the North Pacific, where the scope, scale, and stakes are much larger. Some of the plaintiffs were people who had received little or no allocation of individual fishery quota (IFQ) shares because they had not been fishing during the period from 1988 to 1990, which was established as the cutoff for eligibility. At issue was the fact that administrative delays resulted in the IFQ allocation itself being made five years later. People who entered the fishery in the interim, between 1991 and 1994, received no IFQ, and to continue they were forced to purchase or lease an IFQ from others. In addition, other plaintiffs had fished consistently during that period but did not own or lease the boats on which they fished.

The court decided that the Department of Commerce and other agencies involved had not been "arbitrary and capricious" in using the 1988–90 period, having done so to curtail speculative investment in an already overcapitalized fishery, albeit in a way that stretched the bounds of reasonableness. It also backed the agencies for having allocated the IFQ solely to vessel owners and their lessees, on similar grounds, recognizing the need to balance many objectives, including the importance of controlling investment in boats. Nonetheless, the decision shows recurrent uneasiness at being bound by statutory law and thus not able to address what the court saw as valid concerns of the plaintiffs: "[t]he plan adopted will undoubtedly have an adverse impact on the lives of many fishermen who have done nothing wrong" (*Alliance against IFQs v. Brown* 1996: 22). The court concluded by saying, "This is a troubling case. Perfectly innocent people going about their legitimate business in a productive industry have suffered great economic harm because the federal regulatory scheme changed" (*Alliance against IFQs v. Brown* 1996: 29). Its unease echoes earlier and other worries about the legitimacy of alienating public trust lands and waters.

Chapter 13 Luddites, Sunbathers, and the Public Trust

The public trust doctrine in tidewater property law seemed to serve two masters, including the powerless, at a time when great fortunes and properties were being accumulated during the rise of industrial capitalism with the help of legal institutions that could be bent and molded to suit the process. Although far less well known, it would seem to rank with the 1787 Northwest Ordinance, the 1862 Homestead and Morrill Acts, and the 1944 GI Bill (Hyman 1986) as part of a linked public policy to give special chances to otherwise diffuse and to some extent powerless groups of citizens. But it is telling that a synonym for the public trust doctrine is "state ownership." As I have shown, the meaning of this ownership was altered to support industrial growth and entrepreneurship and to alienate public trust. Nineteenth-century courts and legislatures embraced and reshaped the public trust doctrine as part of the general trend to remove barriers to commerce and communication, which were essential to the development of industrial capitalism (see Rose 1986; Friedman 1973, 1985; Horwitz 1971).

The other reading of public trust remained alive and well in the regulatory regimes of the region's shellfisheries, particularly in the Luddite-like arrangements and rules that protected small-scale harvesters from competition and through the oyster wars. Arguably, the "trying the right" actions of the shellfishers kept it "on the books," so to speak, for use in other domains. After exploring social and conservation bases for regulated inefficiencies in shellfish management, I discuss the resurrection of the public trust doctrine in environmental law in general and in New Jersey beach access cases in particular.

Regulated Inefficiency and Social Relations

In the twentieth century, oyster wars continued, but the weighty court cases about common rights and the public trust began to veer toward issues of transportation, wetlands development, and public access to the state's beaches. From the perspective of the shellfishers, the right was adequately tried and encoded in state law and practice by the early decades of this century. Broad and mutually agreed upon rules of the game were written into the laws and administrative rules of the state's fish and shellfish agencies, which set seasons and conservation laws and dealt with allocation issues by clearly demarcating areas that could and could not be leased. In addition, once shellfish management became a clearly defined responsibility of the state, the government set up commissions, boards, and councils made up of shellfishermen, dealers, and influential citizens who helped arbitrate the kinds of disputes that had gone to court before. Shellfishermen had other arenas for trying to strike acceptable balances between public and private claims on the commons.

The new institutions have also maintained the culture of the commons in their policies. Thus, the Delaware Bay shellfish council maintains a sacrosanct distinction between the public beds up the bay and the planting grounds in Maurice River Cove, even in the face of destructive epidemics of oyster disease. The Atlantic coast shellfish council, which covers the rest of the state and is more concerned with clams and crabs than oysters, also maintains such a distinction. In its decisions about applications for shellfish leases from the state, it relies on state biologists' surveys to determine whether or not an area is "productive" ("natural" in the old terminology). Its industry members are also disinclined to grant leases to people who have not shown some sign of being "true fishermen," acting upon the old equity principle that emphasized historical dependency.

Inshore shellfisheries in North America are notorious for what economists, and some biologists, see as inefficient, if not foolish, regulations. Most obvious is the proliferation of regulations, at the levels of municipalities, counties, and states, forbidding the use of certain tools, such as motor-powered dredges, or forbidding or sharply restricting private property claims in shellfish beds. New Jersey provides one example among many. Except in the oystering regions of the Delaware Bay (and, until the 1960s, in the deep-water clamming areas of Raritan Bay), dredges cannot be used for clamming or oystering, and motor-powered dredges can be used only in the Delaware Bay. What this means is that most bay shellfishermen can use only rakes, tongs, and their toes in their pursuit of clams and oysters.

The social meaning and community implications of the regulations are fairly clear. They are about the distribution of access to shellfish resources, supporting the populist and utilitarian view that as many people as possible should be able to benefit (McHugh 1972; Santopietro and Shabman 1992). Here is how Bill Jenks, a retired bayman and close informant and collaborator, put it: "[t]his clamming, hand clamming, is the thing for the people of the earth. I don't believe it's meant to be mechanized. . . . The resource is finite; we only have so many tens of thousands of acres, it's not like the ocean" (McCay and Jenks 1997: 153).

Over the past two hundred years these regulations were articulated—and challenged and altered—in the context of attempts by local entrepreneurs as well as outsider firms to "develop" the industry along more industrial lines, where efficiency of production, in the short term, is what counts the most. As we have seen, hovering around and sometimes entering these arguments is the common law idea of public trust, the idea that there is something very special about property rights in navigable rivers and tidewaters. In some readings this is little more than a statement that public rights of fishing, navigation, and maybe recreational bathing cannot be curtailed without some justification that doing so is in the public interest. But in other readings one can find the notion that the poor are particularly deserving of protection from privatization of public trust waters, or that the public trust rights are absolutely inalienable. The life-style of the shellfishermen is founded upon those rights.

Baymen today usually express their opinion about these matters in a way that makes no distinction between conservation and social goals. For example, Jenks spoke to the issue of power dredging in New Jersey's bays this way: "I feel very strongly about it. . . . It's a conservation measure. Our bays are limited in size, and if power was ever used, only the big outfits would survive, and then not for long." In competition for a limited resource, only the "big outfits," the ones able to use advanced technology or to make it through a competitive scramble, will survive; the smaller operations will disappear. That is the chain store versus mom-and-pop grocery store problem or the industrial factory versus artisan problem, and no small one at that. But the argument goes farther, claiming that bigness is not better for shellfish conservation. Jenks added, "It would wipe out the resource" (McCay and Jenks 1997: 153).

Neither argument has been thoroughly addressed in research or policy for U.S. shellfisheries, even though the issue is central to most shellfish policy. It may be that the conservation part of the argument is really a front for the social distribution part, as it has been very difficult for people to raise social questions of this sort at least since the onset of the Industrial Revolution in the early nineteenth century. For example, in debates in New Jersey about whether one should be able to use a powered dredge on one's own lease (to take up clams that have been planted in a hatchery or "grow-out" aquaculture operation or perhaps from a relay from polluted waters), it is difficult to make a conservation argument against the practice. One concern expressed is that it may be a way for leaseholders to illegally use a dredge on natural rather than planted clams if the former are in the leasehold. But that is really a distribution issue: the leaseholder is not supposed to have exclusive rights to natural clams (or oysters). For broader conservation issues, it is possible to argue that those natural shellfish should stay on the lease or be taken up more slowly, because they provide a "sanctuary" that helps replenish the waters of the larger bay. But that seems forced. The only direct biological conservation argument concerns the effects of dredging on the bottom, another contentious matter.

More likely, the concerns behind the argument are grounded in fears about changes in competitive position (i.e., being able to take up large quantities and hurt local and regional markets in the short term) as well as the stubborn insistence that it is better to have more employed than fewer. The act of taking up clams on leased grounds has social meaning. If the leaseholder's practice is, as it often is or was, to pay people to take up planted clams, then forbidding the use of powered dredges is, as Bill Jenks concluded in our conversation, "a way to keep the money local. If the dealer had a rig to take them up, he would do it himself and these guys would not make any money" (McCay and Jenks 1997: 154).

Today in the bay shellfisheries of New Jersey, privatization is an important fact. The comanaging shellfish councils routinely consider applications for leaseholds from the state or for transfers of existing leases. In the Delaware Bay, even in the near absence of viable oystering, property in leaseholds in the traditional oyster-planting grounds is actively maintained, traded, and accumulated. In the Atlantic coast area old "barren" oyster leaseholds are still held, inherited, traded, bought, and sold, but most are used for private clamming or, increasingly, the growing out of clams raised in private hatcheries. The councils also allow the creation of new leases, but by the old rules: no larger than two acres; granted only to individuals, not corporations; and only in submerged lands that are neither productive nor potentially productive of shellfish naturally. The 1808 ruling that shellfish found where shellfish naturally grow are the common property of everyone remains intact.

Enough has been written to suggest the sentiments and situations behind the shellfish management rules. Two points are worth raising, however, to add to their defense against those who see such rules as irrational if not irresponsible. The first is that problems in oyster and clam productivity may not in fact be solved by privatization. Privatization is advocated as the best way to manage oystering because the private owner has pecuniary incentives to engage in wise and conservationist practices as well as smart marketing. But privatization can do little to solve the problem of predation (MacKenzie 1977) and rarely if at all can address the problem of shellfish disease. In the Delaware Bay today, all that is left are oysters on the public beds up the bay. The second point is that social relationships of production are critical to people dependent on that production.

The rules support certain ways of life or social relationships to production that are seen as depending on equal rights of access and restrictions on competition from firms with large amounts of capital (see Townsend 1985; Santopietro and Shabman 1992). The Luddite-like rules of the fisheries and the public trust doctrine thus give constitutional support to the fundamental conditions of the bayman and waterman way of life, including open access to the natural resources of the sea. Thereby they help create the imperfections that have made the shellfisheries so anomalous in a capitalist economy, as discussed in chapter 1.

Readings of the Public Trust Doctrine

In 1972 the chief justice of the New Jersey Supreme Court dusted off *Arnold v. Mundy* and underscored how modern the public trust doctrine is compared with other common law remedies for public access problems, namely, prescription and custom (cf. Havey 1994). He emphasized its broad and flexible nature, open to changing interpretation; it is not "fixed or static" but can "be molded and extended to meet changing conditions and needs of the public it was created to benefit" (*Neptune City v. Avon-by-the-Sea* 1972: 306). As we have seen, the doctrine indeed has had different and changing interpretations. One of its readings in America emphasizes common use rights and distributional equity. A second emphasizes the proprietary rights of the state. The third, evident in recent cases, focuses on the state's role as steward of ecologically valuable resources. I briefly summarize the first two and then discuss the third in New Jersey beach access cases.

Common Use Rights and Equity

Although the courts based their rulings on Roman law, natural law, the Bible, and a few cases of English common law, the public trust doctrine reflected as much as anything the tradition of the agrarian commons in medieval Europe and England and the understanding that some classes of people and rural economies in general depended on the common use of wild places and things (see Sax 1980: 189–92; Thompson 1991). The linkage of this dependence to common use rights, an instrument of distributional equity (Sax 1970; Macinko 1993), is central to what I loosely call the culture of the commons.

Accordingly, equity principles are often invoked in conflicts about limiting access to the commons and privatizing erstwhile common resources, including the oyster-planting disputes and the ITQ systems. Rhetoric about the needs of the poor, dramatized by mention of the evils of enclosure and Game Laws in England or images of noble Saxon barons at Runnymede defending the rights of the common man, was often used by lawyers and judges to construct powerful narratives about equity and common use rights. But there is more, as Kirkpatrick pointed out in his *Arnold v. Mundy* decision: the history of England after the Magna Carta was a history of gradual encroachment on common rights. A "free people," he said, would never stand for that.

The emphasis on equity, freedom, and common use rights associated with the public trust doctrine is linked to a particular view of nationhood (Macinko 1993), one that is echoed in current debates about fisheries policy. The question, as shown in chapter 4, was recognized by the courts as having national significance. Is the settlement and social evolution of New Jersey (and, by extension, the nation) to be construed as based on speculative trading in landed (and tidal) property, or is it defined instead by the features of civilization, which included protection for common use rights in fisheries, as part of the compact of the Magna Carta? The question is familiar today. Is our nation to rest entirely on the workings of markets and the behavior of business firms, or is it defined as well by other values, including the right of everyone to a chance to make a living?

State Proprietorship

Echoing the New Jersey Supreme Court's decision in *Arnold v. Mundy* in 1842, Chief Justice Roger Taney of the United States Supreme Court stated the public trust doctrine: "when the Revolution took place, the people of each state became themselves sovereign; and in that character hold the absolute right to all their navigable waters and the soils under them for their own common use" (*Martin et al. v. Waddell's Lessee* 1842: 262–63). However, he left ambiguous what that ownership meant. The ruling could mean that the states serve as trustee for the sovereign people, safeguarding common uses of the people; but it could also mean that as representatives of the people, state legislatures could dispense with the property as they saw fit.

By the 1860s, the second reading became very evident. State legislatures apparently felt free to dispose of the public trust tidelands and submerged lands, often through special agencies like New Jersey's riparian commission, which issued private grants to individuals and corporations, typically for the purpose of filling in wetlands and building docks and wharves to benefit industrial development, transportation, and commerce. Common rights to fishing and navigation did not go away, but attempts to protect them, on the water and in the courts, merely nibbled at the edges and helped clarify the methods of privatization.

In New Jersey and elsewhere, it was tacitly assumed that legislatures and state agencies acted on behalf of the public, but the public had little say and no legal standing in what went on (Jaffee 1971). Yet, as highlighted in this book, the shellfisheries were a major exception. People worked separately and together to protect common use rights to oysters and clams as well as to create and defend private rights. The oyster wars of the end of the nineteenth century and beginning of the twentieth century helped restore the trusteeship notion of state ownership, at least for the shellfish beds, and by so doing helped keep alive the equity reading of public trust.

Environmental Stewardship and Public Access

Part of the modern environmental movement, the third incarnation of the public trust doctrine began to appear in the 1960s and took shape and some force in the 1970s and 1980s (Coastal States Organization 1990). From the inception of an earlier American environmental movement during the 1880s, courts and legislatures occasionally used the general language of public trust when talking about the meaning of state and federal government ownership (Wilkinson 1980: 282). For the federal government, in particular, it meant that the government's extensive lands were not just to be disposed of but that the government had an obligation to protect and manage some of them for future generations (Wilkinson 1980; see also Dana and Fairfax 1980). Beginning in the 1970s, the older, stricter sense of the public trust doctrine, still associated with tides and navigability, was revived and reshaped to be useful in a newly vigorous environmental law (Sax 1970; Anonymous 1970). Navigable fresh waters were recognized as part of its scope, bringing the doctrine squarely into the arena of water rights and water pollution (Johnson 1989; Johnson et al. 1992). In the meantime, tidelands and submerged beds gained new social respect as valuable marine, lake, and wetland ecosystems and as coastal habitats and scenery. The notion of a *public* trust also resonated with the rise of public claims to be involved in decision making and to have legal standing in courts.

This third incarnation of public trust has expanded its scope considerably. One recent listing of 192 cases from the late 1960s to 1991 in which the public trust doctrine has been considered includes not only traditional matters such as tidelands, navigation, and access via adjacent lands to navigable waters but also subsistence fisheries, tidelands, artifacts and archaeological sites, environmental and aesthetic considerations, aquaculture, and dredge and fill (Reis 1991: 27). Charles Wilkinson notes that there are fifty-one public trust doctrines in the United States, because each state has one and the federal government has its

Illinois Central–based doctrine (Wilkinson 1980: 425).[1] However, the importance and role of this doctrine vary greatly among the states. In some states, such as New York (Government Law Center 1991, 1992, 1993, 1994, 1995) and California (Wilkinson 1980), the public trust doctrine has emerged as a major source of state power for environmental protection. Although the doctrine has a long and important history in New Jersey, as I show in this book, the basis of state power over environmental matters in New Jersey has changed. In 1970, when environmentalism led to the creation of the Department of Environmental Protection, a decision was made to attempt to pass legislation specific to the task of protecting the state's vulnerable waters and coastlines rather than to rely on common law principles such as public trust (W. Goldfarb, personal communication, February 1996).

The issue of beach access is an important exception in New Jersey. The state supreme court revived the stronger sense of public trust enunciated in *Arnold v. Mundy* in several beach access cases, including the 1972 ruling of *Neptune City v. Avon-by-the-Sea* (Jaffee 1974) and the 1987 ruling of *Matthews v. Bay Head Improvement Association, Inc.* Wrapped up in a broader attempt on the part of the governing administrations to increase the power of the state executive in relation to the municipalities in a state where home rule is very important, these cases challenged the powers of local municipalities to decide who should have what kind of access to the beaches they controlled and under what conditions. The specific issue was the right of people who do not own property in shore municipalities to enjoy the beaches. In the *Neptune* case, the town of Avon had doubled its nonresident beach fees, prompting representatives of neighboring Neptune to file suit. A lower court denied the public trust argument of Neptune—their common law right of access to navigable waters—by taking the second reading of the public trust doctrine, the state ownership view that grants major powers to the legislature, including those that might abrogate public rights. Once the legislature granted the municipalities the right to charge beach fees, any public right was thereby restricted. The state supreme court heard the case quickly, recognizing the importance of the issue to a burgeoning Jersey shore population, and it came out in favor of Neptune. It ignored several approaches available to it, choosing instead the Kirkpatrick reading of the public trust doctrine, as enhanced by the *Illinois Central* case.

The court was strongly influenced by Joseph Sax, who proposed a strengthened environmental law in which the public trust doctrine would be applied to situations "in which a diffuse public interest needed protection against tightly organized groups with clear and immediate goals" (1970: 556). New Jersey's court was the first to extend public trust to recreational uses: "[w]e have no difficulty in finding that, in this latter half of the twentieth century, the public rights in tidal lands are not limited to the ancient prerogatives of navigation and fishing, but extend as well to recreational uses, including bathing, swimming and other shore activities" (*Neptune v. Avon-by-the-Sea* 1972: 309).

It was clear that the public had rights to the "wet sand" area, between high and low tides, through the public trust doctrine. But how to get there? The court decided that it was up to the municipalities to make this happen: "where the upland sand area is owned by a municipality—a political subdivision and creature of the state—and dedicated to public beach purposes, a modern court must take the view that the Public Trust doctrine dictates that the beach and the ocean waters must be open to all on equal terms and without preference and that any contrary state or municipal action is impermissible" (*Neptune v. Avon-by-the-Sea* 1972: 309). Subsequently, cases were heard that challenged differential access to changing lockers, toilets, parking, and clubs as well as the practice of making lower beach access fees available only to early purchasers (thereby, the state's public advocate argued, discriminating against members of the general public) (e.g., *Lusardi v. Curtis Point Property Owners Ass'n* 1981).[2]

Could the public trust doctrine be applied to privately owned beach property? Litigation on this question began in 1974. Bay Head is an affluent residential community, developed in the 1890s, where all of the beach (about 1.25 miles long) is privately owned, and some of the private property extends a thousand feet into the Atlantic Ocean through riparian grants. The Bay Head Improvement Association (BHIA) was established in 1910 to manage beaches for the property owners, and over the years it acquired some dry sand beaches and leased others. This example of local-level commons management was quite exclusionary: only members of BHIA were allowed on the beaches, and there were no facilities for parking, changing, and so on, for outsiders. However, the practice was to allow residents of neighboring boroughs to obtain beach badges; in 1974, the BHIA decided to stop this, and the neighboring borough of Point Pleasant objected, through Ms. Virginia Matthews, who alleged that she had been denied a beach badge after moving from Bay Head across the street into Point Pleasant. The New Jersey Supreme Court, in *Matthews v. Bay Head Improvement Association, Inc.* (1987), decided that the public right of access to the wet sand area, via the dry sand area, applies not only to property owned by municipalities but also to such "quasi-public" bodies as the BHIA.[3] Moreover, membership in the BHIA should be open to the public at large, and the fees may not discriminate between residents and nonresidents. The opinion was written by Judge Sidney Schreiber, who reviewed the background for the "ancient principle" of public trust: the sovereign owns all land covered by tidal waters but does so for the common use of all the people. He also reviewed the basis for expanding the public trust to bathing, swimming, and other shore activities and hence the need to provide public access to dry sand areas.

After implying that the public should have special rights to beaches because they are unique and irreplaceable resources of high demand, Schreiber turned to a dissent in an English case, *Blundell v. Catterall* (1821). The dissenting judge in that case dwelt on the ancient idea that exclusive property was justified only where private ownership led to improvement of the property, which was not the case for a sandy beach:

> It is useful only as a boundary and an approach to the sea; and therefore, ever has been, and ever should continue common to all who have occasion to resort to the sea. . . . The principle of exclusive appropriation must not be carried beyond things capable of improvement by the industry of man. If it be extended so far as to touch the right of walking over these barren sands, it will take from the people what is essential to their welfare, whilst it will give to individuals only the hateful privilege of vexing their neighbours. (*Blundell v. Catterall* 1821: 283–84, 287, quoted in *Matthews v. Bay Head Improvement Association, Inc.* 1987 [syllabus, 1984: 23–24])

Schreiber took this to mean that there must be some way to satisfy the public's need for access without overly damaging private interests.

Challenges to the Public Trust

The recent revival of the public trust doctrine in New Jersey courts was not simply part of the new environmentalism of the 1970s. There were more particular circumstances as well. From 1973 on, the court that decided the New Jersey beach access cases was particularly liberal and activist, first under Richard J. Hughes, a former governor, and then under Robert Wilentz, who retired in 1996. It took on issues such as school funding and the distribution of low-income housing as well as public trust rights to enjoy the Jersey shore. This was partly at the behest of William Brennan of the United States Supreme Court, who invited the states to "step into the breach" of a newly conservative federal court (Jenkins 1991; cf. Friedelbaum 1979).

The public trust doctrine is on the verge of being recast as archaic; the activism of state and federal courts may be moving in a new direction due to the rise of neoconservative politics and grassroots movements. A series of court cases decided by conservative judges generally upholds the notion that government restrictions on private property owners, for public trust or other reasons, may be considered "takings" and thus require compensation (Belsky 1992; see in particular the case of *Lucas v. South Carolina Coastal Council* 1992).[4] The issue rapidly spread to local and national political arenas, linked to deeply rooted sentiments about the rights of landowners and other citizens as against the powers of government. This is evident in the recent development of the wise use and property rights movements (Echevarria and Eby 1995) and in delays in reauthorizing major environmental legislation on the part of the 103rd and 104th Congresses of 1994 to 1996. The public trust doctrine has been a particular target in these antiregulatory efforts.

The idea that those dependent on common resources have particular use rights has also weakened. The common right of fishing was once imbued with the notion that fishing, like navigation, was an economic pursuit and thus worthy of protection even with the rise of industrial capitalism. With the rise of recreational and environmental interests, this has changed. In the 1980s politically active sports fishers and their lobbyists began to argue that since all fish within U.S. waters are a public resource, no one should have the privilege of profiting from fish. It became a rallying cry for groups trying to outlaw commercial fishing through state legislatures and public referendums. The ability of someone to fish for a living is now seen at law as a privilege rather than a right. In other arenas of conflict over rights to scarce marine resources, it is increasingly seen as an unacceptable privilege.

Chapter 14 Conclusion

A reigning idea in human ecology and natural resource management is that the lack of well-defined exclusive property rights in resources causes people to overexploit these resources. Formalized in the 1950s by economists who focused on fisheries, it also found expression in Olson's analysis (1965) of the social dilemma whereby a group of people with the same interests will not necessarily act collectively to realize those interests because of the incentive each has to "free ride" (Olson 1965) the efforts of the others. The idea was popularized as the tragedy of the commons in 1968 by Hardin, who extended it to the problem of overpopulation.

One consequence of the popularity of this body of thinking and the assumptions behind and generalizations derived from it is that numerous situations of resource abuse are analyzed almost entirely in terms of "common property" or "open access," justifying policies that restrict and privatize access to natural resources. This may be so even when property rights are not the issue at all (Emmerson 1980; Franke and Chasin 1980), where the social dilemma and free riding are not demonstrably at play, or where the property rights that make a difference are not those being analyzed (McCay and Acheson 1987b). As pointed out in chapter 12, the "pirates" of Raritan Bay remained the villains of the saga of declining oysters despite accumulating evidence of habitat destruction and pollution. The property rights at issue were not so much the fishing rights of clammers or the leased ground rights of planters but the freedom of municipalities and industries to treat what they did to the environment as cost-free "externalities."

Theoretical models can be misleading if not harmful (McCay and Vayda 1992). The blinders created by the tragedy of the commons way of understanding fisheries problems are astounding. In the history I have sketched, the issue was less open access to the shellfisheries than it was mismanagement by local and state governments—the tragedy of a mismanaged commons (Marchak 1988–89)—as they responded to the clashes of very different interests and classes and the challenges of complex and generally unpredictable ecological circumstances.

The testimony of the seeders in chapter 12 shows the value of a more nuanced and contextualized view of what tragedies of the commons can be about than is usual in a literature dominated by institutional economics and public choice. For the Newark and Raritan Bay oyster tongers, a certain social relationship to production meant an important, and understandable, stake in maintaining relatively unimpeded access to depleted natural beds of oysters. The tragedy of *that* commons (it is important to be specific) was that the seedmen were forced to work year-round and keep the beds virtually depleted in order to maintain the value of their labor.

This has been an institutional analysis. Economists tend to cast institutions, including property rights, as background conditions or as outcomes of individual choice. In contrast, the anthropological approach I have taken, which can be found under many labels ranging from "social constructionism" to "political ecology" and, yes, "cultural ecology," views institutions in a more dynamic, contingent, and problematized light. It is a more actor-based, social, and contextual take on how institutions are created, challenged, maintained, and changed. Focusing on issues in institutional analyses of the commons, in this conclusion I return to the question of why the oyster fisheries are not all privatized. This concluding chapter also raises the question of the role of rights versus privileges in fisheries management and ends with a summary discussion of the cultural ecology of the public trust.

The Problem, Revisited

Oyster planting galvanized most of the conflicts I depict. Property issues were controversial in part because oystering is on the border between fishing and farming. The key solution to the problem of depletion was seen to lie in "scientific cultivation," and this in turn required the protections and incentives of private property (Brooks 1891). Both technology and will were inadequate to the task.

The farming nature of oyster planting was highlighted by Julius Nelson in 1892 in the following passage written to obtain support from the farming community for oyster research through the New Jersey Agricultural Experiment Station:

> It will broaden a farmer's sympathies to learn that off on the coast there are men who call themselves "oyster-farmers"; who "cultivate" oysters on "farms," who "sow" oyster "seed," and "plant" and "transplant" oyster "plants"; who let their "ground" lie "fallow" to "rest" now and then, because it has raised so many "crops" as to be exhausted; who have to "survey" their "land" and find the "corners" and "fence" it, though it be under the water; who hold such and so many "acres"; who, after having "harvested" a "crop," have to "drag" the "field" to "clean" it prepara-

> tory to receiving the new "seed," and even have to "mow" it with a genuine submarine "mowing machine";[1] and so we might go through the vocabulary of oyster operations and show that the cultivation of oysters is more like the cultivation of potatoes than of animals, for the oyster can no more "locomote" than can a potato. (Reprinted in Woodward and Waller 1932: 196–97)

The potatolike nature of oysters—their immobility, together with the fact that they were usually planted within sight of some point of land—made it easier to claim private property in oysters than in swimming fish. And given the investments involved, profit-seeking oyster planters wanted exclusive claims to the submarine acreage and the transplanted resource. They usually got them, but not without trouble and sharp constraints. The institution that resulted was one of dual property: private property for aquaculture in places known to be barren of shellfish, and common property for natural shellfish and places known to be naturally productive.

But the process was incomplete. Around the turn of the century numerous observers of the fisheries of New Jersey, all clearly in favor of oyster culture as the source of littoral progress, bemoaned the evident fact that while hundreds of thousands of acres of submarine land appropriate to oyster culture were available, only a tiny portion of such lands were actually used for that purpose (Hall 1894; Stainsby 1902). The rest remained common property, or "the wilds," as New Jersey baymen say. Half a century later, at the outset of World War II, Isaiah Bowman, a renowned scientist and president of Johns Hopkins University, addressed the American Association for the Advancement of Science. He posed three cases of failure in relating science to the needs of society, one being peacekeeping, another preventing soil erosion in tropical lands, and the third, the failure of oyster culture in the Chesapeake Bay and north (Bowman 1940). Almost another half century later, a scientist hired to develop shellfish aquaculture in the bays of Long Island, New York, found to his dismay that the privatization required was not acceptable in most areas (cf. Siddall 1988), and Virginia scientists argued once more for a rational approach to the problem of shellfish resource management, including privatization for aquaculture (Hargis and Haven 1988).

Institutionalist Perspectives

The question of why it is difficult to get others to agree to changes in property rights and other institutions is a particular case of the larger question of how institutions respond to individual incentives and choices. It has drawn a large and diverse body of scholarship. Besides "new institutionalists" who underscore collective action problems and transaction costs are "free market environmentalists" who advocate privatization or quasi-privatization of rights to use natural resources and ecosystem services and who therefore see the persistence of public trust claims as problematic.

From this perspective, a reasonable expectation, based on rational action and economizing principles, is that as the oysters get scarcer or demand for them increases, property rights in them will become more precise and secure. For some kinds of things, as for migratory and diffuse resources like air, water, and some fish, the transaction costs of such definition and its enforcement are too high for this definition to take place. As Coase said, "[I]t would cost too much to put the matter right" (1960: 39). But if the resource is capable of being bounded and within view of people with the power to enforce rights, as are oyster beds, then we should expect the development of more precise property claims. This expectation is strengthened by the analyses of economists who have created models, based on the dual property rights systems of the Mid-Atlantic region, which show that private or leased property rights in oyster resources result in improved price structures and labor efficiency (Agnello and Donnelley 1984).

Why, then, haven't all the oystering (and clamming) grounds become private property? In the terms of a new institutional economist, the more general question is "[t]he persistence of seemingly perverse property rights in the face of what would appear to be obvious alternatives" (Libecap 1989: 3), and answers would include how factors such as the heterogeneity of firms in an industry and the physical attributes of the resource affect the transaction costs of making decisions about and implementing new property rights regimes (see also Anderson and Hill 1977; Williamson 1985). Reasons for the halting and limited privatization of the shellfish grounds of New Jersey and other states would thus include difficulty getting agreement among a large number of independent-minded and geographically dispersed people, using different techniques and with different social relations to production. Added is the fact that one cannot always predict where and when oysters and clams (in particular, clams) will successfully reproduce themselves with large "sets" and consequently the importance to harvesters of maintaining options in "the wilds." Other reasons for incomplete privatization include difficulties seeing what others are doing out on the water—the ever-present problems of monitoring and enforcement.

Beyond Rational Action: Culture and Context

In the economic and public choice forms of institutional analysis, sources of change or resistance to change reside in economic measures and calculi, such as transaction costs, or in gamelike structural obstacles to cooperative choice, such as the free rider and prisoners' dilemma problems. As helpful as they can be, they have limitations. Among them are high and sometimes misleading levels of abstraction from empirical cases, which thereby omit the often key fact of embeddedness. Another problem is an overly narrow perspective on institutions. Within economic and public choice schools, institutions are seen as constraints, the "rules of the game" that affect human behavior for collective purposes. A more satisfying view of institutions is that they not only restrain (i.e., through laws) but also enable and empower, establish mandates and values, and create sense and meaning (Giddens 1984; Scott 1995; Douglas 1986).

Turning to the oyster question: attempts to argue for the superiority of private property over common property or open access on the grounds of economic efficiency are flawed because they ignore the embeddedness of economic processes in culture and society (Polanyi 1957; Granovetter 1992). Efficiency measures like Pareto optimality *assume* certain distributions of property rights or institutions. They cannot, therefore, be used to *compare* the performance of different regimes (Bromley 1982). Consequently, arguments for privatization that use economic efficiency gains as the reason are defective, even though they are cloaked with the transparent objectivity of analytic rigor. They do not recognize the critical social fact that through collective processes—political, legal, social—people have decided that some things and places should be public and others private.

Making this argument, Daniel Bromley offers an explicit answer to our question about why there is such resistance to privatization:

> The proper perspective on access to, and control of, the public lands would start with our European heritage wherein only a very few could avail themselves of hunting and fishing activities. Private-property advocates overlook this institutional heritage in their quest to convince us of the current "inefficiencies" of public land administration. . . . After all, it was with a particular social welfare function in mind that our founders determined that certain natural resources would remain the common property of all—not the private property of a fortunate few. (1982: 842)

The only problem with Bromley's otherwise valuable point is that it creates an image of a singular moment of institutional innovation. In contrast to his suggestion of a constitutional moment, the New Jersey cases I present suggest a long, bumpy process, one with many such moments of "institutional innovation" as well as other kinds of events.

In very broad outline, the American institution of common property in the fisheries owes something to moments at the founding of North American colonies, like Rhode Island, Massachusetts, and West New Jersey, where common rights to fish and hunt were written into charters. There and elsewhere the common law, and the cases that constituted it, supported common use rights from time to time. In important cases such as *Arnold v. Mundy* and *Martin v. Waddell,* appellate courts recognized the common law principles protecting public rights of fishing and navigation and the principle of state ownership. But it was not until 1892, in the *Illinois Central* case, that the principle of public trust for common rights such as fishing and navigation gained constitutional status. And as the sagas of New Jersey's oyster wars show, maintaining some resources as common property was an ongoing struggle in particular industries and places. The specification of tenure as common or private took place over a long period of time, involved many different actors, and was never settled once and for all. It is this process, of contesting and specifying institutions such as property rights, that interests the anthropologist.

"A Whole People Were Swept into Exile"

The accounts in this book show far more resistance and legal action than one would expect if the problem could be reduced to the transaction costs of heterogeneity and uncertainty and the free rider problem. In that sense they reflect the preoccupations of political economy or political ecology with class and conflict, or what might be recast as the "romance of the commons" (McCay 1995a). "Commoners" nibbled away at the edges of the private plots and leaseholds, pilfering oysters and clams, sometimes with the effect of "trying the right" in court, always with the effect of trying the patience and pocketbooks of the planters on the water and thereby constraining the expansion of private property. They also organized themselves in what I have called "class acts" to raid disputed oyster beds and again bring their claims to court. The "wars" that resulted brought the issue to the legislature and the public. What might have seemed very local and particular conflicts over small patches of muddy ground were cast in the populist rhetoric of the rights of small producers versus "trusts" and monopolies, a rhetoric that made sense at a time when the Vanderbilts, Rockefellers, and others were accumulating fortunes and wielding economic power. To appreciate the importance of these actions and rhetoric calls for the broader social science perspectives that emphasize relationships of social class and political power as well as the embeddedness of economic calculi in fields of social relations and cultural meaning.

Why did some people say "no," whether through the political process, the courts, organized conflicts, or subtler forms of resistance? Who were these people? What was at stake? How are their actions related to the creations of the law, such as the public trust doctrine? Answering these questions is not easy, given the paucity of historical information about the fisher folk of the region, and I have had to rely heavily on texts such as court cases and legislative acts that carried their own semantic and political weight. However, the general answer seems to be that most of those who said "no" to privatization were relatively poor people who depended on common property rights of access to marine resources to make a living. These "commoners" stole, cheated, fought, and organized collective raids and legal defense to protect their common rights from what they saw as threats to them. Privatization of shellfish resources, like enclosure of the open fields and meadows of agrarian societies, was a "tragedy of the commoners."

This reading, which draws causal links between social class and property rights, is not original. It can be found in the populist dissent of William Pennington in *Yard v. Carman* (1812: 501), where he linked exclusive shad-fishing rights to the infamous Game Laws of England (chapter 7). It can be found in a poem written in 1884 by a young girl from a small town near the Maurice River Cove of New Jersey about the riparian wars of the Delaware (chapter 10):

> *Riparian Rights*
> They staked out what they had no right to claim,
> And said, Bother the poor folks, it's just the same.
> And now when we try to claim our rights,
> They put us in prison to prevent a fight.
> Is this the state that we call free?
> They say law is law, but when wrong it ought not to be.
> Rich men are taking our bread and rights;
> Do you wonder then that we show fight?[2]

It is also evident in the 1909 case about rights to a natural oystering bed in the Mullica River, where one of the judges cast the situation as analogous to the tragic evictions of crofters from the Highlands of Scotland, "when a whole people were swept into exile, to make way for sheep walks and pasture lands" (chapter 11). Rhetorical reference to the Game Laws, enclosure, and the plight of the poor, like debates about the meaning of the Magna Carta and the Proprietors, gave dramatic shape to this argument.

It is tempting to stop here, but there are other ways to address the question, and as scientists we must beware of letting our models restrict our gaze. For instance, privatization could also be a way to help small-scale shellfishers gain some control over their natural and marketing environments; it was clearly a prerequisite for oyster planting, and oyster planting was an extremely important way to maintain some control over supply and quality to meet market conditions, in contrast with harvesting of shellfish in the wilds, which required rapid sale of the shellfish whatever the market demand. The issue was not privatization per se; it was control over the natural processes involved in the reproduction of shellfish and the social processes at play in the reproduction of opportunities for shellfishers. The key issue was whether or not the *natural* shellfish beds should remain open access or become the property of private firms. It was a difficult issue, because around the time of the oyster wars, attempts to manage the natural beds through local commissions (primarily by "shelling" them with oyster shell returned to the water from the shucking houses) did not seem to work or to be sustainable (given difficulties getting appropriations from the legislature and cooperation from the industry). Although it might be—and always has been—arguable that the problem was the lack of adequate state support for public trust property, many insiders and outsiders argued that private owners would do a better job. Accordingly, the people who abused the riparian commission (which they clearly did) to obtain private rights to erstwhile "natural" shellfish beds had some "right" on their sides. The recorded history in shellfish commission reports is silent about this side of things for the oyster war cases, although it does record privatization of the Raritan Bay natural shellfish beds in 1917, a last-ditch and ultimately failed effort to protect the reproductive capacity of that much-abused region, and a similar, also disappointing attempt in the late 1980s to relax the ancient rule against private access to the oyster beds up the bay in the Delaware (chapter 13).

A Different Question

The idea of a tragedy of the commons is difficult to shake. It has roots in both antiquity and the free-market liberalism of early industrialization (e.g., Lloyd 1968 [1837]). The story is easily understood and retold (Rose 1994), and it expresses some truths about the dilemmas of open-access situations. Thus, in the context of a discussion of the limitations of local control of oystering, a New Jersey oysterman, unlikely to have read Hardin's article in *Science* (Hardin 1968) but very much involved with the politics of fisheries management, offered an almost exact rendering of Hardin's way of explaining the tragedy of the commons:

> We've got to have somebody to lead us just a little bit, at least watch us some. We'd soon wipe ourselves out. You know that old story: where there's one field that

> supports 100 sheep and that's all it would support so this one guy decides "I'm better off to put a sheep in there." Well, he is better off but the whole hundred's gonna lose and he isn't gonna worry about the field. And each one of us will want to put that one more sheep in. See what I mean, because it would improve our own position. It takes an outsider, just like baseball or anything else. (Taylor 1983)

Easily retold, the story can draw attention from potentials for effective management of the commons by the commoners, as well as for social and ecological tragedy under privatized or government-managed regimes. Interdisciplinary work on property rights has coalesced on a different take on the question. Rather than asking why all the oystering grounds have not become private property, we might instead investigate how common pool resources are used, allocated, and managed under any given property rights regime, whether "private," "common," "state," or "open access" (Feeny et al. 1990; McCay 1995a).

One would then put aside the question of why there is so little privatization (with its implicit but self-evident agenda) and explore at greater length the genesis, workings, and changes of New Jersey's numerous fishery institutions: informal, "gentlemen's agreement" systems of management; local committees and customs; systems of open-access management, sometimes side by side with systems of leasehold management; legislation; commissions, councils, and agencies of the state; the common law; and the courts.

In this book I have not developed the detailed analysis that can be made of all of this, having selected major legal cases as the framework and thereby having slighted the rich history of fish and shellfish management that could be told. However, I have offered clues. For example, the "turn and turn about" customs of the shad fishers of the Delaware are examples of particular and enduring solutions to conflict and congestion problems, sanctioned by the legislature but clearly local and crafted by the fishing industry itself (chapter 7). Custom was also the (often shaky) basis of most claims to exclusive property in oystering until the end of the nineteenth century. Attempts to get securer property rights, against the objections and raids of common-right shellfishermen, were not always successful, as shown in the saga of the Shrewsbury River (chapter 3). However, where they were successful they led to more formal systems with the backing of the state. Some of these were highly localized. Shark River, the site of one of the important cases that helped reinterpret public trust as alienable state property (chapter 9), was an important example of a locally run common property management institution, where the power to collect fees, survey and allocate leases, and enforce the rules was held at the county level of government and administered by a committee representing the local oyster industry.

New Jersey is not, however, like New York, Massachusetts, and other states where some of the coastal towns hold title to shellfish waters. In New Jersey the public trust doctrine clearly granted "ownership" to the state, and thus even the local systems of management depended on the state legislature to set the rules. They eventually disappeared. The Cape May associations, in which the citizens of the townships held exclusive rights in common to the "natural privileges" of fishing, hunting, hawking, and so on (once the Spicers turned them over to them), depended on acts of the legislature for their regulatory powers. By the end of the nineteenth century, even they were gone, casualties of the legal and political battles between the remnant Proprietors and the state that revitalized the doctrine of state ownership of tidal lands. However, as shown in chapter 13, local-level comanagement, with high levels of participation by members of the industry, became the standard, best realized in the Delaware Bay, where it continues. Although the problem of declining oyster abundance is most evident, highlighted by the dismal fate of the Shrewsbury and Raritan Bay oysters, the story is also one of the exceptional resilience of oystering in the Delaware Bay and the Mullica River until the past forty years or so of epidemic and endemic oyster disease. No small contributor to its resilience has been the science-based, comanagement system.

Central to the comanagement process were scientists who worked closely with members of the industry and politicians, a story that has yet to be adequately told for the distant past and the larger picture of fisheries management in either New Jersey or the United States, although it has been told in part in the documents used in chapter 13 and in case studies such as my own of comanagement in the 1980s hard clam "spawner sanctuary" experiments in New Jersey (McCay 1988, 1989b) and Priscilla Weeks's work on oystermen and scientists in Texas (Ward and Weeks 1994). The comanagement structure of fishery administration continues in New Jersey and other states, and it contributes another answer to the question of why there has been so little privatization of the shellfish grounds: shellfishers who objected are often in positions to say "no" and be heard. They also envisioned more communal and collaborative alternatives.

The Exclusive Right to Fish, in Common?

One of the goals of this study is to raise questions about things we take for granted, like the idea that open access is the cause of overexploitation. Another now taken for granted but worth reconsidering is whether common property fishing should be viewed as constituting a private right or a public privilege. It is now a public privilege. A version of the question appeared in the first set of court cases reviewed, which followed the capture of a law-breaking oyster dredger owned by a Philadelphia lawyer by New Jersey oystermen in the Delaware Bay (chapter 2). Recall that in *Corfield v. Coryell* (1825) a federal district court affirmed states' rights to impose residency rules in the fisheries based on the notion—grounded in the institution of the Delaware River "fisheries"—that just as owners of private fisheries had exclusive rights, so co-owners of common property fisheries had exclusive rights. States were the equivalent of English manors or towns, empowered to manage the property of the tenants in common, who had exclusive use rights. In 1876 the United States Supreme Court upheld a Virginia statute that prohibited citizens of other states from planting oysters in the tidal beds of Virginia on the grounds that the state owned the beds, tidewaters, and even the fish "so far as they are capable of ownership while running" (*McCready v. Commonwealth of Virginia* 1876: 394). The state could appropriate the oyster beds for exclusive use of its citizens because such action was "in effect nothing more than a regulation of the use by the people of their common property" (*McCready v. Commonwealth of Virginia* 1876: 395). The argument rested on a distinction between public and common fisheries similar to that found in the New Jersey case. The court held that fishing rights are not mere privileges or immunities of citizenship but are genuine property rights. Citizens of one state do not have vested interests in the common property of citizens of another state. Therefore, the state can give exclusive use of oyster-planting lands to its own citizens, in this case, Virginians. It is "not different in principle from that of planting corn upon dry land held in the same way" (*McCready v. Commonwealth of Virginia* 1876: 395).

The court of *Corfield v. Coryell* saw fishing rights as property rights, not privileges or immunities, much the same way that the clammer versus oyster planter nuisance cases of the late nineteenth century worked on the question of whether clammers had private cause against the oyster planters (chapter 12). In *Brown v. De Groff* (1888) the state supreme court took the position that each bayman held the private right to clam in the public highways of the state's navigable water. Thus the public nuisance of oyster-planting grounds in Raritan Bay became a private one. But the rendering of fishing rights as exclusive property rights, not privileges or immunities, now seems forgotten in American law. The idea disappeared, together with most *res communes* rights not attached to clearly defined private property (Coquillette 1979). In recent years, the administrative courts used by the National Marine Fisheries Service and lawyers working for the National Atmospheric and Oceanic Administration have construed fishing as a privilege, not a property right (see Milliken 1994). The alternative idea deserves reconsideration as a reading that may help interpret the past and shape the future.

The view that fishing rights are true property rights, not privileges (or immunities), would be much closer to the experienced reality and expectations of participants in the ITQ fisheries (chapter 13) as well. The risk, and the major reason it is not accepted by the government, is that it creates expectations that are not only unrealistic, given the vagaries of fisheries, but that may lead to "takings" cases, where fishermen expecting certain returns from their property and not getting them—say, due to concern about the effect of a fishery on an endangered marine mammal species—have a chance of being compensated for their losses. However, thinking of fishing rights as property rights rather than privileges would have benefits, including benefits to common property rights holders. One is that it might give surer standing in actions of trespass or nuisance when some citizens are deprived of their common or public rights (as when a fishery has been changed to one in which only a few are allowed to hold licenses) or of the value of those rights (as when pollution, habitat change, or overfishing result in resource decline) (cf. Abrams and Washington 1990 on the problem of public and private nuisance law). It also might help create bases for devolving responsibilities to participants in fisheries (Scott 1993) as well as deciding among competing claimants in multiple-stakeholder conflicts.

A related benefit to seeing fishing rights as property rights, not privileges, is that it would give substance to the notion of common property (*res communes*) as well as private property, in contrast with vaguely defined public property. This would be an important change in public policy, one that would help achieve the goal of respecting the experiential and institutional reality of many smaller-scale, locality-oriented fisheries of North America (see Matthews 1993) and help provide an incentive structure for more effective participation of people in fishing industries in the management process. That process includes monitoring and enforcement, not just making decisions, and the legitimacy of the process is arguably both dependent on effective participation and critical to compliance. As noted earlier, this would buck a long and fairly thorough trend toward dismantling the legal importance of *res communes*, a process that was enhanced when lawyers and legal scholars shifted their attention to Hale's distinctions between *jus privatum* and *jus publicum*, or private ownership and ownership subject to the rights of the "public," leaving out common rights. An open question and challenge is whether such a "rights-based" approach to fisheries (Neher, Arnason, and Mollett 1989) requires commoditization and marketability or whether it can be developed within a more community-oriented framework.

The Cultural Ecology of Public Trust

Freedoms to fish and use the foreshores of tidal waters and navigable rivers are often claimed as natural, but they arise from specific political, social, and legal experiences. They have been created and re-created, shaped and challenged and altered in human encounters and deliberations. Consequently, the oyster tongers, shad fishers, beach party goers, and others featured in the stories I have told played no small role in assuring that social goals and the interests of both the public and very special classes of people do matter.

The American public trust doctrine supports and is refueled by the outrage people feel when they find their way to the beach at Malibu, California, or Beach Haven, New Jersey, obstructed by fences and "No Trespassing" or "beach badge required" signs. It took shape, as I have shown, in a number of nineteenth-century oyster wars and court cases: in 1808, when the state's supreme court recognized and elaborated on the rule that shellfish planted where shellfish naturally go are "abandoned" to the commons; in 1812, when William Pennington, one of the state supreme court judges, worried about whether the private fishing rights being disputed in a Delaware River case actually existed, given the free right to fish; in 1821, when Andrew Kirkpatrick decided a case based on the raid on a bed of oysters planted by a farmer on one side of the Raritan River by a rowdy group of oystermen from the other side; in 1842, when Roger Taney of the United States Supreme Court defended the state's property claims in oystering lands, and hence the rights of oyster leaseholders, against the claims of the Board of General Proprietors of East New Jersey; in the "riparian wars" of the Delaware Bay and Mullica River in the 1880s to early 1900s; and so on. Challenged by word and deed in many ways, it took shape again and again, as people expressed their outrage at losing access to what they considered theirs by right, whether it was the right of the public or the right of fishers and baymen.

This culture of the commoners is not, however, the same as the public trust doctrine. There was close mapping in some respects, such as the general egalitarian sentiment of common rights of navigation and fishing. There was more divergence in others, that is, readings of state ownership to mean anything from trusteeship to proprietorship. Oystermen and clammers claimed general, natural, and fundamental rights of free access to fish and shellfish in their natural state. In some cases they also seem to have argued for specific kinds of community, where the many rather than the few could be productively engaged as free agents. It is possible (although unlikely, given the obscurity of public trust law) that ordinary people in the shellfish industry recognized the extent to which the public trust doctrine had been reinterpreted to favor the state legislature's right to "give away" or alienate tidewater lands. More likely, they simply saw that something they thought they had and that made sense to them—the right to harvest naturally productive shellfish—was threatened. When they decided to "try the right" it was up to the lawyers they hired to dredge up and try to give shape and sense to the law.

After undertaking actions on the water to try the right, the shellfishermen gave up control over definition of the essential issues, a phenomenon noted by Merry (1990) in her studies of people using the courts to handle personal conflicts. In the arguments of their lawyers and the opinions of the courts, the notions and concerns of the oystermen and clammers became very specific, precise, mannered readings of very obscure cases and documents of the distant past and the distinct culture of the common law. However, at least some of the time, at critical points in time, and over the long run the definitions of the experts and the decisions of the courts reinforced the claims of those who claimed common rights and made more precise the conditions under which private tenure would be upheld. The shellfishermen, in turn, by their actions and based on their own understandings, retried the right, forcing courts to exhume and re-create the law.

The public trust doctrine and related rulings in state and federal courts offered some protection for the relatively poor and powerless marine commoners. Law is widely recognized as part of hegemony. For law to be effective as an ideological instrument of a ruling class, it must appear impartial and just. To do so it must have some autonomy; it must sometimes *be* impartial and just, and as such it can serve the interests of the powerless as well (Thompson 1975: 266). This idea is nicely summed up by Merry: "[a]s an ideology, law contains both elements of domination and the seeds of resistance. It provides a way of legitimating property and privilege as well as a way of challenging property and privilege" (1990: 8). The public trust doctrine is a case in point.

The "public trust" idea in the doctrine is separable from the "state ownership" idea. It suggests inalienability and deep suspicion about the wisdom of any given legislature to protect it. Through the common law court cases on which it was based and the circumstances that brought shellfishermen to court, the idea was also linked to the notion of inalienable common rights of fishing. No wonder that the organized violence on the oystering grounds of New Jersey was arranged to try the right in the courts. Oystermen and clammers felt that they had a real chance there, and they sometimes did.

When rights come into competition, the outcome is frequently arrived at by arranging them in a hierarchy, making some secondary to others (Peters 1987: 192). As recent public trust cases about property rights in the Hackensack Meadowlands of New Jersey (Keys 1986) and in the oil-rich bayous of Mississippi (Burrowes 1988) show, when rights come into competition it is not inevitable that private rights will come out on top. Sometimes public rights do. That this happens at all is remarkable. As E. P. Thompson (1975, 1976: 339–40) pointed out in reference to the long process of enclosure of the English agrarian commons, the rights most likely to become secondary, and vulnerable, are those based on impermanent, nonmonetary use rights, that is, the customary common rights of the manor and the freeholder. Common rights rarely had the documentary and legal backing that private rights did. In relation to fishing, navigation, and tidewater lands, they had to rely on very suspect interpretations of passages in the Magna Carta and a tiny body of case law; common rights did not do very well in English common law courts. Nor did customary rights do well in American courts (Delo 1974; Rose 1986). Nonetheless, the common rights of navigation and fishing were substantiated in the public trust doctrine and later broadened. They may still be secondary, but they now have some weight.

Earlier I spoke to the theme of resistance to privatization of the commons. I also suggested that the institutional economics approach to the question is valuable in noting that privatization may not always be technically or economically feasible, given the transaction costs of bounding, claiming, monitoring, trading, and enforcing exclusive rights. Schreiber's use of an old English case to argue that surely some of the beachfront is not really worth keeping from the public at the cost of the "hateful privilege of vexing their neighbours" is a case in point. I then pointed to the fact that there are other issues, as the courts keep remembering when they bring up the public trust doctrine, the narrative of which includes messages about equality and fairness. Will giving exclusive use rights to private interests or favoring one group over the other meet public goals? These goals are numerous, variable, and often conflicting but likely include resource conservation, community development, and economizing. Some of these goals refer to economics and some do not, but what is telling is the claim that social goals and public interests matter.

Reference Material

Notes

Introduction

1. Jacob Spicer was born in 1716 and entered the colonial assembly in 1745, remaining in it until his death in 1765. He is best known for working with his friend and political colleague Aaron Leaming to compile 126 volumes of the original grants, concessions, and other state papers concerning New Jersey (Leaming and Spicer 1758). Like Leaming, Spicer was by almost all counts a successful, public-spirited, and accomplished colonist. He was also one of the two "really rich men in the county" (Stevens 1897: 137). My sources are Stevens's eclectic and disorganized local history (1897) and selections from the Spicer and Leaming papers published by the Cape May Historical Society (Stevens 1935, 1943). Thomas L. Purvis, in *Proprietors, Patronage, and Paper Money* (1986), using much the same sources, tells a similar story about Spicer, albeit from the perspective of eighteenth-century New Jersey politics.

2. Major sources include Whitehead (1875), Pomfret (1964), Fleming (1977), and Purvis (1986). The nineteenth-century history of the Proprietors of East and West New Jersey has not, to my knowledge, been written; most of the records remain in manuscript (Purvis 1986: 337). The cases reported here form part of that history, as do legal opinions commissioned by the Proprietors, especially in 1825 (Board of General Proprietors of the Eastern Division of New Jersey 1825) and 1881 (Anonymous 1881) and state investigations into their operations (New Jersey Riparian Committee 1882; Parker 1885).

3. The West Jersey Society, a trading and land company formed by a group of speculators in London, vied with William Penn's Council of the Proprietors of West New Jersey for the power to allocate vacant lands in the southern and western part of the province. All of the proprietary ventures were traced to a gift from King George II to his brother James, the duke of York, of all the land between the Connecticut and Delaware Rivers in North America as part of the restoration of the Stuart monarchy. James gave half of his domain, south of the Hudson River, to two close friends who had helped him during the English civil war: Lord John Berkeley and Sir George Carteret. Quakers, Scotsmen, and others eventually purchased these properties.

4. Here is Aaron Leaming's account of the same meeting: "[a]bout forty people met at the Presbyterian Meeting-house to ask Mr. Spicer if he purchased the Society's reversions at Cape May for himself or for the people. He answers he bought it for himself; and upon asking him whether he will release to the people, he refuses, and openly sets up his claim to the oysters, to Basses' titles, and other deficient titles, and to a resurvey, whereupon the people broke up in great confusion, as they have been for some considerable time past" (in Stevens 1897: 129).

5. For many years I have searched for instances of communal management of natural resources and fisheries in New Jersey's history. The Cape May Associations, plus associations of meadowland and barrier beach users, are the only examples I have found. Why this is so is another research project.

6. I present these accounts as stories for other reasons too. First, the requirements of causal explanation are very difficult to meet in social and historical research, and narrative explanation, within a framework that recognizes the roles of both interpretation and rational choice in social action (cf. Little 1991), is about all that we can do well. More to the case at hand, information about the oyster wars and other conflicts comes almost entirely from legal arguments and court reports, which are stories themselves. Storytelling is a powerful tool in legal persuasion (Weisberg 1992; La Rue 1995), and it can be very risky to use such accounts as sources of information on what really happened without recognizing their rhetorical functions.

7. For example, using the logic of new institutionalist economics, Acheson (1987) argues that the reason why the lobstermen of Maine, well accustomed to fiercely defended territoriality, are unwilling to go the next step to privatize lobstering grounds has much to do with the transaction costs and ecological uncertainty of making this change. I have applied a similar approach to the explanation of illegal activities in a New Jersey fishing community (McCay 1981b).

8. The "scarcity story" has a much longer history in Western thought and is well represented in the work of eighteenth- and nineteenth-century social theorists who imagined propertyless or communal property relations early in human experience transformed into individual, clan, royal, state, and other forms of private property through one or another mechanism (see Maine 1884; Marx 1946). The fictional movie *The Gods Must Be Crazy* develops another familiar variant, where scarcity is created by new items of value and thereby transforms social relationships and culture.

Chapter 1. Oystering in Eighteenth- and Nineteenth-Century New Jersey

1. "Periauger" and "pittiauger" are among the many forms derived from a Spanish word, *piragua,* derived from the Caribbean term for a dugout boat. It came to be used in America and the West Indies for an open, flat-bottomed, schooner-rigged vessel, "a sort of two-masted sailing barge" (*The Compact Edition of the Oxford English Dictionary* 1971).

2. For example, Jacob Spicer and Aaron Leaming were deputized; their sons are the men featured in the introduction who compiled New Jersey's written records of early settlement and colonization and distinguished themselves in many other ways, some not so grand.

3. Very impressive was the 1798 penalty for taking oysters or shells if one was not a resident or was using a vessel that did not belong to a state resident. A citizen could seize such a vessel and tell the local justices of the peace, who would try the offender and, if he was condemned, see that the canoe, vessel, or whatever was sold, half the profits going to the county and the other half to the person who seized it and prosecuted the case. Moreover, anyone on one of these nonresident craft who resisted being boarded could be

fined thirty dollars. The 1798 bill incorporated the May 1 to September 1 closed season for raking on oyster beds or banks "under pretence of taking clams, or other shell fish, or under any other pretence whatsoever" and the law against using oysters for the sole purpose of burning and converting them into lime. A provision against selling oysters during the closed season disappeared, as therefore did free oyster meals for the poor.

4. Ingersoll, a student of Louis Agassiz, was a prolific natural history writer and lecturer (MacKenzie 1991b). From 1879 to 1881 he was employed by the United States Commission of Fish and Fisheries and the Census Bureau as one of the agents in a large study of the fisheries of North America (Goode 1887). He wrote two monographs about the shellfisheries (1881, 1887).

5. Ingersoll offers a date of 1810 for the earliest New Jersey oyster planting at Bergen Point, Upper New York Bay (cited in Lockwood 1883: 226). But he is wrong too, because the New Jersey Supreme Court case described in chapter 3 confirms that planting was well established in the Shrewsbury and Navesink Rivers by 1808. It is much clearer that there was a diffusionary path in New Jersey from north to south (Nelson 1902, 1: 432). In the northern bays, oyster harvesting had been more intense and in existence longer because the sites were close to the domestic and export markets of New York City and New Jersey cities. Moreover, the natural oyster beds were less extensive than those of Delaware Bay. By the early nineteenth century many of the northern beds were virtually empty of local oysters (Kochiss 1974: 10). On the other hand, when oyster planting began in Delaware Bay it was based on still substantial populations of oysters on the natural beds.

6. "Progging" is a term used from South Jersey to the Chesapeake for the activity of doing whatever comes to mind or is possible to do in the marshlands and bays, including fishing, hunting for birds and ducks, trapping muskrats and turtles, shellfishing, and collecting grasses (see Berger and Sinton 1985: 56). The term is used more widely in the English-speaking fringes of the ocean, as in Newfoundland, with similar meanings of poking about for this and that. The term "baymen" is used in the Long Island and New Jersey area for people who "followed the bays," clamming, fishing, doing whatever they could; the term "watermen" is similar and more common from South Jersey to the Chesapeake Bay.

Chapter 2. Oyster Wars and States' Rights

1. The role of the state in natural resources management is as yet inadequately examined. In debates about the tragedy of the commons paradigm, top-down, science-based, and bureaucratic management by the state is juxtaposed against bottom-up management by local communities, with collaboration between local communities or user-groups and the state, the comanagement position, in between (e.g., Berkes et al. 1989). This analytic framework has limited usefulness insofar as it suggests a unified and reified phenomenon, rather than a complex, often loosely integrated set of laws, procedures, and organizations concerned with policies that are binding on the inhabitants of a specified territory. These may be at cross-purposes. Moreover, it leaves unexamined a series of questions concerning relationships between the state, class conflict, and capitalism, as well as questions of

agency and culture (Sinclair 1989). Even more, that "commons" debate presupposes a state organization that has fully developed administrative, enforcement, and legislative capabilities, capable of top-down regulatory intervention. That surely is not true of New Jersey's fisheries agencies prior to the early twentieth century, nor is it accurate for those of many newly emerging postcolonial states.

2. The New Jersey argument went on: the waters of Maurice River Cove are clearly within the territorial jurisdiction of New Jersey by whatever measure used and could be argued as within Cumberland County jurisdiction, too. Principles of common law could be adduced to show that the whole cove of Maurice River was within Cumberland County, New Jersey; but a more precise measure, drawing a line from Egg Island to the mouth of Maurice River, would form a small and secondary cove, which is where the *Hiram* was captured, "and constituting . . . a place for the process of the *coroner,* to the exclusion of the *admiral*" (*Keen v. Rice* 1822: 13), referring to the distinction between general and admiralty law. Moreover, the protection of fisheries is long and widely acknowledged as proper exercise of national and state power. Finally, the bottom of the cove, where oysters are found, is "literally, a *property, the growth of, and attached to, the soil of New Jersey*" (*Keen v. Rice* 1822: 13), having been formed either by alluvial deposit or sea encroachment.

3. M'Ilvaine interrupted, reminding him of an act of assembly of the last session that declared New Jersey's jurisdiction to extend to the channel of the Delaware River and Bay, to which Ingersoll replied that he was "sorry to find New Jersey forgetting her accustomed comity" but that that law was passed after the 1820 law, the object of his discussion.

4. The circuit court would not let Corfield recover damages on the grounds that he himself did not suffer damages, having hired the vessel out to a Mr. Hand, who in turn had hired it out to John Keen, who was at the helm at the time of the incident.

5. The 1825 court also deliberated on the difficult question of New Jersey's boundaries in the Delaware Bay and decided, as did many courts and legislatures before and after, not to give a "decided opinion" on the matter. The terms of the proprietorships of the region were vague in the Delaware River and Bay region, and after the Revolution boundaries were still not settled among the new states; Pennsylvania and New Jersey entered into a compact in 1793 that seemed to have divided the Delaware River down the middle, but rights to Delaware Bay, involving also the state of Delaware, remained contested and ill defined until the end of the nineteenth century.

6. The court cited English common law and may also have been thinking of situations where the common rights to fish, cut peat, take fuel, and pasture animals were ascriptions of residence in particular villages or towns in England, not public.

Chapter 3. River Pirates of the Shrewsbury

1. In most of the period under study, the higher courts of New Jersey were the court of errors and appeals, the supreme court, a court of chancery, and a court of impeachments. The supreme court had the powers of the Court of King's Bench in England, for both civil and criminal law: "the great prerogative writs of the King's Bench: certiorari, mandamus,

and quo warranto" (Bebout 1931: 13). It included a chief justice and eight associate justices. They sat as the court of errors and appeals as well (see also Clevenger 1903).

2. New Jersey history and geography buffs will recognize the surnames of the attorneys and judges, who were from or founded prominent families, are commemorated in place-names, and had generally distinguished careers, enough so to warrant places in biographies of the state's notables. The names of Leverson, Shepard, and Layton are perhaps more obscure, although there are still Laytons who depend on the bounties of the tidal rivers and bays of northern New Jersey.

3. If a several fishery were being claimed, Kirkpatrick said that the questions that would have to be addressed were whether the purchase of riparian land on banks of navigable, tidal waters gave the landowner "the right of soil between high and low water mark," whether the landowner might have exclusive rights to shoals or flats too shallow for navigation, and whether the landowner might have exclusive rights to the center of the river channel, a rule applied to nonnavigable waters in English common law ("the right of the soil *usque ad filum aquae*" [*Shepard and Layton v. Leverson* 1808]). Another possible basis for a several fishery would be "long usage and general content," a comment that may acknowledge the Delaware River shad fisheries, the subject of another supreme court case heard by the same people in 1812 that is described in chapter 6. Kirkpatrick said that these questions "in no way come in view in this case. If it should become necessary to agitate them hereafter, they must rest upon their own merits" (*Shepard and Layton v. Leverson* 1808: 371).

4. *State v. Taylor* (1858) was situated in South Jersey. Thomas Taylor was charged with stealing eighteen bushels of oysters, worth eighteen dollars, from George Hildreth, who had brought seed oysters from the Chesapeake Bay, to the south, and from Great Egg Harbor, just to the north, to one of the sounds of Lower Township, Cape May. Hildreth placed these transplants between low- and high-water mark and staked the ground. The report of this case shows that the general rule about protecting natural beds for common-right fishing was thoroughly accepted by that time, having been legitimated in the most important American legal treatise on tidewater law (Angell 1826: 139). The case also provides another interesting discussion about the place of oysters in nature: were they part of *ferae naturae* or chattel? (*State v. Taylor* 1858: 120). On Taylor's side was the familiar argument that letting someone stake out and defend an exclusive claim to a tidewater flat for oyster planting was tantamount to letting loose a process of enclosure, creating "the exclusive appropriation of public navigable waters to private purposes" (*State v. Taylor* 1858: 122). However, by this time it was understood that the tidewaters were the property of the state, and it would be up to the legislature to establish policy about appropriation.

Chapter 4. Arnold v. Mundy and the Public Trust Doctrine

1. The property in question was originally granted to Peter Sonmans in 1685; then it was bounded on the Raritan River and later on low-water mark. It was called "Nevill's Farm" by the time Coddington and then Arnold had it.

2. In fact, the 1669 Woodbridge charter was vague about these rights; the section that

might indicate them, after describing the metes and bounds of the new town, reads in part: "together with all Rivers, ponds, creeks, Islands, Inlets, Bays, Fishing, Hawking, Hunting . . . to continue and Remaine with the Jurisdiction, Corporation or towneship of the said towne of Woodbridge. . . . To be holden by the said Corporation or Township their heirs and successors as of the manner of Eastern Greenwich in free and common soccage [*sic*]" (reprinted in Ludewig 1971: 12–13).

Chapter 5. Proprietors, Oyster Wars, and the Invention of Tradition

1. In 1803 Elisha Boudinot went to the Board of Proprietors in Perth Amboy to have 54.5 acres of Harsimus Cove, near Jersey City, surveyed and deeded over, a fact that did not get much attention until the case of *Gough v. Bell* in 1847 (see chapter 7). In 1806 Robert Morris obtained or "located" Crab Island in West New Jersey this way (New Jersey Riparian Committee 1882: 67, testimony from one of the Proprietors familiar with the records). Evidently the record keeping of the Proprietors was so inaccessible and poor that these cases were not known to the early-nineteenth-century courts dealing with the question of the rights of the Proprietors versus common rights and the rights of the state.

2. The stakes were high. New York's claim to the Hudson River was connected with political battles between Federalists and Republicans, some of which coalesced in Andrew Hamilton's disastrous duel with Aaron Burr, in the background of which was a plan to develop Jersey City (see Fleming 1977: 93). The validity of *all* New Jersey claims to waterfront and tidewater property along the Hudson River and beyond to New York Bay had been challenged by the city of New York. In 1807 Robert Fulton built his famous steamboat, and he and his partner, Robert Livingston, obtained a twenty-year monopoly on steam navigation from the New York legislature, driving out New Jersey boats from the Hudson River and New York Harbor. In 1812 the Federalist governor of New Jersey, Aaron Ogden, got a similar monopoly from New Jersey's legislature and made a deal with Fulton and Livingston. Both were challenged by another steamboat owner whose pilot happened to be Cornelius Vanderbilt. The matter went to the United States Supreme Court and became the source of federal government power to regulate interstate commerce (Fleming 1977: 98; Horwitz 1977). How the Proprietors fit into this is hard to see, but there they were.

3. It was easy to find ways around residency rules. By the middle of the nineteenth century the "market dealers" based in New York City were known to provide "a large part of the capital which operates beds from Keyport, N.J. to Norwalk, Conn. . . . It is very rare, however, that this planting is done in the capitalists' name" (Ingersoll 1887: 558). To avoid citizenship requirements a share-cropping system was used: in a typical arrangement, the dealer advanced money, the planter provided the labor, and they split both the costs of taking up oysters and the profits (Ingersoll 1887: 558).

4. The action of ejectment is a famous example of the use of a legal fiction as a shortcut in English common law (Friedman 1973: 18–19). The claimants to disputed title each pretended to have leased the land to someone (or if one really had leased the land, the

other pretended). Everyone, including the court, knew the mummery for what it was, but it served to bring the issue of title before the court in a much less cumbersome way than was otherwise available in common law until past the middle of the nineteenth century.

5. Waddell was well enough situated to be engaged in lengthy lawsuits and complex and seemingly shady proceedings, including one where he got the federal district court to agree that he should receive the property and effects of a bankrupt person rather than the receiver appointed under a creditors' bill (*Ex parte* Waddell, District Court, S.D., New York, October 1842).

6. Unfortunately, the report focuses almost entirely on one issue, the meaning of the colonial letters patent from King Charles II to the duke of York and of the deed of surrender made by the Proprietors in 1702, even though many other arguments and issues were actually addressed. This is because the court reporter, Robert Peters, decided to exclude all else. Generally displeased with this reporter, the next year four justices of the United States Supreme Court agreed to replace him (Siegel 1987) but not in time to leave history and this account with a truncated view of the issues discussed.

7. See note 1.

8. Wood also anticipated the objection that the Proprietors of West Jersey had granted common rights to the people of West Jersey; hence, the Proprietors of East Jersey could grant private rights. He countered by observing that the early law that made the Delaware "a common fishery . . . grew out of the controversy with Pennsylvania [over boundaries], and was the assertion of a right as against them" (*Martin et al. v. Waddell's Lessee* 1842: 387).

9. The case of the *Prior of Tynemouth* (1291) was ambiguous; it could be interpreted as supporting the local prior's ownership of the foreshore as against a group of burgesses holding a crown franchise in a dispute over towing rights on the Tyne River. The other, *Sir Henry Constable's Case* (1601), about rights to wreck found on the foreshore, actually supports private ownership in its debate about whether the admiral or the county had jurisdiction.

10. The interpretation did not preclude public rights of navigation, citing Lord Hale, who observed that some rivers are public rivers although owned privately, namely, the Wey, Severn, and Thames in England. But it also accepted private rights of alienation in the Hudson River where it was not navigable, which was, by definition but not by fact, where it was no longer tidal. In fact, to this day private riverside landowners can successfully keep boaters from using navigable but freshwater waterways in New York and some other states.

Chapter 6. Local Custom in the Delaware Shad Fisheries

1. Pennington said that according to Sir William Blackstone, a "free fishery" meant an exclusive right to fish in a public river, a "royal franchise derived by royal grant" (*Yard v. Carman* 1812: 499). The Magna Carta forbade the creation of free fisheries. However, Sir Edward Coke had argued that a free fishery was the same as a common fishery. In the case

at hand it did not really matter, according to Pennington, because Carman's claim was not backed by a royal franchise.

2. Pennington became governor of the state the following year, and when his term as governor and chancellor ended in 1815 he was appointed by President Madison to New Jersey's federal district court, forced therefore to sit on the sidelines when, in 1821, the issue that he raised in *Yard v. Carman* appeared as the central question in *Arnold v. Mundy,* Chief Justice Kirkpatrick presiding. But he must have been pleased, nine years after the *Yard v. Carman* decision, when his former colleague on the bench upheld the law of common property in tidal, navigable waters in New Jersey. We know that when the Proprietors' challenge to Kirkpatrick's ruling went to the United States Supreme Court in 1842 as *Martin et al. v. Waddell's Lessee,* Pennington's son, then also governor, went to Washington, D.C., to follow the case (Siegel 1987: 136).

3. The original charter of King Charles II to the duke of York was bounded at what was interpreted as the low-water mark of Delaware River and Bay. Similarly, William Penn's charter for Pennsylvania ended at the Delaware. The crown was interpreted in the case of *Bennett v. Boggs* (1831) to have reserved the right to the bed of Delaware River and Bay, and with the American Revolution, the states made their claims.

4. Until 1891, the Wharf Act, which allowed upland owners to build docks or wharves in tidelands in front of their property, applied to the rest of the state; in that year everyone in the state had to have permission of the riparian commissioners, or a separate "king's grant," to fill in and build on tidelands (Goldschore 1979).

5. The legislature first passed acts to tax these fisheries in 1779, four years before the end of the Revolutionary War. In subsequent tax acts and war taxes it referred to them as "accustomed fisheries, the property of private persons" and later, by 1801, as "fisheries" alone. The Faunces, for instance, paid tax for over 60 years, and "fisheries" were taxed annually for at least 106 years. The state, therefore, could be interpreted as having intended to recognize the right of private property in Delaware River fisheries.

Chapter 7. Local Custom on the Banks of the Hudson

1. They were required to get permission in writing from owners of riparian land to construct wharves, and so on, between high- and low-water mark. They had one year to raise $1 million in subscriptions and five to construct this new "capacious, safe, and convenient harbor opposite the city of New York" (New Jersey Laws, March 18, 1837, 443). A year later the period of time required to raise the money was extended to three years. By 1849 nothing had happened, and some people tried to repeal this and related acts.

2. According to Abraham Zabriskie, who claimed special knowledge because he had served as counsel in the earliest hearing of the case, in 1844 Mary Bell actually bought a strip of land along the shore from the Coles family because the presiding judge in the lower court had said that although she might own the underwater property, she had no right to exclude the adjacent landowners from access to the water or even to fill up the land (Zabriskie 1871: 34). The fact that she did this was offered as yet another proof of

how people accepted what the chancellor called "rights of adjacency" (Zabriskie 1871: 34–35).

3. In his annual message, the New Jersey governor also said that he concurred with the recommendation of the riparian commissioners to give Jersey City ample frontage for constructing public wharves and piers (Randolph 1871: 11). By this time corporations had almost completely taken over the city's waterfront, and municipal officials tried to persuade the state to help them provide public amenities from public trust lands.

Chapter 8. Alienation of the Public Trust

1. *Townsend v. Brown* (1853) was based on a conflict in South Jersey waters near Little Egg Harbor Bay. The case illustrates the persistence of another local custom, this one holding the public trust line at low- rather than high-water mark. It was also notable in being held by Chief Justice Green, who also heard the *Gough v. Bell* cases of the time and applied some of the same logic. At issue was an ambiguity in a legislative act; Green noted that in such a case "the interpretation shall be most favorable to the public, and most strongly against the grantee. The rule is founded in wisdom. All experience teaches that public rights are yielded to private interests with sufficient alacrity" (*Townsend v. Brown* 1853: 87).

Chapter 9. Riparian Rights and Oyster Wars on the Delaware Bay

1. Legislation protected public trust use rights by stipulating that the grants were to be used for purposes of property improvement and development, not for creating exclusive shellfish preserves, and that they were not to encroach upon natural shellfish beds.

2. As of 1902 there was no shelling at all in the Newark Bay and Staten Island Sound (New Jersey Oyster Commission 1902: 8). In Tuckerton Bay experiments in creating "shelled or cindered ground" to enhance seed oysters had failed, although many persons, especially planters, remained optimistic (New Jersey Oyster Commission 1902: 13). In the Atlantic County grounds (e.g., Great Bay, the Mullica, etc.), shells had been planted in numerous places, but one commentator observed that production had actually declined since the shell commission was appointed in 1893 (New Jersey Oyster Commission 1902: 20) and suggested that the technique of shelling was not appropriate, largely because by shelling in concentrated areas it was only too easy for poachers to scoop up the lot: "when planted for the spat to catch upon during June and July, [the shells] shall be properly scattered as a farmer scatters his seed over the field, and not be spilled in particular bunches where thieves may readily come in the night and take them away" (New Jersey Oyster Commission 1902: 21).

3. Recall that in 1903 the commission had also gone to the trouble of persuading the legislature to appropriate $9,000 to buy off riparian grants that had been used by certain persons to try to claim private property above the southwest line (New Jersey Bureau of Shell Fisheries 1903: 29).

4. I have not been able to locate the court cases; references to them appear in New Jersey Oyster Commission (1902: 44–45) and New Jersey Bureau of Shell Fisheries (1903).

Chapter 10. Riparian Rights and Oyster Wars on the Mullica River

1. Mott's partners purchased most of the salt marsh around Roundabout Creek in 1903, and Mott helped them plant oysters there, hoping to use the old law that allowed surrounding landowners to stake off oyster and clam beds for exclusive use.

2. Moreover, according to oral tradition, one of the Sooys had gone out west, where he sold shares in his oyster venture in New Jersey to prospectors and miners. When he returned to New Jersey he sold shares in a gold mine to oystermen and others. Many local men lost money (Donald Maxwell, personal communication, June 29, 1983).

3. At least one body was found in the bay, but since it was the body of a foreign immigrant, it was not reported (Donald Maxwell, personal communication, June 29, 1983).

4. In particular, Superintendent Horner pointed to "thousands of acres in the vicinity of the Cedar creek bed, in Barnegat bay, which are useless for anything in the way of oyster culture at the present time, and, in fact, devoid of any natural product" (New Jersey Bureau of Shell Fisheries 1908: 40).

5. The likelihood that persons with propagating leases would be persons with "large capital" seems not to have been great, since only eight of the fifty lessees in 1912 also held leases in planting grounds (one measure of capital), and only fourteen more were held by persons who shared surnames with planting leasehold "owners." In addition, the planting leases held by those who held propagating leases (N = 8) were also small, ranging from 1.44 to 10 acres. Furthermore, as the Board of Shell Fisheries later remarked, the leases were "gambler's chances" and not likely to lead to a strong pattern of wealth accumulation by a few. The turnover from year to year in leaseholders was at least 25 percent.

Chapter 11. Commoners and Other Nuisances on the Raritan Bay

1. In his use of the terms "trespass" and "pretext," Hall reveals his agreement with the planters' arguments that the baymen's claim to the right to take clams was a ruse to get access to planted oysters. The situation could be read differently, though: that they did indeed refuse "to recognize the right of the planters to the possession of bottom for private enterprise" (Hall 1894: 470) as part of a more general protest against enclosure.

2. The state leaseholds in the Raritan area that the court of *Martin et al. v. Waddell's Lessee* upheld were renewed in 1834 for ten years, but after 1844 the legislative record is silent. Were the commoners able to persuade the legislature not to approve a renewal of the leasing system? They had been able to stop leaseholds elsewhere in the state. Or did oyster planters prefer using dubious title through the Proprietors or other vehicles to the involvement of the state? All that is clear is that the private property claims of the planters were not clear. Thus planters' claims to exclusive property were described as "unautho-

rized" and "illegal" by one court (*Brown v. De Groff* 1888), although a lower court had described them as "permitted" (*De Graff v. Truesdale* 1887).

Chapter 12. Comanaging and Enclosing the Commons

1. According to an interview done by Lawrence Taylor in 1983, an oystermen's association had arisen to protect local shippers and planters from outside interests, especially Philadelphia marketers who wanted to buy into the industry. By 1983, with the effects of MSX, there were only a few members left, mostly the larger shipper-planters, and in the minds of most people, this association was the same as the shellfish council. To the extent that was so, it had clearly lost its powers, because a few years earlier the administration of New Jersey's fisheries had changed so that the shellfish councils lost their powers, becoming advisory only. However, the state's chief of shellfisheries, within the Division of Fish, Game, and Wildlife of the Department of Environmental Protection since 1970, usually takes great care to follow that advice.

2. The rule prohibiting marketing oysters directly from the natural beds remained, and consumer culture intervened, making it difficult to market oysters during the summer. Oysters are difficult to market during the summer because their quality is poor, due to the fact that many are breeding at that time. This fact has somehow evolved into a strong consumer notion that oysters are either inedible, unhealthy, or unavailable during the "non-*r*" months of the summer. It should be noted that the situation was considerably more complicated than suggested by this brief account, and the rule against dredging on the planted grounds during the summer was reimposed and then relaxed again during the 1980s.

3. The surf clam fishery is for a large clam, *Spisula solidissima,* found off the coast of New Jersey and neighboring states; the meat of the clam is sold as processed clam chowder or clam strips (for frying). The fishery involves dredging, but with hydraulic gear, and it has developed high levels of technology and capital investment. In 1989 there were 133 vessels in the fishery; in 1996 there were fewer than 40. The fishery is related to one for another large, offshore clam, the ocean quahog, *Arctica islandica,* the story of which is similar to that for surf clams and thus is not developed here. New Jersey is a major center for these fisheries.

4. Disregard of public trust arguments in recent ITQ cases may partly be the result of ambiguity about the status of the public trust doctrine within federal, as opposed to state, law: the major ITQ systems are for federal waters (although comparable systems are found in a few states), whereas the public trust doctrine refers mainly to states.

Chapter 13. Luddites, Sunbathers, and the Public Trust

1. According to Reis (1991: 30), the doctrine that the state holds lands beneath navigable waterways in trust for the public has been explicitly adopted by only thirty-eight states, but these comprise all that have considered the issue.

2. *Lusardi* started as a situation in which Peter Lusardi was angry about loud, late-night parties being held on a beachfront lot by members of an association of homeowners in a residential development that had title to the lot. It was a nuisance, according to the zoning ordinance of Brick Township. The question was, What right did people have to have fun on the beachfront lot? The Supreme Court decided that they did have such a right, particularly since the township had not done anything to realize the state's new coastal zone management policies.

3. The question of whether the *jus publicum* remains with land that has been acquired as private property as an easement was not considered. Rather, the question was whether the property of the association might be construed as sufficiently "public" to justify application of the public trust doctrine. A significant fact was that some property owners made beach badges available to paying guests, suggesting a kind of public recreational use.

4. The conservatism of the courts may be one reason that the public trust doctrine has not emerged as the basis for legal challenges to the most significant attempt to privatize the nation's marine resources since the leasing and sale of shellfish leases: the creation of ITQs in commercial fisheries (chapter 12).

Chapter 14. Conclusion

1. An aquatic mowing machine was developed in 1885 to cut down eelgrass, one of the many "enemies" of the oyster-planting industry (Hall 1894: 477–78).

2. Grace Laws of Dragston, New Jersey, in the *Bridgeton Dollar Weekly News,* May 5, 1884; courtesy of Daniel O'Connor, Port Norris, New Jersey.

References Cited

Note: I found most of the documents concerning New Jersey's riparian issues in the Special Collections / New Jersey Room of the Alexander Library of Rutgers the State University, New Brunswick, New Jersey; I found some items at the New Jersey State Library in Trenton, New Jersey, and a few others in the University of California system during my sabbatical leave. Yet another essay could be written about the bibliographic process, including my belated discovery that the reason for coincidence between the cases I had selected for study and those used by the Board of General Proprietors of East New Jersey for their own advantage in the late nineteenth century had much to do with the fact that the Proprietors and others were responsible for what was published and what was not.

I use the social science rather than the legal method of referring to law cases in the text; however, in the legal citations below, I use the bibliographic custom of the law. The citation system used is generally based on *The Bluebook: A Uniform System of Citation*, 16th ed. (Cambridge, Mass.: Harvard Law Review Press, 1996). See that document for meanings of abbreviations. Where I lack full citations, I give the secondary source I used. I also give fuller publishing information for some cases the reports of which were specially published.

Legal Citations

Alliance against IFQs v. Brown 1996, 84 F. 3rd 343 (9th Cir.).

Arnold v. Mundy 1821, 6 N.J.L. 1 (Sup. Ct.).

Attorney-General v. Philpott 1631 (in MacGrady 1975).

Attorney General v. Richards 1795, 2 Anstr. 603, 3 Rev. Rep. 632.

Attorney-General v. Sooy Oyster Company 1909, 78 N.J.L., 49 Vroom. (E. and A.), 394.

Bateman v. Hollinger et al. 1894, 30 A. 1107 (Court of Chancery of New Jersey, December 13).

Bell v. Gough 1852, 23 N.J.L. 624.

Bennett v. Boggs 1831, 1 Bald. C.C. 60. Published as *The Opinion of the Circuit Court of New Jersey on the Rights of Fishery in the River Delaware; Delivered by Justice Baldwin*. Philadelphia: Printed by Thomas Kite, 1831.

Blundell v. Catterall 1821, 5 B. and Ald. 268, 275, 106 Eng. Rep. 1190, 1193 (K.B.).

Brown v. De Groff 1888, 14 A. 219, 50 N.J.L. 409, 7 Am. St. Rep. 794.

Browne v. Kennedy 1821, 5 Harris and Johnson 195 (Md.).

Carson v. Blazer 1810, 2 Binney 475 (Pa.).

Cobb v. Davenport 1867, 32 N.J.L. 369 (Sup. Ct.).

Commonwealth v. Cyrus Alger 1851 (Suffolk and Nantucket), 52 (Ma.).

Corfield v. Coryell 1825, 6 Fed. Cas. 546 C.C.E.D. Pa. 1825. Published as *New-Jersey Oyster Rights, and Territorial Limits. Circuit Court of the United States for the Eastern District of Pennsylvania. Edward D. Corfield v. Daniel Carrall [sic]*. Philadelphia, 1825.

De Graff v. Truesdale 1887, 10 N.J.L.J. 90, N.J. Sup.

Douglas v. Seacoast Products, Inc. 1977, 431 U.S. 265.

Fitzgerald v. Faunce 1884, Court of Errors and Appeals [Supreme Court]. 46 N.J.L. 536.

Geer v. State of Connecticut 1895, 40 L. Ed 112 (U.S.).

Gibbons v. Ogden 1824, 22 U.S. 1.

Gough v. Bell 1850, 22 N.J.L. 441 (Sup. Ct. 1850), aff'd, 23 N.J.L. 624 (E. and A. 1852), originally tried in 21 N.J.L. 156 (Sup. Ct. 1847); reappeared in federal district court as ejectment case in 1853 (see Grier 1864).

Grace v. Willetts 1888, 50 N.J.L. 414 14 A. 559.

Illinois Central Railway Company v. State of Illinois 1892, 146 U.S. 387.

John Den ex dem. William C. H. Waddell v. Merrit Martin and Others (or *Den, Waddell's Lessee v. Martin et al.*) 1837. Published as *The Decision of the Circuit Court of the United States for the District of New Jersey on the Rights of the Proprietors . . . Delivered at October Term, 1837*. New York: James Van Norden.

Keen v. Rice 1822; *Report of a Cause [sic] Tried in the District Court of Philadelphia . . . April 24, 1822, John Keen v. Phillip Rice, Involving the Right of New Jersey to the Oyster-Beds in Maurice River Cove*. Bridgeton, N.J.

Lucas v. South Carolina Coastal Council 1992, 112 U.S. S. Ct. 2886.

Lusardi v. Curtis Point Property Owners Ass'n 1981, 86 N.J. 217.

Magnuson Fishery Conservation and Management Act 1976 (94-265, as amended). 16 U.S.C. 1801.

Martin et al. v. Waddell's Lessee 1842, 41 U.S. (16 Pet.) 367.

Matthews v. Bay Head Improvement Association, Inc. 1987, 95 N.J. 306, 471 A. 2nd 355 [syllabus, 1984].

McCready v. Commonwealth of Virginia 1876, 94 U.S. 391.

Metzger v. Post 1882, 44 N.J.L. 74, 43 Am. Rep. 341.

Mugler v. Kansas 1887, 123 U.S. 623, 669.

Murphy v. Ryan 1868, Ir. R.-C. L. 143, 152.

National Audubon Society v. Superior Court (Mono Lake) 1983, 333 Cal. 3rd 419, 189 Cal. Reptr. 346, 658 P. 2nd 709.

Neptune City v. Avon-by-the-Sea 1972, 61 N.J. 296, 304, 294 A. 2nd 47.

Palmer v. Mulligan 1805, 3 Caines 307 (N.Y. S. Ct. 105).

Pearson v. Mosbacher 1991, 762 F. Supp. 370 (D.D.C.); decided with and cited as *Seawatch Int'l v. Mosbacher* 1991.

People of the State of New York v. Central Railroad of New Jersey ca. 1871, Court of Appeals, New York State, referenced in Randolph (1871: 961).

Phillips Petroleum v. Mississippi 1988, 484 U.S. 469.

Polhemus v. Bateman 1897, 37 A. 1015, 60 N.J.L. 163.
Polhemus v. State of New Jersey 1894, 57 N.J.L. 348.
Pollard's Lessee v. Hagan 1845, 44 U.S. (3 How.) 212.
Prior of Tynemouth 1291 (MacGrady 1975).
Russell v. Jersey Company 1854, 15 How. 426.
Seawatch Int'l v. Mosbacher 1991, 762 F. Supp. 370 (D.D.C.).
Shepard and Layton v. Leverson 1808, 2 N.J.L. 391 (N.J. Sup.).
Sir Henry Constable's Case 1601 (cited in MacGrady 1975).
State v. Abraham Post 1893, 26 A. 683, 55 N.J.L. 264 (N.J. Sup.).
State v. Mayor of Jersey City 1856, 25 N.J.L. 525, 528 (Sup. Ct.).
State v. Mott. See New Jersey Bureau of Shell Fisheries 1906.
State v. Taylor 1858, 27 N.J.L. 117, 72 Am. Dec. 347.
Stevens v. Paterson and Newark Railroad Company 1870, 34 N.J.L. 532 (E. and A.).
Townsend v. Brown 1853, 24 N.J.L. 80.
Virginia Matthews et al. v. Bay Head Improvement Assoc., Etc. et al. 1984 A-104; Syllabus, J. Schreiber, writing for the Court.
Wooley v. Campbell 1874, 37 N.J.L. 163.
Yard v. Carman 1812, 3 N.J.L. 936.

Other References

Abrams, Robert, and Val Washington. 1990. "The Misunderstood Law of Public Nuisance: A Comparison with Private Nuisance Twenty Years after *Boomer*." *Albany Law Review* 54: 359–99.

Acheson, James M. 1987. "The Lobster Fiefs Revisited: Economic and Ecologic Effects of Territoriality in Maine Lobster Fishing." Pp. 37–65 in Bonnie J. McCay and James M. Acheson, eds., *The Question of the Commons: The Culture and Ecology of Communal Resources*. Tucson: University of Arizona Press.

Agnello, Richard J., and Lawrence P. Donnelley. 1984. "Regulation and the Structure of Property Rights: The Case of the U.S. Oyster Industry." *Research in Law and Economics* 6: 165–72.

Anderson, Lee G. 1995. "A Commentary on the Views of Environmental Groups on Access Control in Fisheries." *Ocean and Coastal Management* 28 (1–3): 165–88.

Anderson, Terry L., and Peter Hill. 1977. "From Free Grass to Fences: Transforming the Commons of the American West." Pp. 200–16 in Garrett Hardin and John Baden, eds., *Managing the Commons*. San Francisco: W. H. Freeman and Company.

Anderson, Terry L., and Donald R. Leal. 1991. *Free-Market Environmentalism*. Boulder, Colo.: Pacific Research Institute for Public Policy and Westview Press.

Angell, Joseph. 1826. *A Treatise on the Right of Property in Tide Waters and in the Soil and Shores Thereof. To Which Is Added an Appendix, Containing the Principal Adjudged Cases*. Littleton, Colo.: F. B. Rothman. Reprinted 1847, 1983.

Anonymous. 1864. *An Appeal to the Legislature, Asking Them to Inquire into the Rights of the State in Lands under Water in New York Bay, Etc.* (Includes Senate Bills nos. 29 and 154 and an editorial from the *Newark Daily Advertiser,* Saturday, March 5, 1864.) New York: John F. Trow, Printer. 30 pp.

——. 1881. *East Jersey Proprietary Rights: Abstract of Title and Opinions of Chancellor Kent and E. Van Arsdale, Esq. 1497–1881.* Trenton, N.J.: Naar, Day and Naar, Printers and Stationers.

——. 1894. "Oysters and the Riparian Grantees." *New Jersey Law Journal* 17: 155–57.

——. 1940. "Oyster Industry Once of Major Importance in Keyport, Vicinity." *Matawan Journal,* October 17.

——. 1970. "The Public Trust in Tidal Areas: A Sometimes Submerged Traditional Doctrine." *Yale Law Review* 79: 762–89.

——. 1982. "*Tangier Sound Waterman's Association v. Douglas:* Chesapeake Bay Blue Crab Restrictions Held Unconstitutional." *Territorial Sea* 2 (2): 2–5, 10–12.

Apparadurai, Arjun, ed. 1986. *The Social Life of Things: Commodities in Cultural Perspective.* Cambridge: Cambridge University Press.

Archer, John E. 1990. *By a Flash and a Scare: Incendiarism, Animal Maiming, and Poaching in East Anglia, 1815–1870.* Oxford: Clarendon Press.

Bates, Robert H. 1992. *Social Dilemmas and Rational Individuals: An Essay on the New Institutionalism.* Duke University Program in Political Economy, Papers in International Political Economy, Working Paper Number 164.

Bebout, John E. 1931. "Documents and Readings in New Jersey Government." Vol. 1. Photo-Lithoprint reproduction of author's manuscript by Edwards Brothers, Ann Arbor, Mich.

Belsky, Martin H. 1992. "The Public Trust Doctrine and Takings: A Post-Lucas View." Pp. 71–93 in The Government Law Center, *The Use of the Public Trust Doctrine as a Management Tool for Public and Private Lands, December 4, 1992.* Albany, N.Y.: Albany Law School.

Berger, Jonathan, and John W. Sinton. 1985. *Water, Earth and Fire: Land Use and Environmental Planning in the New Jersey Pine Barrens.* Baltimore: Johns Hopkins University Press.

Berkes, Fikret, ed. 1989. *Common Property Resources: Ecology and Community-Based Sustainable Development.* London: Belhaven Press.

Berkes, Fikret, David Feeny, Bonnie J. McCay, and James M. Acheson. 1989. "The Benefit of the Commons." *Nature* 340 (July): 91–93.

Blackford, Eugene G. 1885. "Report on an Oyster Investigation in New York with the Steamer *Lookout.*" Pp. 157–63 in *Report of [United States] Commissioner of Fish and Fisheries.* Washington, D.C.: Government Printing Office.

Blaikie, Piers M. 1994. *Political Ecology in the 1990s: An Evolving View of Nature and Society.* CASID Distinguished Speaker Series no. 13, Michigan State University, Center for Advanced Study of International Development, Ann Arbor, Mich.

Board of American Proprietors of East New Jersey. 1885. *Bi-Centennial Celebration of the Board of American Proprietors of East New Jersey. At Perth Amboy, Tuesday November 25, 1884.* Newark, N.J.: Press of the Advertiser Printing House.

Board of General Proprietors of the Eastern Division of New Jersey. 1825. *The Case of the Proprietors of East New-Jersey with the Opinions of Counsel on the Same*. Newark, N.J.: Printed by W. Tuttle and Company.

Board of Proprietors of East New-Jersey. 1837. *The Decision of the Circuit Court of the United States for the District of New Jersey on the Rights of the Proprietors of the Eastern Division of the State of New-Jersey. Delivered at October Term, 1837. Printed by Order of the Proprietors of East New-Jersey*. New York: James Van Norden.

Bowman, Isaiah. 1940. "Science and Social Effects: Three Failures." *Scientific Monthly* 50: 289–98.

Bromley, Daniel W. 1982. "Land and Water Problems in an Institutional Perspective." *American Journal of Agricultural Economics* 64: 834–44.

Brooks, William K. 1891. *The Oyster: A Popular Summary of a Scientific Study*. Baltimore, Md.: Johns Hopkins Press.

Burrowes, Todd R. 1988. "Supreme Court Reinvigorates the Public Trust while Settling Its Boundaries." *Territorial Sea* 8 (1): 1–10.

Bush, Bernard, comp. 1986. *Laws of the Royal Colony of New Jersey*. Vol. 3: *1760–1769*. Trenton, N.J.: New Jersey State Library, Bureau of Archives and History.

Calabresi, Guido, and F. Bobbitt. 1978. *Tragic Choices*. New York: Norton.

Christy, Francis T., Jr. 1973. *Fishermen's Quotas: A Tentative Suggestion for Domestic Management*. University of Rhode Island, Law of the Sea Institute, Occasional Papers 19. 7 pp.

Ciriacy-Wantrup, S. W., and Richard C. Bishop. 1975. "'Common Property' and Natural Resources Policy." *Natural Resources Journal* 15 (4): 713–27.

Clark, Eleanor. 1964. *The Oysters of Locmariaquer*. Chicago: University of Chicago Press.

Clevenger, William M. 1903. *The Courts of New Jersey: Their Origin, Composition and Jurisdiction. Also, Some Account of Their Origin and Jurisdiction, by Edward Q. Keasbey*. Plainfield: New Jersey Law Journal Publishing Company.

Coase, Ronald H. 1960. "The Problem of Social Cost." *Journal of Law and Economics* 3: 1–44.

Coastal States Organization. 1990. *Putting the Public Trust Doctrine to Work*. Ed. David Slade. Washington, D.C.: Coastal States Organization.

Coquillette, Daniel R. 1979. "Mosses from an Old Manse: Another Look at Some Historic Property Cases about the Environment." *Cornell Law Review* 64 (5): 761–821.

Cordell, John, ed. 1989. *A Sea of Small Boats*. Cultural Survival Report 26. Cambridge, Mass.: Cultural Survival.

Coudert, Frederick R. 1909. "Riparian Rights: A Perversion of Stare Decisis." *Columbia Law Review* 9: 217–37.

Cox, Susan J. B. 1985. "No Tragedy on the Common." *Environmental Ethics* 7: 49–61.

Creed, Carolyn F. 1991. "Cutting Up the Pie: Private Moves and Public Debates in the Social Construction of a Fishery." Ph.D. dissertation, Department of Anthropology, Rutgers the State University.

Cronon, William, Jr. 1983. *Changes in the Land: Indians, Colonists, and the Ecology of New England*. New York: Hill and Wang.

Cushing, John D. 1978. *The Earliest Printed Laws of New Jersey, 1703–1722,* with editorial notes by John D. Cushing. Wilmington, Del.: M. Glazier.

Dana, Samuel Trask, and Sally K. Fairfax. 1980. *Forest and Range Policy: Its Development in the United States*. 2nd ed. New York: McGraw-Hill.

Delo, Lew R. 1974. "The English Doctrine of Custom in Oregon Property Law: *State ex rel. Thorn v. Hay*." *Environmental Law* 4: 383–417.

Del Sordo, Stephen G. 1985. "Oysters and Bayshore Towns." Paper presented at the conference Man and Bay Together, cosponsored by Lehigh University and the Wetlands Institute, Newark, Del., May 18.

Demsetz, Harold. 1967. "Toward a Theory of Property Rights." *American Economic Review* 62 (2): 347–59.

Doner, Henry L. 1987. "Riparian Land Rights in New Jersey." *New Jersey Law Journal* 119 (3): 1, 23–24.

Douglas, Mary. 1986. *How Institutions Think*. Syracuse, N.Y.: Syracuse University Press.

——. 1994. "Institutions Are the Product." Talk delivered at the Sixth International Conference on Socio-Economics, Jouy-en-Josas, France, July 15–17.

Dryzek, John S. 1987. *Rational Ecology: Environment and Political Economy*. Oxford: Basil Blackwell.

——. 1990. *Discursive Democracy: Politics, Policy and Political Science*. Cambridge: Cambridge University Press.

Echevarria, John, and Raymond Booth Eby, eds. 1995. *Let the People Judge: Wise Use and the Private Property Rights Movement*. Covelo, Calif.: Island Press.

Elmer, Lucius Quintus Cincinnatus. 1872. *The Constitution and Government of the State of New Jersey, with Biographical Sketches of the Governors from 1776 to 1845 and Reminiscences of the Bench and Bar during More Than Half a Century*. Newark, N.J.: M. R. Dennis.

Emmerson, Donald K. 1980. *Rethinking Artisanal Fisheries Development: Western Concepts, Asian Experiences*. World Bank Staff Working Paper no. 423. Washington, D.C.: World Bank.

Fee, Walter R. 1933. *The Transition from Aristocracy to Democracy in New Jersey 1789–1829*. Somerville, N.J.: Somerset Press.

Feeny, David, Fikret Berkes, Bonnie J. McCay, and James M. Acheson. 1990. "The Tragedy of the Commons: Twenty-Two Years Later." *Human Ecology* 18 (1): 1–19.

Fegley, Stephen R., Susan E. Ford, John N. Kraueter, and Harold H. Haskin. N.d. "The Persistence of New Jersey's Seed Beds in the Presence of MSX Disease and Harvest: Management's Role." Typescript, 27 pp. Bivalve, N.J.: Haskin Shellfish Research Laboratory, Rutgers the State University.

Fleming, Thomas. 1977. *New Jersey: A Bicentennial History*. New York: W. W. Norton and Company.

Ford, Susan E. 1996. Personal communication, Port Norris, N.J., July 10.

——. 1997. "History and Present Status of Molluscan Shellfisheries from Barnegat Bay to Delaware Bay." Pp. 119–40 in Clyde MacKenzie, Victor Berrell, Aaron Rosenfeld, and Willis Hobart, eds., *The History, Present Condition, and Future of the Mollusk Fisheries of North and Central America and Europe,* vol. 1. NOAA Technical Report 127. Washington, D.C.: Government Printing Office.

Franke, Richard W., and Barbara H. Chasin. 1980. *Seeds of Famine: Ecological Destruction and the Development Dilemma in the West African Sahel.* Montclair, N.J.: Allenheld, Osmun.

Friedelbaum, Stanley H. 1979. "Constitutional Law and Judicial Policy Making." Pp. 197–228 in R. Lehne and A. Rosenthal, eds., *Politics in New Jersey.* Rev. ed. New Brunswick, N.J.: Eagleton Institute of Politics, Rutgers University.

Friedman, Lawrence M. 1973. *A History of American Law.* New York: Simon and Schuster.

——. 1985. *A History of American Law.* 2nd ed. New York: Simon and Schuster.

Gabriel, Ralph Henry. 1921. *The Evolution of Long Island: A Story of Land and Sea.* Port Washington, N.Y.: Ira J. Friedman.

Gersuny, Carl, and J. J. Poggie, Jr. 1974. "Luddites and Fishermen: A Note on Response to Technological Change." *Maritime Studies and Management* 2: 38–47.

Giddens, Anthony. 1971. *Capitalism and Modern Social Theory: An Analysis of the Writings of Marx, Durkheim and Max Weber.* Cambridge: Cambridge University Press.

——. 1984. *The Constitution of Society.* Berkeley: University of California Press.

Goldfarb, William. 1996. Personal communication, New Brunswick, N.J., February.

Goldschore, Lewis P. 1979. *The New Jersey Riparian Rights Handbook, Prepared for the County and Municipal Government Study Commission, State of New Jersey.* 2nd ed. Trenton, N.J.

Goode, George Brown. 1881. *The First Decade of the United States Fish Commission: Its Plan of Work and Accomplished Results, Scientific and Economical.* Salem, Mass.: Salem Press.

——. 1887. *A Geographical Review of the Fisheries Industries and Fishing Communities for the Year 1880.* The Fisheries and Fishing Industries of the United States, sec. 2, ed. G. B. Goode. Washington, D.C.: Government Printing Office.

Gordon, H. Scott. 1954. "The Economic Theory of a Common Property Resource: The Fishery." *Journal of Political Economy* 62: 124–42.

Gordon, Thomas F. 1834. *A Gazette of the State of New Jersey.* Trenton, N.J.: Daniel Fenton.

Government Law Center. 1991. *The Public Trust Doctrine.* Conference proceedings, December 6. Albany, N.Y.: Albany Law School.

——. 1992. *The Use of the Public Trust Doctrine as a Management Tool for Public and Private Lands.* Conference proceedings, December 4. Albany, N.Y.: Albany Law School.

——. 1993. *After "Lucas": The Public Trust Doctrine and Public Nuisance Law in New York.* Conference proceedings, December 10. Albany, N.Y.: Albany Law School.

——. 1994. *The Public Trust Doctrine on Long Island: Public and Private Rights in Coastal Areas.* Conference proceedings, December 15. Albany, N.Y.: Albany Law School.

——. 1995. *The Public Trust Doctrine: Protecting Public Resources for the Needs of Today and for Future Generations*. Conference proceedings, December 15. Albany, N.Y.: Albany Law School.

Granovetter, Mark. 1992. "Economic Action and Social Structure: The Problem of Embeddedness." In M. Granovetter and R. Swedberg, eds., *The Sociology of Economic Life*. Boulder, Colo.: Westview Press.

Greenhouse, Carol. 1986. *Praying for Justice*. Ithaca, N.Y.: Cornell University Press.

Grier, [Robert C.]. 1864. *Notes of Charge of Chief Justice Grier. Den ex Dem. Mary Bell, vs. J. B. Coles et al., Ejectment, tried Sept. 28, 1853. Published with Report of the Commissioners on the Extent and Value of Lands under Water in the County of Hudson, Read January 25, 1849, and Ordered to be Printed*. New York: John F. Trow, Printer. Pp. 83–86.

Grumet, Robert Steven. 1979. "'We Are Not So Great Fools': Changes in Upper Delawaran Socio-Political Life, 1630–1758." Ph.D. dissertation, Department of Anthropology, Rutgers University.

Habermas, Jürgen. 1984. *The Theory of Communicative Action*. Vol. 1, *Reason and the Rationalization of Society*. Boston: Beacon Press.

Hahn, Steven. 1982. "Hunting, Fishing, and Foraging: Common Rights and Class Relations in the Postbellum South." *Radical History Review* 26: 37–64.

Hale, Sir Matthew. 1787. *A Collection of Tracts Relative to the Law of England: From Manuscripts Now First Edited by Frances Hargrave*. London: Printed by T. Wright and Sold by E. Brooke.

Hall, Ansley. 1894. "Notes on the Oyster Industry of New Jersey." Pp. 463–528 in *Report of the Commission (U.S. Commission of Fish and Fisheries) for the Year Ending June 30, 1892*. Washington, D.C.: Government Printing Office.

Hammond, John L., and Barbara Hammond. 1920. *The Village Labourer 1760–1832: A Study in the Government of England before the Reform Bill*. Rev. ed. London: Longmans, Green and Company.

Hanna, Susan. 1990. "The Eighteenth Century English Commons: A Model for Ocean Management." *Ocean and Shoreline Management* 14: 155–72.

Hardin, Garrett. 1968. "The Tragedy of the Commons." *Science* 162: 1243–48.

Hargis, William J., Jr., and Dexter S. Haven. 1988. "Rehabilitation of the Troubled Oyster Industry of the Lower Chesapeake Bay." *Journal of Shellfish Research* 7 (2): 271–79.

Haskin, Harold H. 1991. Personal communication, Bivalve, N.J.

——. 1996. Personal communication, Bivalve, N.J., July 10.

Haskin, Harold H., and Susan Ford. 1979. Development of resistance to *Minchinia nelsoni* (MSX) mortality in laboratory-reared and native oyster stocks in Delaware Bay. *Marine Fisheries Review* 41 (1–2): 54–63.

Havey, Melody F. 1994. "*Stevens v. City of Cannon Beach:* Does Oregon's Doctrine of Custom Find a Way around *Lucas?*" *Ocean and Coastal Law Journal* 1: 109–22.

Helgason, Agnar, and Gísli Pálsson. 1996. "Contested Commodities: The Moral Landscape of Modernist Regimes." Paper presented at the European Association of Social Anthropologists, Barcelona, July 12–15.

Hobsbawm, Eric, and Terrence Ranger, eds. 1983. *The Invention of Tradition.* Cambridge: Cambridge University Press.

Horwitz, Morton J. 1971. "The Emergence of an Instrumental Conception of American Law, 1780–1820." Pp. 287–326 in Donald Fleming and Bernard Bailyn, eds., *Law in American History.* Boston: Little, Brown and Company.

——. 1973. "The Transformation in the Conception of Property in American Law, 1780–1860." *University of Chicago Law Review* 40: 248–90.

——. 1977. *The Transformation of American Law, 1790–1860.* Cambridge, Mass.: Harvard University Press.

Howkins, Alun. 1979. "Economic Crime and Class Law: Poaching and the Game Laws, 1840–1880." Pp. 273–87 in S. B. Burman and B. E. Harrell-Bond, eds., *The Imposition of Law.* New York: Academic Press.

Hull, H., comp. 1924. *Oke's Fishery Laws.* 4th ed. London: Butterworth and Company.

Humbach, John A. 1993. "Evolving Thresholds of Nuisance and the Takings Clause." *Columbia Journal of Environmental Law* 18 (1): 1–29.

Hurst, J. Willard. 1960. *Law and Social Process in the United States.* Ann Arbor: University of Michigan Law School.

Hyman, Harold M. 1986. *American Singularity: The 1787 Northwest Ordinance, the 1862 Homestead and Morrill Acts, and the 1944 G.I. Bill.* Athens: University of Georgia Press.

Ingersoll, Ernest. 1881. *A Report on the Oyster-Industry of the United States.* Monograph B, Tenth Census of the United States. Washington, D.C.: Government Printing Office.

——. 1887. "The Oyster, Scallop, Clam, Mussel, and Abalone Industries." Pp. 505–626 in G. B. Goode, ed., *Fisheries and Fishing Industries of the United States. Sec. V. History and Methods of the Fisheries, Vol. II.* Washington, D.C.: Government Printing Office.

Jaffee, Leonard R. 1971. "State Citizen Rights Respecting Great-Water Resource Allocation: From Rome to New Jersey." *Rutgers Law Review* 25 (4): 571–710.

——. 1974. "The Public Trust Doctrine Is Alive and Kicking in New Jersey Tidalwaters: *Neptune City v. Avon-by-the-Sea*—A Case of Happy Atavism?" *Natural Resources Journal* 14: 309–35.

Jenkins, John A. 1991. "Strong Arm of the Law." *Rutgers Magazine* 70 (3): 30–35.

Jentoft, Svein. 1989. "Fisheries Co-management: Delegating Government Responsibility to Fishermen's Organizations." *Marine Policy* 13: 137–54.

Jentoft, Svein, and Bonnie J. McCay. 1995. "User Participation in Fisheries Management: Lessons Drawn from International Experiences." *Marine Policy* 19 (3): 227–46.

Johannes, Robert E. 1978. "Traditional Marine Conservation Methods in Oceania and Their Demise." *Annual Review of Ecology and Systematics* 9: 349–64.

——. 1981. *Words of the Lagoon: Fishing and Marine Lore in the Palau District of Micronesia.* Berkeley: University of California Press.

Johnson, Judith Jones, and Charles Fremond Johnson III. 1975. "The Mississippi Public Trust Doctrine: Public and Private Rights in the Coastal Zone." *Mississippi Law Journal* 46 (1): 84–117.

Johnson, R. D., and G. D. Libecap. 1982. "Contracting Problems and Regulation: The Case of the Fishery." *American Economic Review* 72: 1005–22.

Johnson, Ralph W. 1989. "Water Pollution and the Public Trust Doctrine." *Environmental Law* 19: 485–513.

Johnson, Ralph W., Craighton Goeppele, David Jansen, and Rachael Paschal. 1992. "The Public Trust Doctrine and Coastal Zone Management in Washington State." *Washington Law Review* 67 (3): 521–97.

Keasbey, Edward Q. 1912. *The Courts and Lawyers of New Jersey 1661–1912*. New York: Lewis Historical Publishing Company.

Keifer, David R. N.d. [1993]. "Surf Clam and Ocean Quahog Vessel Allocations, 1977–1992." Typescript. Dover, Del.: Mid-Atlantic Fishery Management Council.

Kennedy, Victor S., and Linda L. Breisch. 1983. "Sixteen Decades of Political Management of the Oyster Fishery in Maryland's Chesapeake Bay." *Journal of Environmental Management* 16: 153–71.

Kent, James. 1826. *Commentaries on American Law*. New York: Published by O. Halsted. Facsimile ed., New York: Da Capo Press, 1971.

Keys, Moya. 1986. "The Hackensack Meadowlands—State or Private Interest?: An Analysis of the Tidelands Doctrine." *Rutgers Law Review* 38 (2): 377–401.

Kochiss, John M. 1974. *Oystering from New York to Boston*. Middletown, Conn.: Wesleyan University Press for Mystic Seaport.

La Rue, L. H. 1995. *Constitutional Law as Fiction: Narrative in the Rhetoric of Authority*. University Park: Pennsylvania State University Press.

Leaming, Aaron, and Jacob Spicer, comps. 1758. *The Grants, Concessions and Original Constitutions of the Province of New-Jersey*. Philadelphia: W. Bradford.

Lévi-Strauss, Claude. 1963. *Structural Anthropology*. Trans. Claire Jacob. New York: Basic Books.

Lewis, Thomas B., and Ivar E. Strand, Jr. 1978. "*Douglas v. Seacoast Products, Inc.*: The Legal and Economic Consequences for the Maryland Oystery." *Maryland Law Review* 38 (1): 1–36.

Libecap, Gary. 1986. "Property Rights in Economic History: Implications for Research." *Explorations in Economic History* 23: 227–52.

——. 1989. *Contracting for Property Rights*. New York: Cambridge University Press.

Little, Daniel. 1991. *Varieties of Social Explanation: An Introduction to the Philosophy of Social Science*. Boulder, Colo.: Westview Press.

Lloyd, William Forster. 1968 [1837]. *Lectures on Population, Value, Poor-Laws, and Rent, Delivered in the University of Oxford during the Years 1832, 1833, 1834, 1835, and 1836*. Reprints of Economic Classics. New York: Augustus M. Kelley.

Lockwood, Samuel. 1882. "The Oyster Interests of New Jersey." Pp. 217–350 in *The Fifth Annual Report of the Bureau of Statistics of Labor and Industries of New Jersey*. Trenton, N.J.

——. 1883. "The American Oyster, Its Natural History, and the Oyster Industry in New

Jersey." Pp. 219–350 in *The Fifth Annual Report of the Bureau of Statistics of Labor and Industries of the State of New Jersey*. Trenton, N.J.

Ludewig, Dorothy F. D. 1971. *Timely Told Tales of Woodbridge Township*. Woodbridge, N.J.: Woodbridge Township Board of Education.

Lund, Thomas A. 1975. "British Wildlife Law before the American Revolution: Lessons from the Past." *Michigan Law Review* 74 (1): 49–74.

——. 1980. *American Wildlife Law*. Berkeley: University of California Press.

MacDonald, Marshall. 1887. "The Fisheries of the Delaware River." Pp. 654–57 in G. B. Goode, ed., *Fisheries and Fishing Industries of the United States. Sec. V. History and Methods of the Fisheries, Vol. II*. Washington, D.C.: Government Printing Office.

MacFarquhar, Neil. 1996. "Court Hears Two States Claim a Piece of History." *New York Times*, April 12, B1, B2.

——. 1997. "Ruling like Solomon's Splits Ellis Island in Two." *New York Times*, April 2, A1, B4.

MacGrady, Glenn J. 1975. "The Navigability Concept in the Civil and Common Law: Historical Development, Current Importance, and Some Doctrines That Don't Hold Water." *Florida State University Law Review* 3: 511–615.

Macinko, Seth. 1993. "Public or Private?: United States Commercial Fisheries Management and the Public Trust Doctrine, Reciprocal Challenges." *Natural Resources Journal* 33: 919–55.

MacKenzie, Clyde L., Jr. 1977. "Predation on Hard Clam (*Mercenaria mercenaria*) Populations." *Transactions of the American Fisheries Society* 206 (6): 530–37.

——. 1991a. *The Fisheries of Raritan Bay*. New Brunswick, N.J.: Rutgers University Press.

——. 1991b. "The Literary Contributions of Ernest Ingersoll." *Explorers Journal* (Spring): 25–28.

Maine, Sir Henry. 1884. *Ancient Law*. 10th ed. New York: Henry Holt.

Marchak, M. Patricia. 1988–89. "What Happens When Common Property Becomes Uncommon?" *BC Studies*, no. 80 (Winter): 3–23.

Martin, Irene. 1994. *Legacy and Testament: The Story of Columbia River Gillnetters*. Pullman: Washington State University Press.

Marx, Karl. 1946. *Capital: A Critique of Political Economy*. Trans. Samuel Moore, ed. Frederick Engels. New York: Modern Library.

Matthews, David Ralph. 1993. *Controlling Common Property: Regulating Canada's East Coast Fishery*. Toronto: University of Toronto Press.

Maxwell, Donald. 1983. Personal communication, Leeds Point, N.J., June 29.

McCay, Bonnie J. 1978. "Systems Ecology, People Ecology, and the Anthropology of Fishing Communities." *Human Ecology* 6 (4): 397–422.

——. 1980. "A Fishermen's Cooperative, Limited: Indigenous Resource Management in a Complex Society." *Anthropological Quarterly* 53: 29–38.

——. 1981a. "Development Issues in Fisheries as Agrarian Systems." *Culture and Agriculture: Bulletin of the Anthropological Study Group on Agrarian Systems* no. 11, pp. 1–8.

——. 1981b. "Optimal Foragers or Political Actors? Ecological Analyses of a New Jersey Fishery." *American Ethnologist* 8: 356–82.

——. 1984. "The Pirates of Piscary: Ethnohistory of Illegal Fishing in New Jersey." *Ethnohistory* 31: 17–37.

——. 1987. "The Culture of the Commoners: Historical Observations on Old and New World Fisheries." Pp. 195–216 in Bonnie J. McCay and James M. Acheson, eds., *The Question of the Commons: The Culture and Ecology of Communal Resources*. Tucson: University of Arizona Press.

——. 1988. "Muddling through the Clam Beds: Cooperative Management of New Jersey's Hard Clam Spawner Sanctuaries." *Journal of Shellfish Research* 7 (2): 327–40.

——. 1989a. "Sea Tenure and the Culture of the Commoners." Pp. 203–26 in John Cordell, ed., *A Sea of Small Boats*. Cambridge, Mass.: Cultural Survival.

——. 1989b. "Co-Management of a Clam Revitalization Project: The New Jersey 'Spawner Sanctuary' Program." Pp. 103–24 in E. Pinkerton, ed., *Cooperative Management of Local Fisheries*. Vancouver: University of British Columbia Press.

——. 1993. "The Making of an Environmental Doctrine: Public Trust and American Shellfishermen." Pp. 85–96 in Kay Milton, ed., *Environmentalism: The View from Anthropology*. London: Routledge.

——. 1995a. "Common and Private Concerns." *Advances in Human Ecology* 4: 89–116.

——. 1995b. "Social and Ecological Implications of ITQs: An Overview." *Ocean and Coastal Management* 28 (1–3): 3–22.

McCay, Bonnie J., and James M. Acheson, eds. 1987a. *The Question of the Commons: The Culture and Ecology of Communal Resources*. Tucson: University of Arizona Press.

——. 1987b. "Human Ecology of the Commons." Pp. 1–34 in Bonnie J. McCay and James M. Acheson, eds., *The Question of the Commons: The Culture and Ecology of Communal Resources*. Tucson: University of Arizona Press.

McCay, Bonnie J., and Carolyn F. Creed. 1990. "Social Structure and Debates on Fisheries Management in the Mid-Atlantic Surf Clam Fishery." *Ocean and Shoreline Management* 13: 199–229.

——. 1994. "Social Impacts of ITQs in the Sea Clam Fishery." Final Report to the New Jersey Sea Grant College Program, New Jersey Marine Sciences Consortium, February.

McCay, Bonnie J., Carolyn F. Creed, Alan Christopher Finlayson, Richard Apostle, and Knut Mikalsen. 1995. "Individual Transferable Quotas (ITQs) in Canadian and U.S. Fisheries." *Ocean and Coastal Management* 26 (1–3): 85–116.

McCay, Bonnie J., John B. Gatewood, and Carolyn F. Creed. 1990. "Labor and the Labor Process in a Limited Entry Fishery." *Marine Resource Economics* 6: 311–30.

McCay, Bonnie J., and William P. Jenks, III. 1997. "The Importance of Shellfisheries to Coastal Communities: A View from New Jersey Clamming." Pp. 145–55 in Clyde MacKenzie, Victor Berrell, Aaron Rosenfeld, and Willis Hobart, eds., *The History, Present Condition, and Future of the Mollusk Fisheries of North and Central America and Europe*. NOAA Technical Report Series. Washington, D.C.: USGPO.

McCay, Bonnie J., and Svein Jentoft. 1996. "From the Bottom Up: Participatory Issues in Fisheries Management." *Society and Natural Resources* 9: 237–50.

McCay, Bonnie J., and A. P. Vayda. 1992. "The Ecology of Natural Resource Management." Paper presented at the annual meeting of the American Anthropological Association, San Francisco, December 3.

McEvoy, Arthur F. 1986. *The Fisherman's Problem: Ecology and Law in the California Fisheries, 1850–1980*. Cambridge: Cambridge University Press.

McGinnis, William C. 1959. *History of Perth Amboy, N.J., 1651–1959*. Perth Amboy, N.J.: American Publishing Company.

McGoodwin, James R. 1990. *Crisis in the World's Fisheries: People, Problems, and Policies*. Stanford, Calif.: Stanford University Press.

McHugh, J. L. 1972. "Jeffersonian Democracy and the Fisheries." Pp. 134–55 in Brian J. Rothschild, ed., *World Fisheries Policy*. Seattle: University of Washington Press.

Meadows, Dennis L., Thomas Fiddaman, and Diana Shannon. 1991. *Fish Banks, Ltd.: Game Administrator's Manual*. 2nd ed. Durham: Institute for Policy and Social Science Research, University of New Hampshire.

Menzo, Julia. 1996. "Industrial Organization Impacts of ITQs in the Mid-Atlantic Surf Clam and Ocean Quahog Fishery." M.A. thesis, Department of Agricultural Economics, Cook College, Rutgers the State University, New Brunswick, N.J.

Merry, Sally Engle. 1990. *Getting Justice and Getting Even: Legal Consciousness among Working-Class Americans*. Chicago: University of Chicago Press.

Milliken, William J. 1994. "Individual Transferable Fishing Quotas and Antitrust Law." *Ocean and Coastal Law Journal* 1 (1): 35–57.

Moloney, David G., and Peter H. Pearse. 1979. "Quantitative Rights as an Instrument for Regulating Commercial Fisheries." *Journal of the Fisheries Research Board of Canada* 36: 859–66.

Moore, Stuart A. 1888. *A History of the Foreshore and the Law Relating Thereto; with a Hitherto Unpublished Treatise by Lord Hale, Lord Hale's 'De Jure Maris,' and Hall's Essay on the Rights of the Crown in the Seashore*. 3rd ed. London: Stevens and Haynes.

Moss, George H., Jr. 1964. *Nauvoo to the Hook: The Iconography of a Barrier Beach*. Locust, N.J.: Jersey Close Press.

Munsche, P. B. 1981. *Gentlemen and Poachers: The English Game Laws 1761–1831*. Cambridge: Cambridge University Press.

National Research Council. 1986. *Proceedings of the Conference on Common Property Resource Management, April 21–26, 1985*. Washington, D.C.: National Academy Press.

Neher, Philip A., Ragnar Arnason, and Nina Mollett, eds. 1989. *Rights Based Fishing*. Dordrecht: Kluwer Academic Publishing. Proceedings of the NATO Advanced Research Workshop on Scientific Foundations for Rights Based Fishing, Reykjavík, Iceland, June 27–July 1.

Nelson, Thurlow C. 1933. "Report of the Biologist." Pp. 16–22 in *Annual Report for 1932–33 of the New Jersey Agricultural Experiment Station,* New Brunswick, N.J.

——. N.d. *Our Friend the Oyster.* Trenton, N.J.: Department of Conservation and Economic Development, Division of Shellfisheries.

Nelson, William, ed. 1902. *The New Jersey Coast in Three Centuries: History of the New Jersey Coast with Genealogical and Historic-Biographical Appendix.* 3 vols. New York: Lewis Publishing Company.

Netboy, Anthony. 1968. *The Atlantic Salmon: A Vanishing Species?* Boston: Houghton Mifflin.

Netting, Robert McC. 1976. "What Alpine Peasants Have in Common: Observations on Communal Tenure in a Swiss Village." *Human Ecology* 4: 135–46.

Neustadt, Maxine Fern. 1968. *Proprietary Purposes in the Anglo-American Colonies: Problems in the Transplantation of English Patterns of Social Organization.* Ann Arbor, Mich.: University Microfilms International.

New Jersey Board of Commissioners on Lands under Water. 1864. *Report of the Commissioners on the Extent and Value of Lands under Water in the County of Hudson. Read January 25, 1849, and Ordered to be Printed.* New York: John F. Trow, Printer. (Outside cover: *Report of the Commissioners on Lands under Water, 1849. Opinions of Mssrs. Parker, Zabriskie, Frelinghuysen, and Browning, 1864. Notes of Charge of Chief Justice Grier, Bell vs. Coles. Act Appointing Commissioners, 1864. Synopsis of All Grants of Land under Water Made by the State of New Jersey.*)

——. 1865. *Report of Commissioners Appointed to Ascertain the Rights of the State and of Riparian Owners to the Lands Lying under Water.* Trenton, N.J.: Printed by J. R. Freese, State Gazette Office.

New Jersey Board of Health. 1908, 1916. *Annual Reports.* Trenton, N.J.

New Jersey Board of Shell Fisheries. 1909–19. *Annual Reports.* Trenton, N.J.

New Jersey Bureau of Shell Fisheries. 1901–8. *Annual Reports.* Trenton, N.J.

New Jersey Bureau of Statistics of Labor and Industries. 1897. *Nineteenth Annual Report, for Year Ending October 31st, 1896. Trenton.* Part 1: *The Oyster Industry of New Jersey.*

New Jersey Department of Environmental Protection. Division of Marine Services, Office of Coastal Zone Management. 1977. *Riparian Law and Coastal Zone Management in New Jersey: A Staff Briefing Paper.* Trenton, N.J.

——. 1982. *Tidelands Maps and the Coastal Property Owner: A Fact Sheet, Questions, Answers and Where to Turn for Help.* Trenton, N.J.

New Jersey General Assembly. 1799. *Acts of the General Assembly of the State of New Jersey, 1799.* Trenton, N.J.

New Jersey Laws. Various dates, published as *Legislative Documents of New Jersey.* Trenton, N.J.

New Jersey Oyster and Shell Commission. 1901. *Report.* Trenton, N.J.

New Jersey Oyster Commission. 1902. *Report of the Commission for the Investigation of the Oyster Industry, New Jersey Legislature.* Camden, N.J.

New Jersey Riparian Association. 1870. *Facts for the Shore Owners of the State of New Jersey.* New York: V. Seymour, Kennard and Hay.

New Jersey Riparian Commissioners. 1870. "Report." Pp. 1017–20 in *Legislative Documents for 1870*. Trenton, N.J.

——. 1890. *Report of the Riparian Commissioners of the State of New Jersey*. Trenton, N.J.

New Jersey Riparian Committee. 1882. *Report of Joint Committee to Investigate the Acts and Proceedings of the Board of Proprietors of East Jersey Touching the Rights and Interests of the State, and of the Citizens Thereof*. Trenton, N.J.: John L. Murphy, Book and Job Printer.

——. 1906–7. *Testimony Taken before the Committee of the Senate and House of Assembly of the State of New Jersey to Investigate the Granting of Riparian Lands by the State, Etc.* Paterson, N.J.: Chronicle Print.

New Jersey State Oyster Commission. 1899. *Annual Report for the Year Ending October 31st, 1899*. Documents of the State of New Jersey, no. 45.

North, Douglass. 1981. *Structure and Change in Economic History*. New York: W. W. Norton.

——. 1990. *Institutions, Institutional Change and Economic Performance*. Cambridge: Cambridge University Press.

Ogden, O. W. [1828]. *Memorial to the Honorable the Legislature of the State of New Jersey*. 8 pp. Microfiche JMF-0214, New Jersey State Library, Trenton.

Ohnuki-Tierney, Emiko. 1990. "Introduction: The Historicization of Anthropology." Pp. 1–25 in E. Ohnuki-Tierney, ed., *Culture through Time: Anthropological Approaches*. Stanford, Calif.: Stanford University Press.

Olson, Mancur. 1965. *The Logic of Collective Action*. Cambridge, Mass.: Harvard University Press.

Ostrom, Elinor. 1990. *Governing the Commons: The Evolution of Institutions for Collective Action*. New York: Cambridge University Press.

Parker, Cortlandt. 1864. "Opinion of Cortlandt Parker, Esq." Pp. 49–56 in New Jersey Board of Commissioners on Lands under Water, *Report of the Commissioners on the Extent and Value of Lands under Water in the County of Hudson. Read January 25, 1849, and Ordered to be Printed.*

——. 1885. "Historical Address." Pp. 7–43 in *Bi-Centennial Celebration of the Board of American Proprietors of East New Jersey. At Perth Amboy, Tuesday November 25, 1884*. Newark, N.J.: Press of the Advertiser Printing House.

Peters, Pauline E. 1987. "Embedded Systems and Rooted Models: The Grazing Lands of Botswana and the Commons Debate." Pp. 171–94 in Bonnie J. McCay and James M. Acheson, eds., *The Question of the Commons: The Culture and Ecology of Communal Resources*. Tucson: University of Arizona Press.

Pinkerton, Evelyn, ed. 1989. *Cooperative Management of Local Fisheries: New Directions for Improved Management and Community Development*. Vancouver: University of British Columbia Press.

Plater, Zygmunt J. B., Robert H. Abrams, and William Goldfarb. 1992. *Environmental Law and Policy: A Coursebook on Nature, Law, and Society*. American Casebook Series. St. Paul, Minn.: West Publishing Company.

Polanyi, Karl, ed. 1957. *Trade and Market in Early Empires*. New York: Free Press.

Pole, J. R. 1978. *The Pursuit of Equality in American History*. Berkeley: University of California Press.

Pomfret, John E. 1964. *The New Jersey Proprietors and Their Lands*. Princeton, N.J.: D. Van Nostrand.

Potter, Stephen. 1988. Personal communication, Absecon, N.J., December.

Powell, W., and P. DiMaggio, eds. 1991. *The New Institutionalism in Organizational Analysis*. Chicago: University of Chicago Press.

Power, Garrett. 1970. "More about Oysters than You Wanted to Know." *Maryland Law Review* 30 (3): 199–225.

Purvis, Thomas L. 1986. *Proprietors, Patronage, and Paper Money: Legislative Politics in New Jersey, 1703–1776*. New Brunswick, N.J.: Rutgers University Press.

Randolph, Theodore F. 1871. "Riparian Commission" section of Governor Randolph's address. Pp. 10–11 in *New Jersey Legislative Documents for 1870*. Trenton, N.J.

Reaney, Bernard. 1970. *The Class Struggle in 19th Century Oxfordshire: The Social and Communal Background to the Otmoor Disturbances of 1830 to 1835*. History Workshop Pamphlet 3. Oxford: History Workshop, Ruskin College.

Reis, Robert I. 1991. "The Public Trust Doctrine—The Search for Future Standards." Paper presented at the conference on the Public Trust Doctrine: The Ownership and Management of Lands, Water, and Living Resources, Albany Law School, Government Law Center, Albany, N.Y., December 6. 43 pp.

Robson, Charles, ed. 1877. *The Biographical Encyclopaedia of New Jersey of the Nineteenth Century*. Philadelphia: Galaxy Publishing Company.

Rose, Carol. 1986. "The Comedy of the Commons: Custom, Commerce, and Inherently Public Property." *University of Chicago Law Review* 53 (3): 711–81.

——. 1994. *Property and Persuasion: Essays on the History, Theory, and Rhetoric of Ownership*. Boulder, Colo.: Westview Press.

Rosen, Lawrence. 1989. *The Anthropology of Justice: Law as Culture in Islamic Society*. Cambridge: Cambridge University Press.

Santopietro, George D., and Leonard A. Shabman. 1992. "Property Rights to the Chesapeake Bay Oyster Fishery: History and Implications." *Society and Natural Resources* 5 (2): 165–78.

Sax, Joseph L. 1970. "The Public Trust Doctrine in Natural Resource Law: Effective Judicial Intervention." *Michigan Law Review* 68: 471–75.

——. 1971. *Defending the Environment: A Strategy for Citizen Action*. New York: Alfred A. Knopf.

——. 1980. "Liberating the Public Trust Doctrine from Its Historical Shackles." *U.C. Davis Law Review* 14 (2): 185–94.

Scheiber, Harry N. 1973. "Property Law, Expropriation, and Resource Allocation by Government: The United States, 1789–1910." *Journal of Economic History* 33: 232–51.

Scott, Anthony. 1955. "The Fishery: The Objectives of Sole Ownership." *Journal of Political Economy* 63: 116–24.

——. 1993. "Obstacles to Fishery Self-Government." *Marine Resource Economics* 8: 187–99.

Scott, F. Richard. 1995. *Institutions and Organizations*. Thousand Oaks, Calif.: Sage Publications.

Scott, James C. 1985. *Weapons of the Weak: Everyday Forms of Peasant Resistance*. New Haven, Conn.: Yale University Press.

Seebohm, Frederic. 1926. *The English Village Community*. Cambridge: Cambridge University Press.

Siddall, Scott E. 1988. "Shellfish Aquaculture as a Cottage Industry: A Model for Development in New York." *Journal of Shellfish Research* 7 (2): 295–301.

Sider, Gerald M. 1980. "The Ties That Bind: Culture and Agriculture, Property and Propriety in the Newfoundland Village Fishery." *Social History* 5 (1): 1–39.

——. 1986. *Culture and Class in Anthropology and History: A Newfoundland Illustration*. Cambridge: Cambridge University Press.

Siegel, Martin. 1987. *The Taney Court, 1837–1864*. Millward, N.Y.: Associated Faculty Press.

Sinclair, Peter R. 1989. "Fisheries and Regional Development: Contradictions of Canadian Policy in the Newfoundland Context." Pp. 105–13 in S. J. Thomas, L. Maril, and E. P. Durrenberger, eds., *Marine Resource Utilization*. Mobile: University of South Alabama Publication Services.

Smith, Lincoln. 1950. "The Great Pond Ordinance—Collectivism in Northern New England." *Boston University Law Review* 30 (April): 178–90.

Smith, M. Estellie. 1984. "The Triage of the Commons." Paper presented at the annual meeting of the Society for Applied Anthropology, March 14–18, Toronto, Canada.

Squires, Dale, James Kirkley, and Clement A. Tisdell. 1995. "Individual Transferable Quotas as a Fisheries Management Tool." *Reviews in Fisheries Science* 3 (2): 141–69.

Stainsby, William. 1902. *The Oyster Industry: A Historical Sketch*. Monographs on New Jersey's Industries from the *Twenty-Fifth Annual Report of the Bureau of Statistics of New Jersey*. Trenton, N.J.

Starr, June, and Jane F. Collier, eds. 1989a. *History and Power in the Study of Law: New Directions in Legal Anthropology*. Ithaca, N.Y.: Cornell University Press.

——. 1989b. "Introduction: Dialogues in Legal Anthropology." Pp. 1–28 in June Starr and Jane F. Collier, eds., *History and Power in the Study of Law: New Directions in Legal Anthropology*. Ithaca, N.Y.: Cornell University Press.

Stevens, Jan S. 1980. "The Public Trust: A Sovereign's Ancient Prerogative Becomes the People's Environmental Right." *U.C. Davis Law Review* 14 (2): 195--232.

Stevens, Lewis Townsend. 1897. *The History of Cape May County, New Jersey, from the Aboriginal Times to the Present Day*. Cape May City, N.J.: Lewis T. Stevens, Publisher.

——. 1933. "Memorandum Book of Jacob Spicer, 1757–1764." *Cape May County Magazine of History and Genealogy* 1: 109–18.

——. 1934. "Jacob Spicer's Memorandum Book (Continued), 1754–1764." *Cape May County Magazine of History and Genealogy* 1: 162–73.

——. 1935. "Jacob Spicer's Memorandum Book—1754–1764, Copied by Lewis T. Stevens." *Cape May County Magazine of History and Genealogy* 1: 182–89.

——. 1943. "Cape May's First Land Purchasers." *Cape May County Magazine of History and Genealogy* 2: 229–31.

Stevenson, Charles H. 1894. *The Oyster Industry of Maryland.* Bulletin of the U.S. Fish Commission 12. Washington, D.C.: Government Printing Office.

——. 1899. "The Shad Fisheries of the Atlantic Coast of the United States." Pp. 101–269 in *Report of the U.S. Commissioner of Fish and Fisheries, 1899.* Washington, D.C.: Government Printing Office.

Stewart, Frank H. 1940. "Cape May County Ratables." *Cape May County Magazine of History and Genealogy* 2: 74–84.

Stutz, Bruce. 1992. *Natural Lives, Modern Times: People and Places of the Delaware River.* New York: Crown Publishers.

Sweet, Gordon. 1941. "Oyster Conservation in Connecticut: Past and Present." *Geographical Review* 31 (4): 591–604.

Swisher, Carl Brent. 1961. *Roger B. Taney.* Hamden, Conn.: Archon Books. Originally published, New York: Macmillan, 1935.

——. 1974. *History of the Supreme Court of the United States.* Vol. 5: *The Taney Period.* New York: Macmillan.

Tawney, R. H. 1912. *The Agrarian Problem in the Sixteenth Century.* Facsimile ed., New York: Burt Franklin, 1961.

Taylor, Lawrence. 1983. Tape transcriptions, interviews in Bivalve, N.J., August 1983. Typescript, author's files.

Thompson, E. P. 1966. *The Making of the English Working Class.* New York: Vintage Books.

——. 1975. *Whigs and Hunters: The Origins of the Black Act.* London: Allen Lane.

——. 1976. "The Grid of Inheritance: A Comment." Pp. 328–60 in Jack Goody, Joan Thirsk, and E. P. Thompson, eds., *Family and Inheritance: Rural Society in Western Europe, 1200–1800.* Cambridge: Cambridge University Press.

——. 1978. *The Poverty of Theory and Other Essays.* New York: Monthly Review Press.

——. 1991. *Customs in Common.* New York: New Press.

Tober, James A. 1981. *Who Owns the Wildlife? The Political Economy of Conservation in Nineteenth-Century America.* Westport, Conn.: Greenwood Press.

Townsend, Ralph E. 1985. "The Right to Fish as an External Benefit of Open Access." *Canadian Journal of Fisheries and Aquatic Sciences* 4: 2050–53.

Turner, Michael. 1984. *Enclosures in Britain, 1750–1830.* London: Macmillan Press.

Umbeck, John R. 1981. *A Theory of Property Rights: With Application to the California Gold Rush.* Ames: Iowa State University Press.

United States Commissioner of Fish and Fisheries. 1885. *Annual Report.* Washington, D.C.: Government Printing Office.

——. 1901. *Fisheries of the Middle Atlantic States.* Washington, D.C.: Government Printing Office.

——. 1904. *Fisheries of the Middle Atlantic States*. Washington, D.C.: Government Printing Office.

van Ginkel, Rob. 1988. "Limited Entry: Panacea or Palliative?" *Journal of Shellfish Research* 7 (2): 309–14.

——. 1989. "'Plunderers' into Planters: Zeeland Oystermen and the Enclosure of the Marine Commons." Pp. 89–105 in J. F. Boissevain and J. Verrips, eds., *Dutch Dilemmas: Anthropologists Look at the Netherlands*. Assen: Van Gorcum.

Vayda, Andrew P. 1996. *Methods and Explanations in the Study of Human Actions and Their Environmental Effects*. CIFOR/WWF Special Publication. Jakarta: Center for International Forestry Research and World Wide Fund for Nature.

Wacker, Peter O. 1975. *Land and People: A Cultural Geography of Preindustrial New Jersey; Origins and Settlement Patterns*. New Brunswick, N.J.: Rutgers University Press.

Ward, William, and Priscilla Weeks. 1994. "Resource Managers and Resource Users: Field Biologists and Stewardship." Pp. 91–113 in Christopher L. Dyer and James R. McGoodwin, eds., *Folk Management in the World's Fisheries: Lessons for Modern Fisheries Management*. Niwot: University Press of Colorado.

Weber, Max. 1961. *General Economic History*. New York: Collier Books.

Weisberg, Richard. 1992. *Poethics and Other Strategies of Law and Literature*. New York: Columbia University Press.

Wennersten, John R. 1981. *The Oyster Wars of Chesapeake Bay*. Centreville, Md.: Tidewater Publishers.

Whitehead, John. 1897. *The Judicial and Civil History of New Jersey*. Boston: Boston History Company, Publishers.

Whitehead, William A. 1875. *East Jersey under the Proprietary Governments*. Newark, N.J.: Martin R. Dennis.

Wilkinson, Charles F. 1980. "The Public Trust Doctrine in Public Land Law." *U.C. Davis Law Review* 14 (2): 269–316.

——. 1989. "The Headwaters of the Public Trust: Some Thoughts on the Source and Scope of the Traditional Doctrine." *Environmental Law* 19: 425–72.

Williamson, Oliver. 1985. *The Economic Institutions of Capitalism: Firms, Markets, Relational Contracting*. New York: Free Press.

Wilson, James Grant. 1870. *Memories of Andrew Kirkpatrick and His Wife Jane Bayard*. New York: Privately Printed for Mrs. Dr. How.

Woodward, Carl R., and Ingrid Nelson Waller. 1932. *New Jersey's Agricultural Experiment Station, 1880–1930*. New Brunswick, N.J.: New Jersey Agricultural Experiment Station.

Young, Michael D., and Bonnie J. McCay. 1995. "Building Equity, Stewardship, and Resilience into Market-Based Property Rights Systems." Pp. 87–102 in Susan Hanna and Mohan Munasinghe, eds., *Property Rights and the Environment*. Washington, D.C.: Beijer International Institute of Ecological Economics and the World Bank.

Zabriskie, A. O. 1864. "Opinion of A. O. Zabriskie, Esq." Pp. 57–61 in New Jersey Board of Commissioners on Lands under Water, *Report of the Commissioners on the Extent and Value of Lands under Water in the County of Hudson. Read January 25, 1849, and Ordered to be Printed.*

——. 1871. *Dissenting Opinion of the Chancellor, Court of Errors, November Term, 1870, the Paterson and Newark Railroad Company vs. Stevens.* Pp. [26–46] in *The Riparian Proprietors' Right to Dock Out to Navigable Waters in the State of New Jersey, without Paying the State, Virtually Decided by the United States Supreme Court, January 16, 1871. The Dissenting Opinion of Chancellor Zabriskie in the Riparian Case Really Confirmed and the Opinion of Chief Justice Beasely [sic] Set Aside by the Court. Water Laws of All the Other States. The Riparian Laws of New Jersey Are Contrary to the Decisions of the United States Supreme Court.* Jersey City, N.J.: Evening Journal.

Index

About the Author

Bonnie J. McCay grew up in southern California, a bodysurfer and reluctant fisherperson. In her later studies in the Pacific Northwest she was captured by issues in culture and ecology, an interest that she carried with her to the easternmost part of North America, Newfoundland. Somewhere along the line she became interested in the problems of "the commons" from an academic as well as a policy perspective, and this has informed much of her work since she began teaching and doing research at Rutgers University in 1974. At Rutgers, she belongs to the very innovative Department of Human Ecology as well as a more traditional Anthropology Department, and she is associate director of a new Ecopolicy Center.

Dr. McCay has published extensively on fishing communities and their adaptations to ecological and socioeconomic changes, on problems with "the commons," on the application of ecological theory to social phenomena, and on many aspects of ecosystem and natural resources management. She has been a member of many national and international organizations and is currently president-elect of the International Association for the Study of Common Property.